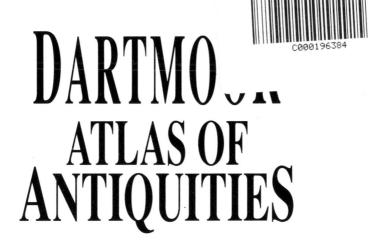

DARTMOOR
ATLAS OF
ANTIQUITIES

C000196384

JEREMY BUTLER
VOLUME TWO
THE NORTH

DEVON BOOKS

First published in Great Britain in 1991 by Devon Books

Copyright © 1991 Jeremy Butler

All rights reserved. No part of this publication may be reproduced,
stored in a retrieval system, or transmitted in any form or by any means,
electronic, mechanical, photocopying, recording or otherwise, without
the prior permission of the copyright holders.

British Library Cataloguing-in-Publication Data
Butler, Jeremy
    Dartmoor: atlas of antiquities.
    Vol. 2: The North.
    I. Title
    936.2353

ISBN 0-86114-870-3

Devon Books
397 Topsham Road
EXETER EX2 6HD

Designed for Devon Books by
Topics Visual Information
397 Topsham Road
EXETER EX2 6HD (0392) 87680

Printed and bound in Great Britain by BPCC Wheatons Ltd, Exeter

SALES
Direct sales to Tormond House, 84 Abbey Road,
Torquay, Devon TQ2 5NP

CONTENTS

DARTMOOR – ACCESS TO THE MOOR

The author reminds readers of this work that public access to much of the land within the National Park boundaries is restricted. No right of access is implied through the provisions of the text or mapwork in this publication. Permission should be sought from landowners before attempting access to restricted areas.

Readers will also appreciate that Dartmoor is one of the most important archaeological landscapes in Britain. Many sites are protected under the Ancient Monuments and Archaeological Areas Act and you may be breaking the law if you disturb them. Please take care to protect them.

INTRODUCTION

Volume Two covers the northern part of Dartmoor, from the Commons of South Tawton, Belstone and Okehampton southwards to the Tavistock-to-Moretonhampstead road and Dartmeet. The area includes the highest and most remote parts of the moor from which the walker may often return from a long day's hike without having sighted a single fellow traveller. The vast and stoneless rolling hills at the centre are covered by blanket bog, hollowed and deeply fissured in places, but never enclosed in ancient, or modern, times. Here no man-made barriers impede the walker's slow and laborious progress, restricted only by the red flags warning of activity on the firing ranges. Only the turf ties on the hillsides, the cause of much of the walker's difficulties and occasional imprecations, and the half-hidden pebble mounds along the still minor streams tell of the former presence of peat cutter and tinner.

Even during the greatest expansion of the prehistoric enclosures around the edge of the high ground those hardy early farmers of the second millennium B.C. found this central area too inhospitable for settlement. Few of their round houses and stone-walled fields reach even to the 500m contour, and these at first are widely separated, sited in the more sheltered hollows beside the upland streams. Lower down the settlements become larger and more numerous, eventually to merge into the network of rectangular fields bounded by parallel reaves along the eastern side of the moor. The latter form a continuous band some 50m higher than much of the present moorland boundary, from the River Dart northwards as far as Cosdon Hill. Here are some of the most complex settlements on the moor, wonderfully preserved and easily accessible, though in places obscured by bracken during the summer. The larger villages and hut groups are separated by the eastward-flowing streams and their tributaries, supplemented by reaves in places and extending for an uncertain distance below the moorland edge. Probably little has been lost on the east side of Buttern Hill where the present margin dips to its lowest level, later enclosure apparently having been discouraged by the damp ground. East of Kes Tor a few isolated huts and the orientation of the field walls suggest that here the earliest settlement continued for a considerable distance downhill. Further north on the east side of Cosdon Hill where enclosures now climb to the 400m contour in places, there is very little to see of the prehistoric settlement at all. The ancient field pattern is still preserved here but only some fragmentary banks and a few huts survive, too troublesome to remove or doing duty as wall supports.

The northern river valleys held little appeal for the early colonists despite the generally easy gradients. A few sites were occupied high above the east bank of the Taw but apart from one doubtful site the moorland courses of both East and West Okement and their tributaries seem to have been avoided. Perhaps not surprisingly other prehistoric remains are also less frequent, with fewer cairns and not a single stone row or free-standing stone circle between Little Hound Tor and the possible site south-east of Sourton Tors. Cairns re-appear in numbers on Longstone and Homerton Hill, presumably associated with settlements now lost within the enclosed lands below the moorland edge, for prehistoric fields appear to underlie much of the farmlands to the north-west[2]. From here a string of cairns lines the higher ground along the western border of the moor as far as White Hill, a comparatively insignificant rounded hill but the site of at least seventy cairns large and small. The neighbouring valleys of Lyd and Willsworthy Brook are not well endowed with early settlement sites and here also these are likely to have been engulfed within the present fields.

By contrast the next valley southwards, the Tavy, holds some of the largest hut groups on the moor. Seventy-eight huts are linked together at Watern Oke West, seventy on Standon Down and seventy-three along its Colly Brook tributary north-west of Roos Tor. Other large concentrations occur along the West Dart with eighty huts below Littaford Tors, and along the east bank of the Walkham where over a hundred huts are more widely dispersed between Little Mis Tor and Merrivale Bridge.

Parallel reaves re-appear on Cudlipptown Down but are neither so numerous nor so neatly laid out as in the eastern settlements. Their moorside limit is the Great Western boundary reave[2] which winds its way southwards over Roos Tor to Merrivale before eventually being lost within the present enclosures west of Sharpitor. Long rectangular fields, like those within the Youlden newtakes, are rare and hut groups are more typically associated with a number of small and irregularly shaped enclosures. Some of these have been overbuilt, for instance by the outer newtakes of Standon Farm and perhaps Lower Godsworthy; others such as those north of Roos and Cox Tors are simply ignored by the later field walls which cut across them.

Other types of prehistoric structures such as free-standing stone circles are well represented on the north moor. Of stone rows those on Cosdon and Assycombe Hills and Hurston Ridge are exceptionally well preserved and important groups occur at Fernworthy and Shovel Down. In later times not one of the rivers escaped the attention of the tin streamers, particularly the neighbouring valleys of Walla Brook and West Webburn where, by the nineteenth century, there were some of the most productive mines on the moor. Less successful tin mines were opened, and frequently soon abandoned, in several other valleys. Transient industries such as the Sourton Ice Works made a brief appearance but none perhaps had a more widespread effect upon the landscape than the peat cutters' ubiquitous turf ties.

As with Volume One the area maps and plans were initially based on aerial photographs and I would like to thank those members of the Exeter Flying Club who gamely took over the controls at the appropriate moments. Sheila Lemmy not only peered into the screen for countless hours tracing the maps and plans but weeded the text for errors and added many helpful comments. Moira Moore again braved the winter elements to assist with the surveying. I am also grateful to Mary Kitowski and Theresa Isaacs who typed a chapter apiece at short notice and particularly to my mother who undertook the rest of the manuscript.

(Figures in **heavy type** throughout refer to the maps in the centre section.)

LIST OF SITES DESCRIBED WITH MAP REFERENCES

Figures on left refer to maps and text.

LIST OF FIGURES

THE SITES

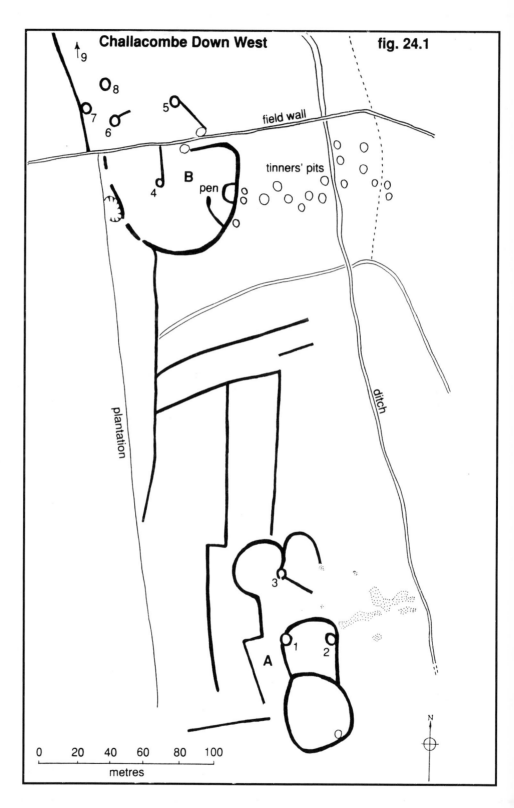

Challacombe Down West   fig. 24.1

field wall

tinners' pits

B

pen

plantation

ditch

A

N

0   20   40   60   80   100

metres

MAP 24

MAP 24 CHALLACOMBE DOWN AND SOUTH BIRCH TOR

1 Challacombe Down West settlement (fig.24.1)

The valleys of the Redwater Brook and the upper West Webburn on either side of Challacombe hill are likely to have been prime sites for early settlement, with easy sheltered slopes down to the streams. Later occupation, which has continued from at least the thirteenth century and probably beyond has obliterated all but a small fragment beside the upper reaches of the Redwater, (fig. 24.1), whilst nothing of prehistoric date survives along the west side of the Webburn valley.

Challacombe, probably the *Cherlecombe* referred to in 1244[20] had a substantial medieval population as the number of abandoned house foundations here testify. At this time the hillside above the village was gradually enclosed by cornditch walls, extending as far as the wall marking the parish boundary above the West Webburn. In the other direction noticeably larger enclosures continued around the southern tip of the hill into Redwater valley, stopping just short of the prehistoric settlement. Much of the summit was enclosed by less substantial banks with ditches, through which a drove road above the village allowed access from the river. The sixteen individual enclosures, known as wares[33], were put under plough, and lynchets were soon formed on the steep slopes. These horizontal terraces are easily seen from the road even when covered in bracken, the best of the many examples to be seen on the moor. The openwork known as Scudley Beam was utilized as a boundary between the second and third wares from the parish boundary, as was a gulley on the opposite slope. Other gerts, probably of sixteenth century date, were cut across the lynchets after the fields had been abandoned.

The village gradually contracted over the ensuing centuries like its neighbour Blackaton, a kilometre down the valley. It temporarily revived during the eighteenth and nineteenth centuries, housing some of the workers from the newly opened mines at the head of the valley, so much so that an inn was established here. Since the mines ceased the workings have reverted to moorland and Challacombe to a house and farm.

Agriculture was not the only reason for the dearth of early remains here. The medieval tin streamers, who widened as well as deepened the river beds, were also no doubt responsible for the loss of some prehistoric structures creating their own interesting antiquities in the process, but the greatest damage has been caused by the Forestry Commission's plantation on both sides of the Redwater. The Commission leased Soussons Farm from the Duchy of Cornwall in 1945, completing tree planting over 220 hectares of the Down by 1949[19]. Unfortunately no preliminary archaeological survey of the area was carried out and little can be expected to have survived the deep ploughing when the densely packed trees are eventually cut down. Part of Challacombe Down settlement has been irrevocably lost but originally it probably extended downhill to the river bank.

Two homesteads can be distinguished, A and B, connected by a number of parallel banks in two groups not quite at right angles. A further series of parallel banks south of A descends the hillside from an indeterminate origin uphill, very slight and difficult to follow even when the bracken is down. These do not seem to be integrated with the farmstead but appear to pre-date it. The wall of the main enclosure of A is still substantial, standing to 1.2 m high uphill but without dwellings inside. A rectangular annexe of similar area was constructed on the north side with a hut, 1 (4.3 m), in the corner and possibly a second hut

MAP 24

opposite, 2, now represented by a few earthfast slabs next to the bank. A pair of semi-circular banks beyond look as though they were additional enclosures, with hut 3 (c.4.0 m) in the angle where they join.

Homestead B is now a single enclosure (57 x 75 m), cut through by the present boundary wall which appears to have claimed at least some of its stones. Its wall is badly damaged next to the plantation but elsewhere is in fair condition showing the usual construction of inner and outer slabs with a rubble in-fill. A circular setting of slabs, 4 (c.3.0 m), many of them leaning inwards, may be a rebuilt hut near the centre of the homestead, the only interior structure apart from a pair of cross walls and a rectangular pen (8 x 9 m) against the uphill side.

Much-damaged remains of four small huts (5-8 m) can be seen on the other side of the boundary wall, all more or less difficult to distinguish from surrounding surface blocks. A much larger one, 9 (8.0 m), partly filled with stones, stands on the edge of the tinners' gully 140 m north of the wall.

2 The Red Barrows, cairns and stone rows on Soussons Down (figs 24.2 and 24.3)

Deep within Soussons plantation a small clearing has been left unplanted around the four burial mounds known as the Red Barrows (fig. 24.2). These are grouped closely together in a line approximately north to south in what was once a prominent position along the ridge of Soussons Down. The remains are still substantial despite being the subject of an excavation by the Dartmoor Exploration Committee in 1902, whose main effort was directed at barrows 1 and 2 which were constructed mostly of earth. Trenches,only partly refilled and still visible, were cut at right-angles across the centre of barrow 1 (20 x 2.0 m), the upcast being thrown out to the south now distorting the shape here. Below the original ground level at the centre, the excavators found a shallow pit containing only some charcoal and a small flint flake, all that remained from an earlier unrecorded excavation. The northern arm of the trench revealed a circular 'kistvaen' about 3 m from the edge of the barrow, constructed of small flat stones and about 0.6 m across,containing partially burnt human bone including part of a skull and a flint flake. The only pottery found was a small shard near the southern edge of the barrow. Part of the circumference at least was surrounded by a kerb of stones, one standing clear of the edge and the tops of several others being visible within the mound on the south-west side. Not mentioned in the excavation report is a slight bank with the suggestion of a ditch alongside running to the base of the uphill edge. This may be a prehistoric reave, the only one found on the Down, as the orientation differs by about 10° on either side of the barrow and so was presumably aligned on it.

Barrow 2 (15 x 1.2 m) a few metres to the north was also trenched, about half the structure being removed. A central pit below ground level contained wood charcoal and small fragments of burnt bone. Alongside this an area paved with flat stones covered more burnt bone and charcoal. A flint arrowhead and two pieces of bronze were also recovered from within the barrow.

The excavation report unaccountably dismisses cairns 3 and 4 as 'mere heaps of stones a few inches above ground level' whereas the former is a substantial monument measuring 21 m across by 1.3 m high. It was 'barren of any result' but apart from the shallow pit off-centre appears to be undamaged and probably still contains the remains of its original occupier. Cairn 4 (10 x 0.4 m) is small, with a flat uneven surface.

The tin mine 500 m to the north was known as Golden Dagger at least as early as 1851 and Greeves[34] makes the interesting suggestion that something similar to the gold-studded dagger found at Two Barrows on Hamel Down twenty-one years later (**map 20**), may have been dug out of one of these barrows shortly before that date.

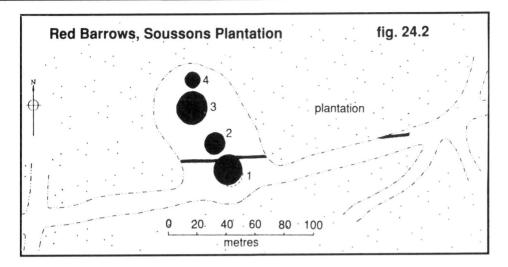

MAP 24

Red Barrows, Soussons Plantation   fig. 24.2

plantation

0   20.   40   60   80   100
                metres

The Committee also carried out a perfunctory excavation 'without success' of cairn 5 (10 x 0.3 m), which lies within the plantation some 300 m north of Red Barrows, their oval pit still visible in the centre of the mound. Trees were at one time planted to the very edge of the cairn, effectively destroying all traces of a triple stone row which descended the hill to the south. The rows had already been partly damaged 1897 when many of the stones were removed to construct the nearby enclosure wall across the Down. By the following year only seven stones remained standing, with others fallen and buried but it could still then be traced for 62 m from the cairn.

On the edge of the plantation, almost a kilometre south of the Red Barrows, is one of the best known cairn circles on Dartmoor, 6 (fig. 24.3), where for once the Forestry Commission has left a generous clearing around it. A circle of 22 earthfast stones with a diameter of 8.6 m surrounds the remains of a cist, of which the two side slabs alone remain visible. An interesting find was made here when the cist was excavated in 1903. A false floor of paving slabs had been laid below the earth infilling, concealing two large coils of human hair. This was taken as a comparatively recent manifestation of witchcraft, belief in which was still prevalent on Dartmoor in the early nineteenth century according to Mrs Bray[22]. She quotes from her husband's journal for 1827 where he records that one of his tenants had recently destroyed a cist, apparently on White Tor, which also contained 'human hair clotted together' amongst the earth and stones.

3. Challacombe Down stone rows (fig.24.4)

This triple stone row descends the heather-covered ridge of Challacombe hill in the direction of the summit of Birch Tor to the north. At the uphill end a bulky standing stone is set across the line of the rows like a General reviewing his troops, tall enough to be visible from Grimspound across the valley. The rows were first reported about 1828 when most of the stones were found to be standing in their present positions, despite Crossing's remark that all were fallen at this date[10]. A few within the rows were re-erected by Burnard and Baring-Gould in 1893, one of them probably set incorrectly across the middle row near its downhill end. Alongside this they also re-erected some fourteen stones in the haphazard position in which they were found making a very strange arrangement. Possibly these were the final stones from the lost north end of the rows, dragged here by the 'Old Men' excavating Chaw Gully who were always respectful of the antiquities in the vicinity of their workings.

MAP 24

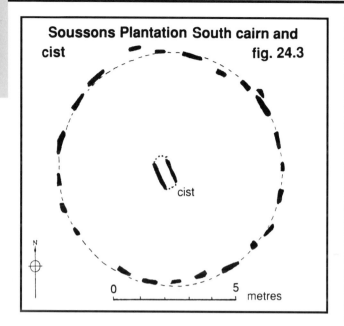

Soussons Plantation South cairn and cist fig. 24.3

0 ____ 5 metres

Unlike most Dartmoor stone rows no trace of barrow or cairn is to be found at the uphill end. Possibly one existed here originally but when, and who was responsible for its removal from this isolated spot, remains a mystery. The heather cover is very thick here and a low cairn could still lie hidden beneath it. The terminal pillar is 0.5m shorter than when it was measured in 1893 and of the 103 stones then recorded only 82 can now be found, the rest presumably sunk below the vegetation.

Total length of the rows is 145.6 m from the terminal stone, which would be increased by 10 m if the fourteen re-erected stones alongside were added to the lower end. Distance between the rows is very close to an average 1.85 m and between the stones along the rows 2.6m, though the latter variation is considerable with the separation sometimes halved. They can be seen to curve slightly to the west as they ascend the hillside.

4 Birch Tor cairn

This cairn, slightly west of the summit, was badly damaged by a road contractor in 1925 and would have been an even greater casualty had not R. H. Worth prevented him carting away the rest. Much material had already been removed from the interior and southern half, exposing a kerb of large slabs leaning inwards towards the centre and set well within the edge, but only two of these remained by the time Worth prevented further depredation. The original dimensions are uncertain, but the present diameter is about 17 m and the cairn stands 2 m above ground on the western side.

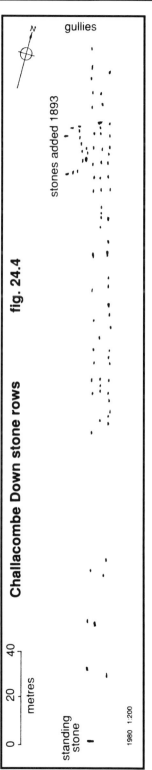

fig. 24.4 Challacombe Down stone rows

gullies

stones added 1893

40
20 metres
0

standing stone

1980 1:200

MAP 24

5-8 The Redwater Brook and Golden Dagger Mine (Fig. 24.5 and Map24)

South of Challacombe Down the Redwater meanders across a flat swampy plain, in no great hurry to effect its junction with the West Webburn a short distance above Grendon bridge. The stream emerges calmly from the dip between the hills of Soussons and Challacombe giving little indication of the enormous scars worked into the upper valley sides by succeeding generations of tinners. Quiet now for over half a century, perhaps for the first time in eight hundred years, the valley once reverberated to the sound of pick and hammer, iron-shod stamps and creaking water-wheels as the tinners scoured the stream bed and burrowed laboriously into its flanks. In the nineteenth century miners and their families were permanent residents in the valley and many more made the daily or weekly journey from surrounding farms and villages. In his book *Tin Mines and Miners of Dartmoor* Tom Greeves reproduces many old photographs depicting life in the valley during the hey-day of the mines.

The earliest evidence of tinning are the mounds of discarded pebbles on the valley floor extending alongside the stream to its source below Birch Tor. The lower leats and wheel pits cut through this rubble, which has also been levelled in places to accommodate some of the mine buildings. The alluvial mounds in the lower end of the valley were re-worked in the 1920s when three buddles and a small water-wheel were constructed to grade the ore, **5**. Two of these, both about 4 m across and retaining their central cones, can be seen alongside the stream below the wheel pit. This concreted structure, for a wheel only about 3 m in diameter, was fed via a wooden launder, which has of course disappeared, from a leat re-using one of the medieval field banks uphill. From here the ore concentrate was carted along the track upstream to the dressing floor next to the engine shed, **6**. Medieval lynchets stand out as steps in the hillside above the track on the right, an extension around the tip of the hill of those above Challacombe but set rather closer on the steeper slopes here. Across the valley the crumbling walls of Soussons Farm are visible amongst the trees, a scene very different from the bare hillside of mining days before the plantation was laid out in the years following 1945.

The concrete foundations of the engine house and the site of the dressing floors lie to the right of the track on the southern edge of the plantation, **6**. Water for a turbine and buddles was provided through the iron pipe emerging from the bank below the trees, taken off the Redwater half a kilometre upstream. Three buddles complete with central cones or 'spreaders', can be found nearby, two in an excellent state of preservation with drains for carrying the 'tailings' down to the river.

From here the roofless shell of Dinah's house, **7**, can be seen alongside the track upstream. It housed several generations of miners during the active life of Golden Dagger mine and its last occupant left only in 1942. The room facing the door was the office, with a sitting room on the left and kitchen and two bedrooms on the right over a large store-room beneath. Below the house is the site of the stamping mills marked on the first edition of the Ordnance Survey (1809). Nothing now remains, but the stamps were probably served by the leat which runs between track and plantation.

About 100 m upstream a path branches off to the left, crossing the river on a clapper bridge. Immediately after this a leat leads off to the old dressing floors, but of these only a few walls are to be found, half buried in the marshy ground beneath the trees. The path continues to a wheel pit (7 x 3 m) on the edge of the plantation, very well preserved with some of the massive beams for supporting the axle still bolted in place. The wheel was exceptionally wide and was used to drive sixteen head of stamps in a shed alongside but these have been cleared from the site.

The valley track continues upstream and itself shortly crosses the Redwater. The sunken

MAP 24

walls of a wheel pit lie hidden in a hollow on the opposite bank, fed by an aqueduct from a leat within the plantation. A hundred metres to the north the trees begin to recede from the stream and the foot of an enormous openwork appears on the flank of Soussons Hill, the Golden Dagger tin mine, **8**, and fig. 24.5.

The openwork probably dates from as far back as the sixteenth century, if not earlier. Interest in the mining potential of the upper end of the valley had been continuous from at least the 1750s but the first recorded mention of the Golden Dagger mine yet found is in 1851. Serious underground working of the sett seems to have begun only in 1879 when Moses Bawden took over the lease, investing a large amount of money in new plant and machinery and most of the shafts date from this period. The mine was successful, producing very fine quality tin, continuing in production under several different owners until 1914. Its best year was 1892 when 41 men were employed producing 26 tons of black tin. After the war only surface work was resumed, reworking the alluvial deposits along the valley bottom.

At the track junction below the openwork are the foundations of a long narrow building divided into three rooms. This was the miners' 'dry' (fig. 24.5.1) where clothes wet from underground could be changed before the long walk home. Behind the 'dry' is a low-roofed tunnel driven into one side of the gully, recently exposed after having been hidden by a landslip for many years. This was the adit level from which the ore was taken on a tramway to be processed at the stamps downstream. The water level inside makes it inaccessible but some wooden props can be seen within and a strong draught at the entrance shows that a connection with the air shafts still exists. A track leads up the gully past four of these, still open unlike all the Birch Tor and Vitifer mine shafts, but now wired off for safety. A short distance above the last an adit connecting with Machine shaft 150 m below the summit, **2**, cuts through the infill of the openwork revealing the extraordinary depth of the earlier workings. The track between the two, blocked here and there by fallen branches, is diverted away from the gully edge before arriving at the shaft, a gaping hole sunk 45 fathoms below the surface. A well-preserved wheel pit lies on the north side of the shaft, fed from a branch off the Vitifer leat half a kilometre away. Because of the adverse contour the further end of the leat was raised on an aqueduct and carried across the South Lodes on a wooden launder. The sett continued westward over the ridge down to the Walla Brook (**map 26**).

Returning to the bottom of the openwork, the valley track continues past the wired-off deep adit from which a stream trickles down to the Redwater, to a gate through the wall on the boundary between the parishes of Manaton and North Bovey.

9 Birch Tor and Vitifer Mines (fig. 24.5)

The Birch Tor and Vitifer setts, north of the wall, were originally separate mines on opposite sides of the Redwater. However, they were usually worked together during most of their recorded history, the first known reference to Vitifer Mine being in 1750[11]. Shafts and adits were being dug before the end of the eighteenth century and the mine operated as a profitable venture until the slump in the price of tin in the 1820s.[30] It was apparently soon after this that the mine captain, Quaker Paul (or Palk) acquired the lease of the mine for a knock-down price, having concealed his knowledge of the most valuable lodes from the owners. According to Baring-Gould[35] Palk soon became a very rich man though he later lost much of his wealth in other mining speculations and was obliged to sell the lease to a group of Plymouth merchants in 1845. Both pay and working conditions were exceptionally poor at this time and the mortality rate underground was high. The consequent shortage of skilled labour led to the recruitment of a criminal element which caused the mine to be described as 'the Botany Bay for miners'[34]. Prospects improved after 1858 when a new company took over the lease employing 150 people in the valley by 1863. The following two

MAP 24

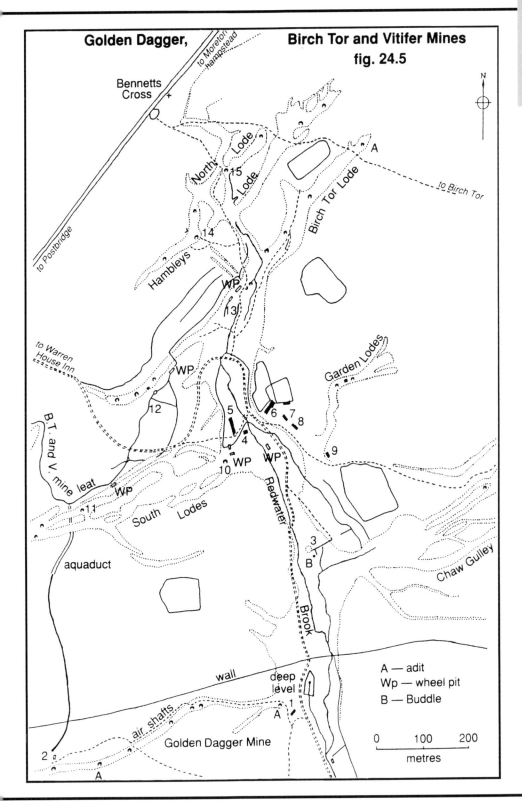

Golden Dagger, **Birch Tor and Vitifer Mines**
fig. 24.5

to Moreton hampstead

Bennetts Cross

to Postbridge

North Lode

15

Lode

14

Hambleys

Birch Tor Lode

to Birch Tor

A

WP

13

to Warren House Inn

Garden Lodes

WP

12

5

6 7 8

9

4

10 WP WP

B.T. and V. mine leat

Wp

11

South Lodes

Redwater

3

B

Chaw Gulley

aquaduct

wall

deep level

air shafts

2

A

Golden Dagger Mine

Brook

A — adit
Wp — wheel pit
B — Buddle

0   100   200
metres

MAP 24

years were the most successful in its history with production reaching 150 tons of black tin, after which it rapidly declined as the best ground became worked out and the mine was abandoned in 1882. A new company took over the sett together with East Birch Tor mine, **10**, in 1903, and it was worked as a moderately successful venture until 1913, employing up to 35 men at one time[32]. A small amount of surface and underground work was resumed after the war until the mine was finally abandoned in 1939.

Proceeding along the track northwards from Golden Dagger the enormous excavation of Chaw Gully opens out on the east side of the Redwater, continuing over the ridge to merge into the sett of East Birch Tor mine. A small stream trickles from the site of an adit about 100 m along the gully and shallow depressions of a number of filled-in shafts can be found higher up. At the mouth of the gully, 3, nothing is to be seen of sheds once housing the stamps and dressing floor of the mine, nor of the two water wheels which provided the power for them. They were destroyed during the last war when unexploded bombs were brought here from Plymouth to be detonated in safety.[34] All that remains is a small overgrown buddle and, uphill, the end of the launder bank and leat which supplied it.

Shortly beyond the dressing floors the track crosses the stream and, after passing a small wheel pit hidden amongst the rubble to the left of the track, enters the centre of the mining village. Most buildings are reduced to their foundations, only the walls of the carpenter's shop, 4, standing more than a few courses high. The long building, 5, divided into five rooms, contained the blacksmith's shop and miners' 'dry'. Across the clapper bridge over the Redwater was a group of buildings, 6, backing onto gardens; a dormitory for the miners above a kitchen and canteen, the mine captain's house, and a cottage. Further along the track were the mining offices, 7, a bungalow for miners and their families, 8, and the manager's house, 9.

The South Lodes: Islands of rock lie marooned along the length of this enormous gully, 500 m long by up to 80 m across at its widest point, excavated by the 'Old Men' probably in the sixteenth century. Work on Dunstan's shaft, 10, named after the mine captain at the time, was started at the lower end of the gully in 1846 eventually reaching 40 fathoms. A water-wheel in the pit a few metres away drained the workings. Lance's shaft, 11, now a deep pit in the highest point of the gully was being worked about the same time. Pump rods for draining the shaft ran back in the twin ditches above the north edge of the gully to a small wheel pit 6 m long, now hidden in the heather. Water from the wheel was taken off the Vitifer leat, though the connection was later blocked when the shaft was abandoned, and drained down the gully before being returned to the main leat at a lower level.

The Birch Tor and Vitifer leat was itself a major undertaking, bringing water to the head of the valley from both the East Dart and North Teign rivers to drive the eight wheels and various ore concentration processes. It was a clever piece of work, falling on average only 1 in 150 throughout its 12.2 kilometre length. Eighty metres beyond Lances wheel the leat expands into a small reservoir with a hatch to divert the flow down the neighbouring gully when necessary. Another reservoir can be seen downhill a short distance before the next wheel pit on the Birch Tor lode. The drainage arch through the lower end of the pit is still well-preserved, the wheel itself being used to pump the shafts uphill. The water had more work to do yet, being carried across the gully on an aqueduct, now crumbling away, to another large wheel pit, 13, on the valley floor, where the supply was supplemented by a branch from the Redwater spring. The forty foot wheel here pumped the lower Birch Tor shafts and others on both Hamblys and North Lodes, the rods to the latter carried in the deep trenches uphill above the wheel pit. The pit drained underground back to the Redwater.

The Birch Tor Lodes: These lodes were being worked from the early part of the nineteenth century, the Walled shaft area being particularly productive. The first thirty metres of this shaft, 12, was found to be neatly lined with stonework from top to bottom, the work of the 'Old Men' centuries earlier in one of their rare ventures into underground mining.

MAP 24

Engine shaft at the lower end of the gully, now completely filled in, was eventually sunk to 84 fathoms, the deepest level at the mine.

More shafts were sunk along the eastern arm of the lode, a miniature canyon on the flank of Birch Tor. Ore was transported up the south side of the gully on a tramway strongly buttressed at its lower end, on its way to the stamps and dressing floors. An adit remains open at the very end of the gully 20 m above the track to the summit of the tor, descending at a steep angle into the hillside but completely blocked by water a short distance from the entrance.

Hamblys and North Lodes: These lodes were being worked during the most prosperous period of the mine, the 1860s and 70s. Hamblys shaft, 14, in particular proving a rich source of ore. The grassy track from the shaft head probably carried a tramway for transporting the ore to the dressing floors. Between here and New shaft, 15, also in production at this time, the eastern side of the openwork has been neatly walled by the tin streamers, a feature often seen alongside stream workings elsewhere.

10 East Birch Tor Mine (fig. 24.6)

The bed of the West Webburn has been streamed from its junction with Redwater Brook upstream to its source above Headland Farm. Half a dozen gerts, washed from leats brought around the hillside, have been driven laterally into the western slopes of Challacombe Hill, following the lodes to high above the river. At the head of the valley Headland Farm and its immediate fields are encompassed by the streamworks at the lower end of a vast openwork which continues over the ridge into Redwater valley. As usual the early tinners responsible for these excavations took great care to avoid unnecessary damage to prehistoric monuments such as the Challacombe stone row which overlapped their workings. They appear to have laid the displaced monoliths alongside the lower end of the row where they were re-erected in a rather curious pattern in 1893.

Interest in the mining potential of the valley seems to have revived in the first half of the nineteenth century, probably in 1836 under the same Captain Paul who made his fortune at Birch Tor and Vitifer[32]. A number of shafts were sunk along the floor and lower valley sides below Headland Farm, eventually reaching 24 fathoms, with adit levels driven east and west along the lodes. As with many mining ventures there were frequent changes of ownership during its short productive life as optimism alternated with disappointment, and work eventually ceased in 1867. The sett was virtually abandoned until 1903 when yet another company resumed intermittent operations until 1927. Details of tin production went mostly unrecorded but Broughton[32] estimates that a mere 55 tons of black tin were removed between 1848 and 1864 during the most active years of the mine.

Immediately below Headland Farm the public footpath to Challacombe passes through the centre of the mine where a few ruined buildings once housed the stamps and dressing floors, 1. Many of the miners were local men attracted by the higher pay at the mines, refreshment being provided for them by the warrener Jan Roberts at the Birch Tor Inn, as Headland Farm was known at this time.[11] Remains are scanty here compared with those in neighbouring Redwater valley, most of the shafts being sunk in the immediate vicinity of the mine buildings. All these have been filled in and are now merely shallow depressions surrounded by a rim of upcast. Two water-wheels can be found nearby supplied by short leats from the Webburn and Grimslake. A third, for draining the shafts, lies a kilometre downstream, the line of trenches visible beside the track having been cut to take the returning pump rods. Unusually, ore was raised from at least one of the shafts, Etheridges, 2, by horse whim.

MAP 24

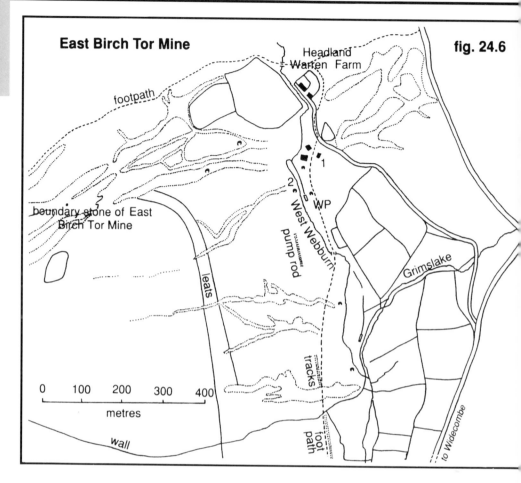

East Birch Tor Mine

Headland Warren Farm

fig. 24.6

footpath

boundary stone of East Birch Tor Mine

West Webburn

pump rod

WP

1

2

Grimslake

leats

tracks

0 100 200 300 400

metres

wall

foot path

to Widecombe

a-k Headland Warren boundary stones and others

A warren was established at Headland at least as early as the late eighteenth century and continued in use well into the present one, the warrener living at Headland Warren Farm. This building doubled as an ale house, re-named the Birch Tor Inn, for a short period in the nineteenth century, catering for the thirsty workforce of the expanding tin mining enterprises in the surrounding valleys.

The warren (250 hectares) extended from the summit of Birch Tor southwards to the wall across Challacombe hill on the boundary between Manaton and North Bovey parishes, and eastwards from the Walla Brook to approximately the line of the present Widecombe road. A series of granite slabs delineated the open side of the warren, all but one with the letters *WB* (for warren bounds) cut on one face. The exception, with the full inscription *Warren Bounds*, is a small slab, not easily noticed, beside the road on the north-east corner of the warren boundary (**map 23, a**). The south-east extent is marked by three slabs, **a-c**, close together on the slopes below Grimspound. The centre one, **b**, has the additional letters *AP and WN* lightly cut above and below the *WB*, supposedly the initials of previous warreners.

MAP 24

This seems unlikely as three generations each of the Roberts and Hannaford families preceeded the last warrener Jim Collins,[11] and the initials are more probably those of the labourers who actually cut and erected the stones.

A further group of 7 slabs, **d-g** and **map 25**, follow the crooked course of the tinners' ditches across the north side of Birch Tor, several being set within them. Bennetts Cross was also labelled as a warren boundary, as were 2 further slabs, **e**, **f**, on the boundary between the parishes of Chagford and North Bovey. The leaning unmarked slab, **j**, across the road from Bennetts Cross continues the parish bound northwards onto Bush Down.

Unlike some Dartmoor warrens such as Vag Hill, it was unnecessary to construct buries as the rabbits easily colonised the broken ground alongside the tinners' gerts. A less obvious task was to feed them, particularly in hard winters, and for this the warreners grew furze within the five enclosures on the side of Birch Tor known as Jan Reynolds' cards. Crossing's tale for the origin of this name relates that they were the aces which dropped from Jan Reynolds' pocket as he was being carried off by the Devil for taking a nap in Widecombe Church. Some of the 'cards' were taken over by the Birch Tor tin miners for growing vegetables.

To provide some protection against stoats two vermin traps were built into the base of the wall across Challacombe hill (**V.T.**). Both are well preserved though they are without their slate shutters.

Stone **k**, a small slab in the floor of Chaw Gully, is inscribed *East Birch Tor* on its eastern face. It was erected about the middle of the nineteenth century to mark the western limit of the sett of East Birch Tor tin mine in the valley below.

Bennetts Cross

This ancient cross served both as a boundary stone on the border between Chagford and North Bovey parishes and as a wayside guide stone for the traveller making his way across the open moorland on the Moretonhampstead to Postbridge track before the present road was constructed in the years following 1772.[19] It stands below the crest of the ridge and would have been of no use to those ascending Hurston Ridge to the north, on the well-used track from Chagford (**map 25**) illustrated in Ogilby's[36] (1675) and later road maps, which joined this route near Statts Bridge.

The cross was first recorded in 1702 but the identity of Bennett remains a mystery, though Crossing has suggested a sixteenth century tinner of that name. Its survival so close to the road is no doubt due to its use as a boundary stone, as two wayside crosses further along the road, on Merripit Hill and at Postbridge, were removed as recently as the middle of the last century. It is visible beside the road not far from the Warren House Inn, crudely shaped with a dainty curve to its shaft like an ancient moorland rowan blasted by the wind. *WB* can just be made out cut into the western face though part of the first letter has flaked away in the last few years.

MAP 25

MAP 25 CHAGFORD COMMON AND BUSH DOWN

1-4 Birch Tor North

Apart from the single cairn which crowns the hill a little to the north of the small rock outcrop of Birch Tor, **map 24.4**, the rounded summit is clear of prehistoric structures. The waterless eastern plain which merges onto Shapley Common held few attractions for early settlers, whilst any settlement that may have existed on the western flank around the head of the Redwater has been sacrificed to the enormous workings of the tin industry here. Only the sheltered northern slope was colonized, above the marshy ground around the little brook which now flows through the modern enclosures of Lakeland farm to join the Bovey in the valley below.

A winding reave forms the southern limit of the settlement, almost following the contour of the hillside, from which four not quite parallel reaves splay out downhill. The west reaves form narrow strips containing individual homesteads and at least two of them continue up the opposite hillside before being lost. The short eastern reave was built of a double line of large slabs, now mostly fallen, presumably dragged from some distance across the noticeably clitter-free slopes. The uphill end was destroyed by tinners pits but the lower terminates on the edge of the mire around the head of the brook, a good example of a stream being used to form part of a boundary.

The pair of enclosures of Homestead **1**, each about 0.2 hectares, straddle the contour reave. Hut 1 (8.4 m) with its well-preserved inner and outer walls partly turf-covered is set across this reave, with an entrance into the field uphill. A few earthfast slabs roughly on the arc of a circle are all that remain of a second hut (c. 7.5 m) built against the wall within the same enclosure.

Homestead **2**, cut through by the main road but probably without loss except for the connecting wall, occupies the uphill end of the western strip. Two fields are built onto the end reave with a pair of huts on the perimeter. A section of the wall above the road can be traced only as a ditch where the stones have been grubbed up, a fate from which the exceptional size of the slabs making up the walls of the huts has preserved them. These are clearly visible from the road, one being particularly large (8.8 x 6.5 m), with most stones remaining though often leaning or flat. A third hut (6.5 m) below the road also retains most of its stones, a tall pillar on the eastern side probably one of the jamb stones. Within, the tops of several small slabs show above the surface probably lining the edge of a raised dais.

Two more groups of huts lie further down the slope, **3**, though thick heather and tinners pits and ditches obscure their field boundaries. The upper pair (7.5, 6.0 m), 13 m apart, are in good condition, the western hut still retaining two jamb stones in position with another fallen across the entrance. Only 3 m separates each of the lower group of three huts, all about 6.5 m in diameter and built of large slabs, many now displaced and overgrown.

On the opposite side of the brook two more huts lie on the edge of the small enclosure, 4, close below the road. The ground is very disturbed here and the lower margin of the field no longer exists. The uphill hut (6.5 m) is constructed of a double skin of very large slabs, the lower (7.5 m) with smaller ones.

MAP 25

5-8 Prehistoric settlements on Chagford Common (fig. 25.1)

The Bovey and South Teign rivers are separated by a ridge of moorland, increasing in height towards the south-west to culminate in the twin hills of Water and Assycombe. The substantial prehistoric settlements which grew around the upper reaches of both these rivers agreed at some stage to a common boundary, and a reave at least 2.5 kilometres in length was constructed along the watershed between them. At its northern end this reave is orientated towards the western edge of the Shapley enclosures, about 50 m away, suggesting that the present field wall may be a continuation of its course in this direction. After about 100 m the reave changes direction southwards, continuing along the west side of the ridge rather than the summit for about a kilometre. It makes a further alteration here, up Hurston ridge and passing close to the stone row before being lost in the heather on the far side of Assycombe Hill. A pair of reaves parallel this latter part of its course, a shorter length some 200 m to the north up Assycombe Hill, and a second 700 m to the south over Water Hill. These end at the source of the Metherall Brook and Bovey respectively, the rivers apparently continuing the land division northwards.

Three independent settlements (**5**, **6**, **7**) developed along the west bank of the Bovey, on the higher slopes clear of the damp ground on the valley floor. There were probably others along the opposite more sheltered slopes now occupied by Lakeland Farm, and more may have existed downstream. They were not confined between parallel banks as are the settlements visible across the valley below Birch Tor, presumably because there was still space for expansion between them.

The ancient field walls (fig. 25.1) stand out starkly on the hillside as a single or occasionally a double line of slabs set in a low bank. Each farmstead contains a number of huts sited around the edges of the fields, some having a small paddock alongside. A flint knife was found within one of these by the Dartmoor Exploration Committee in 1900.

Part of the southern settlement, **5**, has been incorporated within later fields and the walls here are much denuded. Hut 1 is little more than a levelled circular platform and 2 (c. 6.9 m) lies just on the

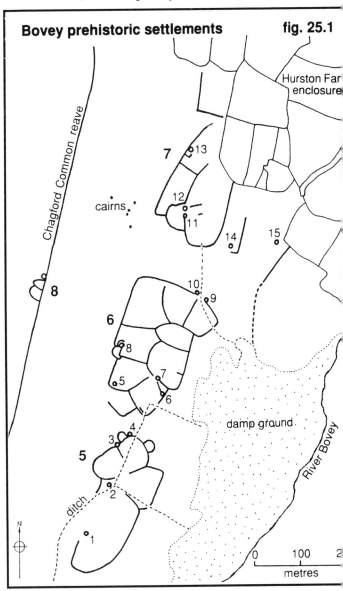

Bovey prehistoric settlements   fig. 25.1

Hurston Far enclosure

Chagford Common reave

cairns

damp ground

River Bovey

ditch

N

0   100   2
metres

MAP 25

outer edge of the enclosure ditch. Hut 3 (6.6 m) is built across the farmstead wall next to a D-shaped paddock, with a much smaller hut, 4, (3.0 m) on the opposite side of it.

Settlement **6**, with half a dozen huts, has expanded to within a few metres of the first settlement. The nearest hut, 5, (6.1 m), lies in the corner of a field with a jamb stone at its eastern entrance. Hut 6 (c. 6.5 m), damaged with much of the wall displaced outwards, is connected by an extra bank to hut 7 (8.1 m), the largest in the group but entirely overgrown. Hut 8 (7.6 m) opens into a D-shaped enclosure on its south side the rest of its wall being closely surrounded by a bank about 1 m outside it. A pair of earthfast slabs, probably on the edge of the dais, show through the turf within the downhill side. Two more huts, 9 and 10 (5.8 and 6.9 m) are separated by a tinners ditch on the northern perimeter of the settlement.

The Hurston enclosures have destroyed the nothern end of settlement **7**, the walls of which become progressively more denuded as they approach the fields. Most of the stones are missing from huts 11 (5.6 m) and 12 (8.0 m) built a few metres apart, and only two large stones remain of 13 (8.8 m), the largest of all the Bovey dwellings. Huts 14 (7.2 m) and 15 (8.0m) appear to be independent but their boundary banks have been entirely removed into the present field walls.

Over the crest of the ridge and invisible from the settlements the Chagford Common reave pursues a course southwards up Hurston ridge. A pair of D-shaped enclosures, with a few set stones alongside as the possible remains of a hut, were added to the far side of the reave and are perhaps the remains of an isolated settlement, **8**. The banks, now much spread and no more than 0.3 m above the turf, were at one time clearly more substantial as the ancient track alongside the reave takes a decided curve around them.

Just out of sight from settlement **7** are a group of at least five low mounds, the nearest about 50 m away uphill. These are about 5 m in diameter and up to 0.3 m high, with other even smaller ones in the vicinity, and most have a shallow pit with a few exposed stones at the centre. These are probably some of the nine cairns excavated by the Dartmoor Exploration Committee in 1900 'on Chagford Common'. The excavators found that several of these mounds covered pits containing wood charcoal, and in one case burnt bones as well.

9 Hurston Ridge stone rows and settlement (figs. 25.2,3)

Remote enough from both the road and the farm enclosures in the neighbouring valleys, the Hurston Ridge double stone row survives as one of the best examples of its kind on Dartmoor. Though the average height of the stones is less than half a metre the two lines descending the hillside from a ruinous cairn at the southern end are still a spectacular sight. The cairn has been thoroughly rifled with the upcast thrown out onto one side forming a miniature cairn of its own. Its shape is irregular, 6.5 x 7.0 m, rising to 0.5 m at the centre but with no sign of the cist at one time visible here. The single earthfast slab facing the rows may be the last of a retaining circle which once surrounded its base.

In contrast with the cairn the integrity of the stone rows seems to have been respected down the ages since the monument was first erected in the early Bronze Age. Some of the stones were re-erected in their original sockets at the end of the last century by the Rev. Baring-Gould, who found a broken stone axe at the foot of the menhir next to the cairn. The re-erected stones are probably the taller ones at the ends of the rows which have packing stones visible around the base.

The 99 stones are arranged in 49 pairs with a final slab set across the lower end from which the cairn is visible on the skyline. The lack of any further stone holes in line indicates that there has been no loss in this direction, at least in recent times, and that the rows are probably complete. Few Dartmoor rows are in such a good state of preservation but most, if

MAP 25

not all, of the double ones probably had similar characteristics before they were despoiled, such as a cairn at the higher end and a slab set sideways terminating the lower. Other common features include the gradual increase towards the ends of both the height of the stones and their distance apart along and between the rows. Many rows also have a similar slight curvature downhill, here amounting to only half a degree, though this of course may not be deliberate.

A more unusual feature is that the wall of a Bronze Age enclosure was built across the line of the rows at a later date including rather less than half within the perimeter. The builders must have held the monument in respect rather than awe

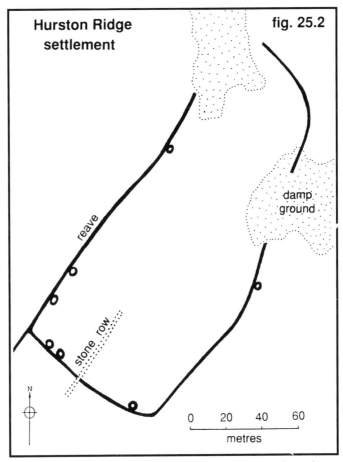

Hurston Ridge settlement

fig. 25.2

damp ground

reave

stone row

0   20   40   60

metres

at this time, causing minimum damage even though the stones would no doubt have been useful in constructing the wall of their own enclosure. The gentle slope above the source of Metherall Brook probably governed the choice of site, when the spring was perhaps more active than now. The settlement was built onto the east side of the watershed reave and enclosed an undivided area of 2.9 hectares. Paltry remains of at least six huts can be identified built onto the inside wall of the enclosure with another outside on the west. A recent plan shows other possible huts[7] but all are low turf-covered banks with a few small stones around the edge and diameters ranging from 3.5 to 4.0 m.

10 Hurston Ridge cairn

This cairn (c. 9.0 x 0.2 m) has a curious history. It was 'lost' soon after it was discovered and excavated by the Dartmoor Exploration Committee in 1900, its position marked on subsequent editions of the Ordnance Survey as 'site of cairn' and excluded altogether from the latest 1:25000 map. The excavators described the cairn as truncated but it was apparently undisturbed at the centre for they found the crushed remains of an inverted cinerary urn resting upside down on a flat stone, protected by a large slab above. The urn, dating from the Middle Bronze Age, was taken to the Plymouth Museum where it has recently (1960-62) been reassembled from over a hundred pieces and put on show. Below the flat stone was a deep pit filled with wood charcoal.

MAP 25

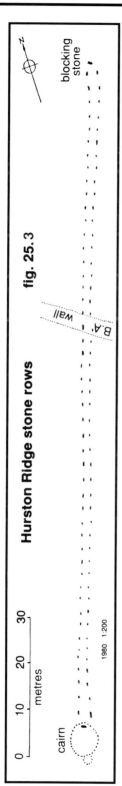

fig. 25.3

Hurston Ridge stone rows

The cairn is still to be found on the west side of Assycombe Hill. It was less than 0.3 m high even before excavation and only a triangular slab lying flat on the south-east edge of a very low mound, apparently the last of a retaining circle, distinguishes it from the surrounding hillside.Until 1986 another slab lay in the shallow pit at the centre, perhaps the stone which protected the urn, but this has since been taken away.

11 West Vitifer cairn

This rather insignificant mound sited just off the ridge north of the stone row was discovered and excavated by members of the Barrow Committee of the Devonshire Association in 1897, and described in their sixteenth report. It contained a cist which had not previously been dug into, an unusual event in Dartmoor archaeology, its survival probably accounted for the small size of the cairn (5.5. x 0.3 m).Below the surface a ring of slabs surrounded the central cist which contained a perfectly preserved 'barbed wire' beaker, dating from around 2000 BC, lying on its side. This almost immediately fell to pieces but has been restored by the British Museum and is now in Plymouth. A cremation had presumably accompanied the beaker, but of this no trace remained. The excavators replaced the earth over the cairn and it has now much the same dimensions as when it was found. A few stones are exposed including one edge of the cist near the centre.

The Heath Stone

The history of the Heath Stone, now identified on Ordnance Survey maps with a large block near the entrance to Fernworthy reservoir, is something of a mystery. This stone, with a biblical inscription cut on one face in 1970, is otherwise undistinguished, being merely the largest in the moorside wall of a prehistoric field and barely worthy of note. The original Heath Stone seems to be that recorded in the first known Perambulation of the Forest of Dartmoor in 1240 when it was known locally as both Langstone and Yessetone. It was depicted as Langestone on the earliest surviving map of Dartmoor illustrating the Perambulation, though the map itself dates from the fifteenth century.[19] Unfortunately the identification of the neighbouring bounds, Heighstone to the north and Alberysheved followed by Wallebroke in the direction of King's Oven are uncertain, so it is not possible to place its precise position between the South Teign and Bovey rivers. The name Hethstone first occurs in the later Perambulation of 1608.

Ogilby's road atlas[36] of 1675, shows only one trans-Dartmoor route which was the most direct way between Exeter and Tavistock via Chagford, joining a branch from Mortonhampstead near Statts Bridge. Heath Stone is marked on the map alongside a tall pillar on the north side of the track near the summit of the ridge and a little over a mile from the bridge. Later road maps based on Ogilby's continued to show the stone, as did many of the county maps such as those of Moll, Hinton, Walpoole and others, throughout the eighteenth century. It did not however appear on

MAP 25

Donn's detailed map of 1765, an entirely new and much more accurate survey for which he won the first award for cartography presented by the Royal Society of Arts, nor in the early editions of the Ordnance Survey maps from 1809 onwards. The stone occasionally resurfaced in various nineteenth-century county atlases such as Cary's New British Atlas (1805) and the British Gazetteer (1852) but now on the opposite side of the track.

The block now labelled Heath Stone would have been useless as a guide stone, standing as it does in a declivity on the edge of the enclosed lands. The traveller using Ogilby's map had a choice of two routes on either side of the Metherall Brook and its surrounding marsh when entering the open moorland from the Chagford direction. Both remain well-defined paths, converging near the top of Hurston ridge (see map) near the standing stone at the upper end of the stone row. This pillar stands out clearly on the skyline from the edge of the moor and would seem a more likely candidate for the original boundary mark and guide post.

West Vitifer Tin Mine

The earliest tinning activity in the valley of the Bovey was, as usual, the streaming of the upper reaches of the river bed. Turf-covered mounds of pebbles accompany the river downstream for nearly 2 kilometres from its source, until it enters the enclosed lands below the miniature tor known as Hurston Castle. In a later period, probably the sixteenth century, a deep gully was excavated into the hillside opposite the southern end of the Lakeland enclosures, extending south-westward onto Bush Down. This gully was later employed as the southern boundary of a pair of fields, now abandoned, which were probably newtakes of Lakeland farm on the opposite side of the valley. Northwards the bank and ditch around these fields, now reduced to little more than the ditch in places, cuts through two of the Bovey prehistoric settlements and further damage was caused by the lines of shallow ditches dug down the slope to improve drainage.

The remains of the buildings on the valley floor belong to the third and last period of tinning activity in the valley when a lease was obtained for the sett in 1850[32]. It seems to have been worked only intermittently over the next twenty-five years with no recorded production, and the company was wound up in 1875[30] after a good deal of money had been spent. What remains of the site lies on the north bank opposite the foundations of the mine buildings and the ford leading onto Bush Down. A wall partly encloses three round buddles 5-6 m across with a subterranean drain, now exposed in places, leading back to the river. Little is to be seen of the stamping floor or wheel pit which were once here but the launder bank survives. This was served by the well-preserved leat taken off 250 m upstream and which must have been carried over the intervening feeder stream on an aqueduct. The depressions of the filled-in Engine shaft can be seen near the buddles and another alongside the lower end of the gully to the west. A number of adits were driven into the hillside to the south-east and though all of these are now blocked, they are easily recognisable from the waste dumps below the entrances.

Bush Down Mine

The Bush Down slopes above the Bovey are scored by numerous ditches and gullies, and a leat which runs northwards around the hillside from near the later mine. These are probably the sixteenth-century workings owned by Chagford Parish which, according to Omerod,[37] were unprofitable. They still were when the sett was re-opened here for a short time in the 1870s in conjunction with the West Vitifer mine in the valley below and Waterhill and King's Oven to the south-west [32]. Several shafts were sunk along the length of an earlier gully, just below the road, and two adits were driven into the hillside 130 m below them. The latter are still open but are no doubt dangerous to enter. Little more remains to be seen apart from a building platform close to the Engine shaft.

MAP 26

MAP 26 Upper Wallabrook and Statts Brook

1 King's Oven (fig. 26.1)

Furnum Regis, or King's Oven, is one of the earliest recorded placenames on Dartmoor, being listed as one of the boundaries of the Forest in the Perambulation of 1240. Its precise position is in some doubt but the name has become associated with the prehistoric pound on the eastern slopes of Water Hill. This is an unlikely location for the boundary mark as the following one is the spring of the Walla Brook which, if the eastern branch is meant, rises only a few metres away. More probably the name originally applied to the cairn with its coursed stonework entrance, **5**, on the summit of Water Hill, a prominent landmark on this part of the moor, and the present boundary point.

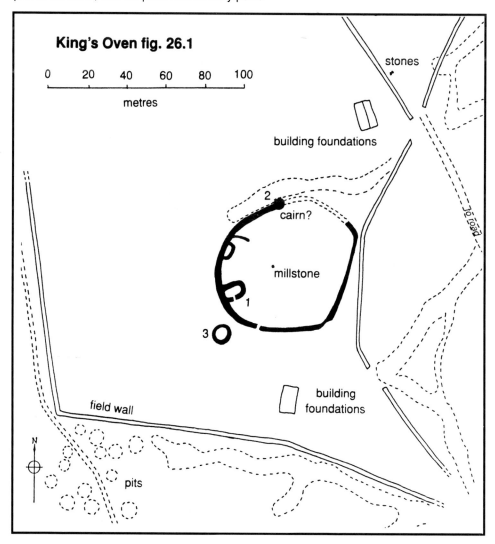

King's Oven fig. 26.1

0   20   40   60   80   100

metres

stones

building foundations

2 cairn?

millstone

1

3

building foundations

field wall

N

pits

MAP 26

Worth[31] suggests that King's Oven refers to a building in the vicinity 'at the hiring of the King' where tin was re-smelted, weighed and taxed, a process later carried out at one of the four stannary towns on the borders of the moor. This has been interpreted as meaning a 'blowing house' but it would be an exceptionally early date for such a building and in any case no leat for powering the bellows approaches the site. Apart from some low banks built onto the western wall and a few tinners' pits and ditches downhill the interior of the pound is quite flat, and some traces at least of such a building could be expected to have survived. A mound of stones once stood at the centre but these were used to construct the mine buildings nearby and only a roughed-out millstone is now to be found here.

In 1895 the Dartmoor Exploration Committee examined the rectangular foundations built onto the south-west side, 1, its walls much spread and with a southern entrance, but were unable to come to any conclusion as to its date or purpose. It is perhaps of prehistoric construction contemporary with the smaller rectangle and bank nearby, or is possibly the remains of a medieval longhouse as the major axis is downhill. The Committee also dug into a mound of stones in the line of the north wall of the pound which was partly surrounded by an arc of upright slabs, two or three of which remain, 2. Charcoal and a flint scraper were found next to the uprights. The structure was interpreted as a cairn, perhaps with a central cist, which had been deliberately slighted by the pound builders. Much of this section of the wall was damaged when the tinners' trench was dug alongside and it seems possible that the excavators were mistaken in this identification.

Outside the pound several circular plots 5-6 m across are levelled into the hillside which may be the remains of associated huts, one of them having traces of a bank part way round the periphery, 3. North and south are the nineteenth-century foundations of buildings connected with King's Oven mine and Bush Down mine. On the other side of the wall opposite the former are a pair of granite blocks with Y-shaped grooves cut in the surface, presumably serving some purpose associated with the workings.

2,4 Assycombe Hill South settlement and cairns (fig. 26.2)

Beyond Statts Farm a rudimentary track continues westwards around the lower slopes of Assycombe Hill, passing between the huts of a settlement on the edge of the damp ground, **2**. Some sixteen small heather-covered huts can be found, most of them in pairs, with single-slabbed walls 3-3.5 m across. The most interesting one is slightly larger, 1 (4.8 m), joined by curved walls to a neighbouring hut and abutting on to another with an annexe. The only enclosure visible (c. 30 x 18 m) is associated with a pair of huts above the track, but much may be concealed beneath the heather. Reaves approach downhill from the east, the slight remains of one passing to the south of the huts but others are so well camouflaged by the heather that they are only visible on aerial photographs.

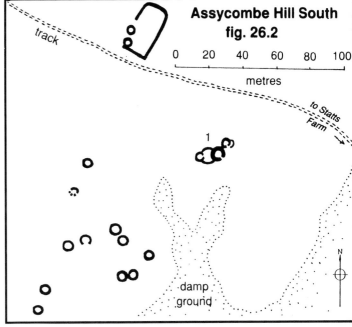

Assycombe Hill South
fig. 26.2

0   20   40   60   80   100
metres

track

to Statts Farm

1

damp ground

N

MAP 26

The proximity of the two cairns **4** on the summit of the ridge 400 m to the south-west suggest these may have been the burial mounds of this community. A few slabs of retaining circles are visible around their edges and shallow central depressions tell of some unrecorded investigation of their contents. Both have a single stone set at right-angles outside the perimeter, a small slab close to the base of the south cairn and a more prominent one about 8 m north-east of the other. One or a very few stones in a similar position are a feature of other Dartmoor cairns, such as those within Stannon Newtake to the west, and might be considered a rudimentary form of alignment.

3 Water Hill East huts

A not very obvious boundary reave runs between North Walla Brookhead and Statts Brook, crossing Water Hill just south of the summit and aligned parallel with the one over Assycombe Hill about 750 m to the north. A cross reave branches off outside the King's Oven enclosure and curves around the side of Water Hill in the direction of the nothern reave, though it cannot be traced quite so far.

In the corner between the two reaves a curved bank cuts off a large area on the side of Water Hill overlooking the Walla Brook valley. Four huts can be found here, spaced around the inside of the curved bank. All are small, no more than 3.5 m in diameter, and are very overgrown with few of their wall stones standing clear of the turf.

5 Water Hill cairns

A modern stone heap caps the large cairn 18 m across on the summit of Water Hill, the stones obtained from an excavation into its north-eastern side. This pit has revealed a stone-lined passage 1.3 m wide from the edge of the cairn towards the centre, apparently blocked by a slab about 2 m in. The passage seems to have been visible at the time of the Rev. Bray's visit in 1831[22] as he describes 'a kind of trench about 6 feet long ... lined with stone', though in the same direction as the line of tinners' pits which are in fact on the opposite side. It may, indeed, have been exposed many centuries earlier and given rise to the name of King's Oven. The cairn, composed of small stones, was probably always flat-topped and apart from the slight central hollow does not appear to be badly damaged.

A few metres from its base on the north side is a much smaller mound (5.0 x 0.3 m), also probably a burial cairn. In 1871 Spence Bate recorded the existence of another, similar in diameter to that on the summit, somewhere near King's Oven but even at this date it had been reduced to little more than the side slabs of the cist.

Tinworks and Leats in the Walla Brook Valley

Both the Golden Dagger sett and the earlier gerts west of the Redwater (**map 24**) continue over the ridge into the Walla Brook valley, though the gunnises and shafts of the former are hidden within the plantation south of Soussons newtake wall. The enormous scale of the streamworks around the head of the Walla Brook, camouflaged by heather and bracken, is best appreciated from the floor of the valley. It was probably the debris washed down from this and the neighbouring valleys of Redwater and West Webburn which caused the long-standing complaints from the inhabitants of Dartmouth, like that noted by Leland (*Itineraries*) about 1538: '... the tinne workes carieth much sand ... and choketh ... the river downward and doth much hurt to Dartmouth Haven'. A short time before, in 1512, Richard Strode, Member for Plympton and himself a tinner, was imprisoned in Lydford gaol 'one of the most annoious, contagious, and detestable places wythin this realm', for introducing a bill into Parliament to prevent this and other harbours from being silted up.

The scale of the workings required additional water supplies and a number of leats were constructed along both sides of the valley. The first was taken off near the source of the

MAP 26

Walla Brook as it re-appears south of the road opposite the site of King's Oven bungalow. The latter was built in the late nineteenth century for Moses Bawden, one time manager of Birch Tor and Vitifer mine, and demolished in 1976.[34] The leat winds around the hillside to the streamworks in Redwater valley but much of its early course has been taken over by a track.

A second left bank leat closely follows the lip of the excavations before returning to the river beside a heather-covered mound, perhaps covering the remains of a blowing house, and lower down yet another disappears into the plantation. The mortar stone (**M.S**) with cavities in both faces, built into the newtake wall 650 m below the corner, shows that at least one such building existed in the valley though a nearer site might have been expected. The foundations on the opposite side of the river seem to be associated with the enclosures here, possibly part of the ancient tenements of Runnage. Ditched banks abound, earlier than the ruined newtake walls, and a wide droveway descends through the abandoned fields to the river. No leats approach the well-preserved little building (c. 4.5 x 3.0 m), closely surrounded by an outer wall in the gert opposite Soussons corner, nor the ruin at the upper end of the valley. The latter (c. 5.3 x 3.8 m) with an entrance facing south was probably a tinners' hut.

Two more leats wind around the slopes of Water Hill on the opposite side of the valley, the lower carrying water from Statts Brook to the right bank gerts. The upper leat negotiates these gullies, on aquaducts in places, to provide the main supply to the Birch Tor and Vitifer mining complex in Redwater valley. It took water from both the East Dart and Varracombe Brook, the latter a tributary of the North Teign (**maps 34, 35**). A curious, but not unique, feature is that much of its course from Sandy Hole on the East Dart is duplicated by an apparently older leat only a few metres away. It was not an error as the second leat remains on the uphill side, crossing the later one in the marsh around the head of Lade Hill Brook. They finally coalesce on White Ridge after emerging from Fernworthy Plantation.

Soon afterwards however a branch is given off on Assycombe Hill. This winds around Coal Mires at the head of Statts Brook to a tin mine on the south-west of Water Hill known as Wheal Caroline. It was one of the less successful ventures and little is to be seen apart from a few gullies and a deep pit at the site of the shaft. A second leat 50 m uphill originating from the spring north of Statts Farm may also once have supplied these workings but continues on to the site of the cottages known, from their exposed postion, as Cape Horn. These were on the south side of the road and were built around the turn of the century to house those working at the nearby mines.

A kilometre along the Postbridge road the Ordnance Survey marks an isolated hut circle beside what appear to be some tinners' pits. The ring of slabs c. 3.5 m across could be of prehistoric date, or perhaps, more likely, contemporary with the excavations.

MAP 27

MAP 27 The Postbridge District

1 Broadun Ring (fig. 27.1)

By the time the first settlers to build their dwellings and enclosures in stone had arrived, the lower East Dart valley had been the home of many previous generations from mesolithic times onwards. These earlier folk lost and discarded thousands of worked flints in the valley which have since been brought to the surface and collected from the surrounding fields. Hundreds were found, all within a few metres, at Greyhound Marsh and over a hundred and fifty at Ringhill a short distance away, sites where they had obviously been fashioned. Other prolific find spots in the area have been Runnage, Huccaby, Brownberry and Lower Merripit.

By three millenia ago the Postbridge district was one of the most densely populated areas on the moor and may never have been entirely deserted after this time. From Lade Hill Brook southwards to Dartmeet, prehistoric banks and enclosures reappear on the few open spaces on the higher ground that here remained undeveloped. A variety of settlement types can be found within the valley, from individual farmsteads with just a pair of huts, such as Bellever Tor North and Laughter Tor West, multiple field systems like those on Riddon Ridge, **map 18**, or, higher upriver, the single enclosures surrounding a large number of huts like Broadun Ring.

Fifty metres above the East Dart the newtake wall alters course around the inside of the uphill edge of Broadun Ring, all but the largest blocks of the ancient wall providing material

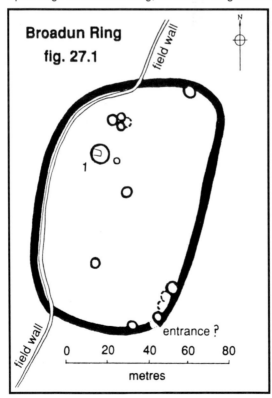

Broadun Ring

fig. 27.1

field wall

N

1

field wall

entrance ?

0   20   40   60   80

metres

for the present one. Elsewhere the wall has collapsed and spread to 3.5 m across except in the south-east corner where several courses of stone still in place show that originally it stood well over a metre high. A gap in the wall nearby may perhaps be the original gateway down to the river as there are no displaced stones on the downhill side. The numerous blocks scattered within show that there was no serious attempt by the inhabitants to clear the interior.

The compound, like neighbouring Broadun, was investigated by Burnard and Baring-Gould in 1893. They excavated ten of the huts and perhaps were also responsible for some of the small pits elsewhere within the enclosures. None of the huts yielded anything exceptional, though five produced some evidence of occupation in the form of a hearthstone or charcoal. A few flint fragments and pot-boilers were also found but not a single shard of pottery.

MAP 27

Apart from hut 1 (7.0 m), by far the largest, all the huts are small (2–4 m). A feature of hut 1 is the interior wall, a platform 0.7 m high by 2 m wide which extends two-thirds of the way across the centre. It is still perfectly visible having been rebuilt by Burnard from the loose stones found on the floor of the hut. Immediately outside it, but now no longer visible, was a small hut barely 2 m in diameter which was thought to have been a storeroom. The curious group of four huts built against each other a few metres away are badly damaged but two were probably dwellings and the other pair identified as store-houses.

2 Broadun (fig. 27.2)

Less than 100 m southward of Broadun Ring is the far bigger prehistoric pound of Broadun, one of the largest single enclosures on Dartmoor. Here also a newtake wall follows the inner edge of the ancient one which has suffered accordingly, being in few places more than 0.3 m high. Only on the south-east side does the modern wall part company to take its own course downhill, but here the pound wall is even more severely damaged by the Powder Mills leat on its long journey towards the Cherry Brook.

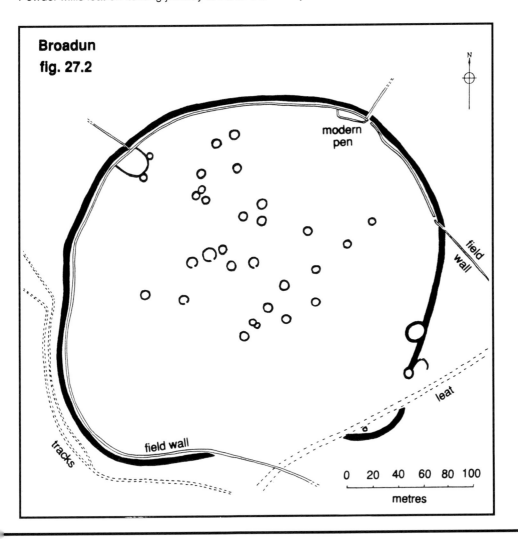

Broadun
fig. 27.2

N

modern
pen

field
wall

leat

tracks

field wall

0   20   40   60   80   100

metres

MAP 27

Some 32 hut circles are clearly defined, and a number of stone heaps scattered about may be the remains of others. They are mainly grouped towards the centre, with a clear area between them and the circuit wall, except on the south-east side where the newtake expands downhill. Probably the outer huts were completely dismantled as another source for the present boundary. Almost all the huts are small (3.0-4.5 m) but as at Broadun Ring one hut near the centre much exceeds the rest in size (7.0 m). Only a few have identifiable entrances.

Following their investigation of Broadun Ring, Burnard and Baring-Gould turned their attention to this settlement. It is not now possible to identify the 11 huts that were dug into as they carefully replaced the soil and turf afterwards. Most of those excavated appear to have been dwellings, if the presence of hearthstones, charcoal and pot-boilers are taken as evidence for it. The charcoal was mainly oak, indicating that it was growing locally at that time. Flints and rubbing stones were also discovered in some of them, as were pebbles of white quartz. The latter are not an uncommon find in huts and Burnard suggested they may have been gaming pieces or slingshots.

3 Lower Broadun (fig. 27.3)

A third settlement lies within shouting distance of the previous two, on the much steeper slope at the base of the hill. Prehistoric enclosures with a river frontage do not usually have a boundary along this side, but this one seems to have been re-used in more recent times when the lower wall was added. The circuit wall has collapsed into a low-spread bank, best seen around the uphill edge but barely visible on the steeper gradient above the river, particularly down the north side. In 1891 Prowse was able to recognise the foundations of 9 huts within the enclosure of which only two (3.5 and 4.0 m) can now be found, connected to the perimeter in the north-west corner. A pile of stones in the opposite corner may be the remains of another.

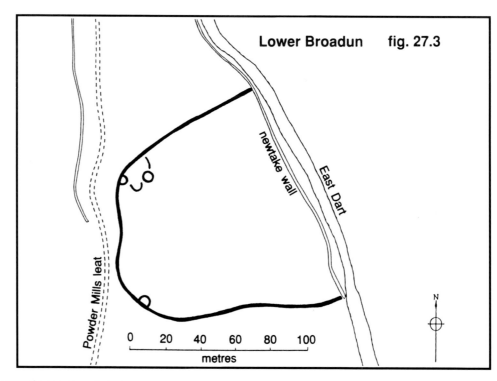

Lower Broadun   fig. 27.3

MAP 27

4 Roundy Park enclosure and cairn (fig. 27.4)

This site is best known for the massive cist outside the north-eastern wall of Roundy Park enclosure, one of the largest cists on Dartmoor. It now stands clear of the much-denuded cairn, its large size necessitating two cover stones and seven side slabs instead of the usual four. When discovered by Burnard in 1893 it had already been emptied and the contents piled alongside. Nothing was found amongst this rubble but he recovered two small fragments of flint and some burnt bones from the debris left inside. He also noticed that one of the end slabs was propped up by a 'cooking stone', perhaps one discarded from the settlement alongside. The cist has been slightly restored as Burnard re-erected two side slabs that had fallen and replaced one of the cover stones.

The cairn lies in contact with the prehistoric circuit wall, now a stony bank 0.3 m high and spread to 4.0 m across, which has been entirely overbuilt by the present dilapidated field wall. Traces of prehistoric occupation have not been completely removed from within the enclosure though no doubt much has disappeared. The probable foundations of at least 5 huts built against the outer wall yet remain, all associated with curved rubble banks which cut off small sections around the edge but leave most of the interior open.

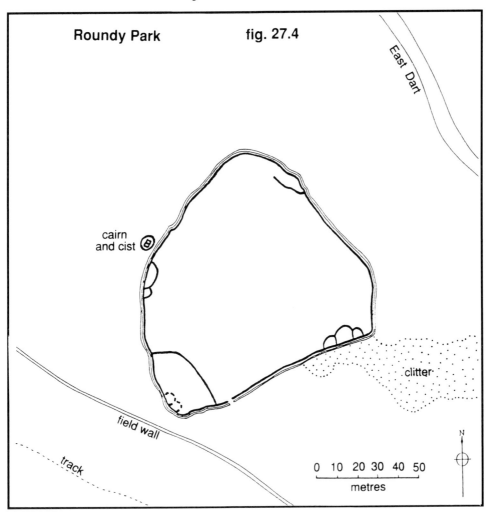

Roundy Park   fig. 27.4

MAP 27

5 Hartland Tor settlement (fig. 27.5)

In contrast to the five single enclosures visible from here on the opposite side of the East Dart valley the prehistoric settlement on Hartland Tor developed a rudimentary parallel field system. There are far fewer huts in this settlement, of which 5 have survived, but like the boundary walls they are of more massive construction. The walls of several huts are similar to those at Metherall, with a neat kerb-like inner face surrounded by much taller slabs around the outside. Banks and lines of slabs, orientated roughly east/west, cross the neck of land between the East Dart and a tributary of the Stannon Brook, extending from north of the Tor southwards probably as far as Hartyland House. North and immediately east of the Tor the walls remain in remarkably good condition and little effort would be necessary to make them once again functional barriers. Further down the eastern slope shallow trenches reveal where the ancient walls have been grubbed up to provide material for the present ones, but some of them have simply been rebuilt and incorporated into the newtakes. The reinforcement of the one nearest the summit was abandoned after 50 m and it continues uphill in the original prehistoric slabwork.

South of the Tor all that survives of the original fields are some shallow steps in the hillside with occasional slabs too large to be of use elsewhere, and a single hut (8.5 m) stranded in the centre of the newtake. North-east of the Tor is an even larger dwelling, 1 (9.0m), built of massive slabs. Beyond the partly rebuilt wall half the perimeter of another hut, 2 (c. 6.5 m), lies inside a concentric outer wall, with a fourth, 3 (5.2 m) built onto the outside. One of the jambs of hut 4 (6.5 m), is in place beside a horizontal slab topping the wall.

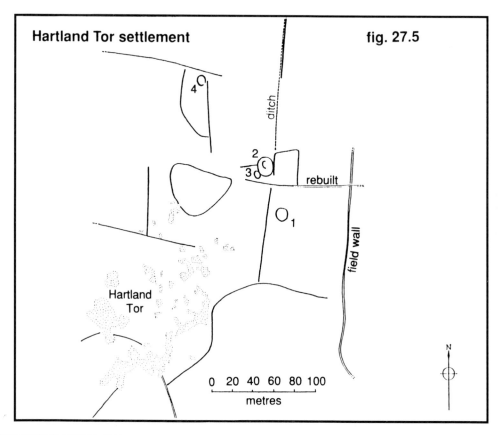

Hartland Tor settlement   **fig. 27.5**

MAP 27

6 Settlements and cairn on Arch Tor

A series of at least five small independent enclosures were laid out along the south-east slope of Arch Tor above Gawler Bottom the damp ground separating it from Lakehead Hill. One or two huts are associated with each enclosure, the paired ones differing noticeably in size. The Powder Mills leat cuts through several huts and most of the enclosures, but the banks are very slight and more sites may yet be found elsewhere on the hillside.

The solitary cairn at the western end has a deep central pit, the upcast thrown outside adding considerably to its diameter.

In 1892 an unusual find, now in Plymouth Museum, was made at Gawler Bottom by peat cutters. The Bronze ferrule of a spear dating from the late Bronze Age was found 1.2 m below the surface. It had been broken at its attachment to the shaft – perhaps the reason for its owner's loss.

7, 8 Prehistoric settlements on Lakehead Hill

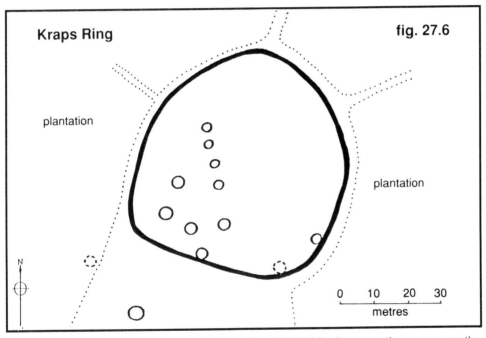

Kraps Ring fig. 27.6

plantation

plantation

0   10   20   30
metres

The greatest single disaster to befall the archaeological heritage on the moor was the afforestation of Bellever Tor and Lakehead Hill from 1930 onwards, rivalled only by the similar treatment of the South Teign valley around Fernworthy. No attempt was made to preserve more than a handful of antiquities, or even to record those that were to be over-planted. These included a number of enclosed settlements along with cairns and stone rows, many of which are unlikely ever to be relocated. Some boundary walls of the former have re-emerged in a sadly mutilated state and, as trees have been felled, their position marked by orange-topped posts.

Only one prehistoric settlement has survived moderately intact on Lakehead Hill, though two more were recorded nearby prior to afforestation. Others very likely occupied the eastern slopes in the area now covered by the Bellever Farm enclosures. Kraps Ring **7**, 120 x 113 m (fig. 27.6), lies at the northern tip of the central open area and was never over-

MAP 27

planted. A plan by Prowse in 1891 depicts 15 huts within the Ring and the tumbled remains of 11 of these are still obvious. The massive enclosure wall, much robbed, is spread to 3.0 m in places, but the original width where both faces are still in place seems to have been 2.0 m, and it must have reached well over a metre in height. The huts are of small-to-medium size (3.0–5.5 m) and several were excavated by the Dartmoor Exploration Committee in 1895. All were found to have been 'dug over' except hut 1 (4.8 m), in which the usual cooking hole and hearth were uncovered, but apparently no artefacts. A much larger hut, 2 (7.8 m), lies, significantly, outside the settlement 35 m uphill, and a fragment of the wall of another lies just within the trees to the west.

Nothing can now be seen of a second enclosure within the plantation 50 m west of the Ring. It had been pillaged for stone before 1891 by which time the hut circles had already disappeared and only the south and west walls of the enclosure were clearly traceable. Recent tree-felling has revealed two short lengths of wall of the other enclosure shown on Prowse's plan 70 m north-east of the Ring. Two huts against the eastern wall were all that remained at that date but neither has been relocated.

A single curved bank about 100 m long orientated towards a hut circle within the edge of the plantation is all that survives of a fourth enclosure which covered the south side of Lakehead Hill, **8**, This hut may be the one excavated by the Dartmoor Exploration Committee in 1896 in which charcoal and three flint flakes were found as well as some pottery shards 'like those at Legis Tor'.

9 Bellever Tor North and north-east settlements (fig. 27.7)

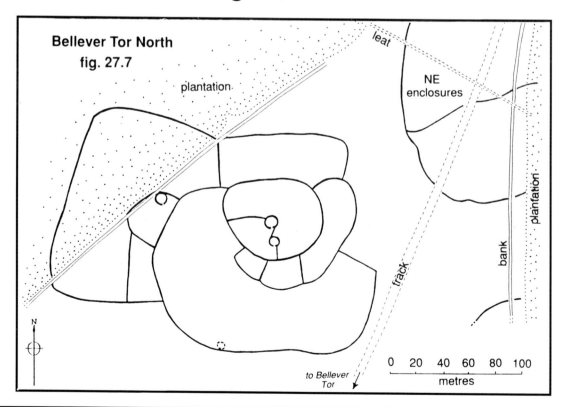

Bellever Tor North
fig. 27.7

plantation

leat

NE enclosures

plantation

bank

track

N

to Bellever Tor

0   20   40   60   80   100
metres

MAP 27

The settlement on the north-facing slope of the Tor shows the rosette type of development, with the huts and smallest fields near the centre and progressively larger enclosures added on to the outside. The largest hut (7.0 m) lies at the hub of the settlement, connected to a smaller one (5.5 m) uphill with jambs supporting each other at the entrance. A third hut (6.5 m) occupies a paddock close to the plantation and the possible remains of another small one can be detected alongside the southern outer boundary. The plan of the settlement appears to be complete but all the banks are slight and the western boundary is difficult to follow within the plantation.

A short distance across the open ground to the east can be seen the upper boundary banks of two more large and apparently independent field systems. The walls soon enter the plantation where they become impossible to trace amongst the trees. At least eight huts can be found alongside a forest path deep within the plantation downhill, but whether associated with these enclosures or part of yet another settlement is at present uncertain.

10 Black Newtake enclosure (fig. 27.8)

A single squarish enclosure occupies the lower western slope of Bellever Tor a short distance from the Cherry Brook. The circuit wall is a low overgrown bank with few stones of any size, incomplete around the northern edge next to the newtake wall. Turf covers the interior perhaps concealing the dwellings, though a flattened area against the south side may be the site of two or more huts from which all stones have been removed.

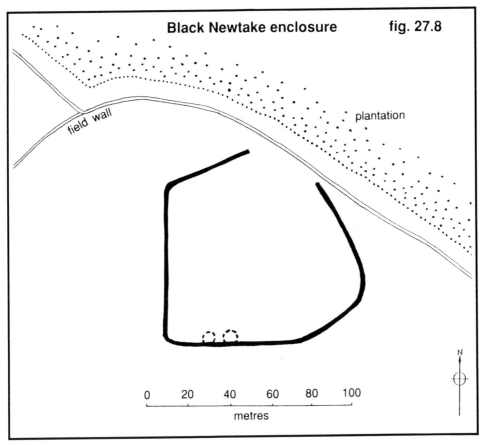

Black Newtake enclosure   fig. 27.8

MAP 27

11 Smith Hill

A prehistoric settlement of unknown size once occupied the promontory between the Cherry Brook and its tributary Smith Hill Brook, but the area has been enclosed as part of Smith Hill Farm and well cleared of obstructions. All that remains is a single hut circle (c. 6.0 m) on the eastern slope and the low banks, nowhere more than 0.3 m high, which once formed part of at least two enclosures over the summit.

12 Dunna Brookhead north and west

Two independent settlements developed on the slopes north and west of the mire around Dunna Brook spring, both of them much damaged by the pillage of stones from their walls. The west settlement was centred around a square enclosure containing a medium-sized free-standing hut (6.0 m) with an annexe (3.2 m) attached, and perhaps a second small building (3.0 m) in the western corner. Separate banks to north and south show that the original area extended further up and down the slope.

The uphill boundary of the north settlement has disappeared next to the newtake wall and much of the rest reduced to a low bank and isolated slabs. Two large fields include a single oval-shaped hut (4.5 x 3.0 m) with a yard attached to the perimeter wall.

13-16 Prehistoric settlement around Laughter Tor (figs. 27.9,10,11)

Laughter Tor is surrounded by prehistoric settlements, sited on the north **13**, north-west **14**, west **15**, east **16**, south and south-west slopes, the latter two described in **map 28**. All are overgrown and in poor condition having lost much of their stonework to the surrounding newtake walls. The best preserved is the farmstead north of the Tor, **13** (fig 27.9), on the other side of the newtake wall where very stony ground has protected it from both stone robbery and the plantation. The walls are difficult to distinguish from the surrounding clitter in places but at the centre is a roughly oval enclosure, A, up to 36 m across, surrounding a pair of huts. Both are in fair preservation, one hut (4.4 m) free-standing near the centre, the other (3.8 m) built onto the perimeter wall. An outer enclosure, B, has been added uphill, attached to a summit rock by a well-defined wall. Two banks originating on the north side of the oval disappear into the plantation and are probably the boundaries of another field, C. About 150 m to the north-west of the farmstead a small number of trees have recently been felled beside a track, exposing a few metres of walling and possible remains of hut circles, **14**.

A larger settlement **15** (fig. 27.10) lies on the easy open slope west of the Tor. A pair of huts are at the hub of at least twelve fields which increase in size away from the centre. Both door posts are present at the entrance of hut 1 (8.2 m) which faces the original gateway opening into its surrounding paddock. A pair of slabs are set across the bank here and walls outside converge to form a passageway. The other hut, 2, only about half the size (4.4 m) is built across the perimeter of an adjoining field.

The Dunnabridge track passes through the lower part of Laughter Tor East settlement **16** (fig. 27.11) which is very poorly preserved. Not only do three newtake walls cut through the site but several ditched banks show that the area was once included within earlier enclosures probably of medieval date. Not surprisingly little remains of the walls particularly on the downhill side and the original extent of the settlement is uncertain. A pair of damaged huts lie next to one of the newtake walls and another pair (3.0, 3.5 m), the larger one with an annexe, can be found a short distance uphill.

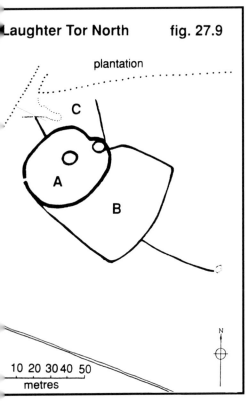

Laughter Tor North   fig. 27.9

plantation

C

A

B

10 20 30 40 50
metres

N

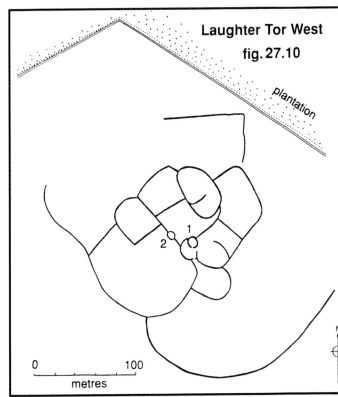

Laughter Tor West
fig. 27.10

plantation

1
2

0   100
metres

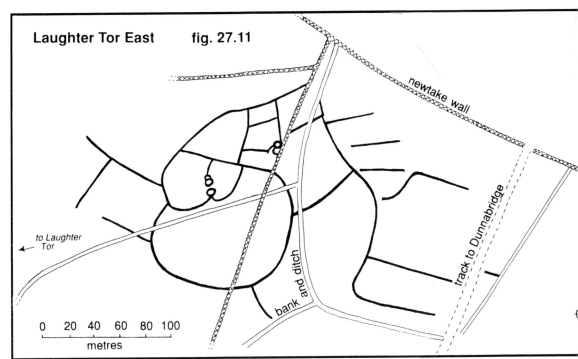

Laughter Tor East   fig. 27.11

newtake wall

to Laughter
Tor

bank and ditch

track to Dunnabridge

0   20   40   60   80   100
metres

MAP 27

17, 18 Cairns on Chittaford Down and Archerton

Three cairns lie on the hillside in the triangle between the Cherry Brook and its eastern tributary draining Rowtor bog, **17**. The lower pair are grass-covered mounds about 8.5 m in diameter with deep central pits. Although they had previously been dug into, the cairns were excavated by the Dartmoor Exploration Committee in 1891, who found that both covered a shallow central pit below the original ground surface which contained wood charcoal. In the east cairn this was mixed with a small amount of burnt bone. The third cairn north of the wall is a more complicated structure. The southern half has been broken into exposing a cist at the centre, three sides of which are still in place. The cover slab is displaced sideways but is still partly hidden under the turf which covers the untouched portion. The mound seems to have been built over an inner circle of tall slabs immediately surrounding the cist, with a second ring forming a kerb around the outside.

Two more cairns, **18**, survive on the eastern side of Chittaford Down separated by the reave known as the Great Central Trackway, but here reduced to a low rubble bank running between the East Dart and Lower White Tor 1.5 kilometres to the west. South of the point where the reave alters course to the north-east is a low irregular mound surrounded by 3 or 4 slabs of a retaining circle. A companion cairn nearby which contained a cist has entirely disappeared since it was first recorded in 1891. The second cairn 300 m to the north-east was excavated by the Dartmoor Exploration Committee in the same year as those beside the Rowtor Brook. In this case the central pit lay beneath a cist, with only three sides remaining, in which was found wood, charcoal and a flint flake. More interestingly, an archer's stone wrist-guard was recovered from under one of the side stones of the cist, no doubt lost by the wearer as he heaved the slab into place.

The cist within the Archerton enclosures was examined by Burnard some time before 1890 but it had already been dug into and nothing was discovered beyond the fact that its floor had been paved.

19 Cairns and stone rows on Lakehead Hill (figs 27.12, 13)

Ancient settlements occupy the lower slopes of Lakehead Hill but the rounded summit seems to have been reserved entirely for burial. Situated on the north side of the hill the most remarkable feature of cairn 1 (fig. 27.13.1) is the retaining circle of 13 stones, with another buried beneath the turf. Most of the cairn has been removed, some of the material having been dumped outside the south-west edge of the circle. The interior now rises only slightly above ground level, its smooth surface suggesting that the damage may have occurred centuries ago. The diameter of the circle is 6.0 m through the centre of the stones which are kerb-set around the southern edge, becoming more widely spaced around the opposite side where one slab is missing. An earthfast stone within the circle may be part of an interior setting.

All that remains of cairn 2 are the four sides of a cist (fig. 27.13.2) at the centre of a very slight mound about 10 m within the plantation. It now appears in much the same condition as when excavated by Burnard in 1898, when not only had practically all the cairn stones been carted away along with the cover slab, but the cist had been emptied of most of its contents. By clearing out the earth remaining around the sides and floor of the cist Burnard recovered a surprisingly large haul of artefacts including six flint knives and scrapers and numerous fragments of pottery from at least two vessels, one of them a much-decorated example of Beaker type. Some wood charcoal was also found but no human remains.

A stone row, 3 (fig. 27.13.3) lies close to the summit of the hill, orientated very nearly

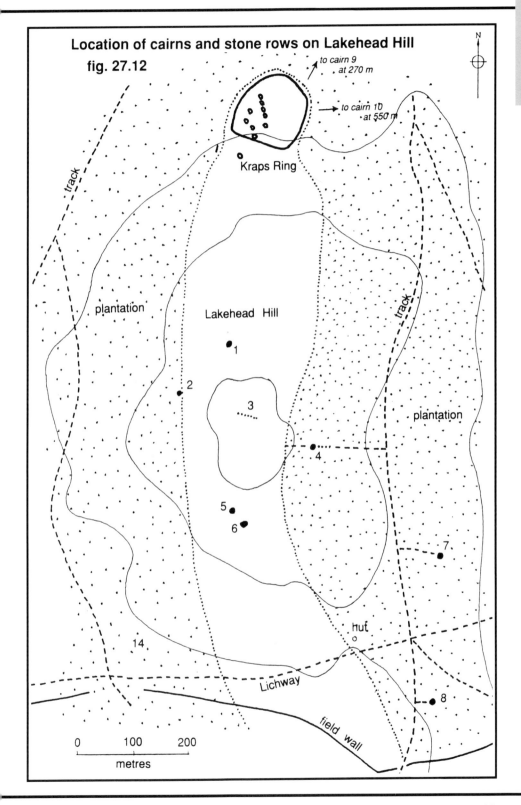

Location of cairns and stone rows on Lakehead Hill
fig. 27.12

MAP 27

MAP 27

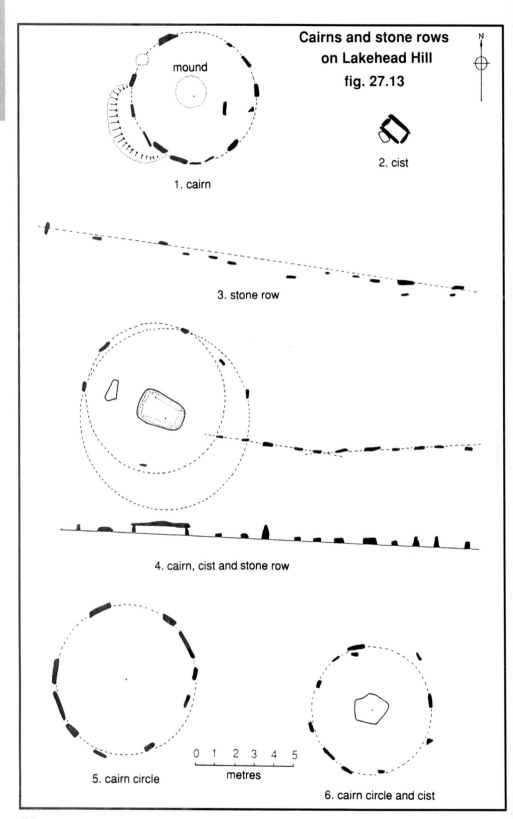

Cairns and stone rows
on Lakehead Hill
fig. 27.13

N

mound

1. cairn

2. cist

3. stone row

4. cairn, cist and stone row

5. cairn circle

0 1 2 3 4 5
metres

6. cairn circle and cist

MAP 27

east/west. Only 12 stones stand in line, with spaces for another 3 or 4. Two slabs on edge alongside the eastern pair are more likely to be packing stones than the remains of a second row. The irregular spacing and remarkably poor alignment suggests that the stones may have been re-erected out of position by some unknown antiquary in the past. If a cairn once terminated the row it had been completely removed before the monument was first recorded and no trace of it now remains. The site is level and the cairn could have been at either end, the stone at right-angles to the end of the row being either a blocking stone or the remaining slab of a retaining circle.

A muddy track leads through the plantation to the circle, cist and stone row 4 (fig. 27.13.4). The row runs downhill from the cist of five slabs topped with a massive capstone and surrounded by a retaining circle of which six stones remain. The cairn material had been entirely removed long before the Dartmoor Exploration Committee re-erected the cist and many of the stones in 1895. The restoration was probably inaccurate and at least one of the circle stones seems to have been misplaced outwards giving the impression that the row starts from within the circumference. The smaller circle shown on the plan best fits the majority of stones (diam. 6.7 m) but places the cist well off-centre. In addition to the 11 stones of the row the sockets of two more were uncovered in 1895 but these are no longer visible. An exceptional feature is the marked alteration of course northwards after the fifth stone. Rather surprisingly, although the Committee's description of the cist as 'perfect' must be taken as an exaggeration considering all the stones were flat when found, there was no mention of any artefacts being recovered during the restoration.

Two well preserved circles are conspicuous on the hillside south of the summit. The upper circle, 5 (fig. 27.13.5), 6.8 m in diameter, consists of 10 erect slabs with spaces for perhaps 4 others surrounding an almost flat interior. There is no sign of a central cist but about 40 m to the south-east of the circle 3 or 4 slabs in line are probably the remains of a stone row. Individual slabs of similar size are however fairly numerous in the vicinity. The second circle, 6 (fig. 27.13.6) diameter 5.6 m, and also with 10 slabs, lies 16 m to the south-east. Much of the interior is taken up by the large cover slab of a cist, excavated by the Dartmoor Exploration Committee in 1896, but 'nothing was found'. Like its companion circle a stone row 'apparently' led away to the south-east for 50-60 m but this can no longer be traced.

Cairn 7 (c. 19.0 x 0.9 m) lies in a clearing deep within the plantation on the east side of the hill. It seems to have been large but has been so badly damaged that its original size is impossible to estimate. The stones and earth have been scattered in all directions exposing two sides of an exceptionally large cist in a hollow now well off-centre. Both cover and end stones are gone though the only large slab lying on the edge of the mound may be one of the latter. The tops of a few stones on an arc around the north edge of the mound seem to belong to an outer ring. Worth (Barrow Report 54) supposed this cairn to be identical to one recorded in the *Transactions of the Devonshire Association* for 1895 and 1896, but the latter was described as in fine condition within a double circle and having a stone row orientated to the north-west. It seems possible that this one still remains hidden within the plantation. Also awaiting re-discovery are the 3 ruined cairns (11-13) excavated by the Dartmoor Exploration Committee in 1901 'near the large cairn on Lakehead Hill' which presumably refers to cairn 7. One of these, 40 m to the east of the large cairn, covered a shallow pit containing wood charcoal but the others yielded nothing at all.

All that remains of cairn 8 are the two sides and an end slab of a cist on a very slight mound in a clearing in the plantation. Burnard re-erected the side slabs which were lying flat and excavated the cist in 1914, but it had already been thoroughly rifled. No artefacts were found but the infill contained charcoal, and more was recovered from a shallow pit dug below floor level at the centre of the cist.

Even less survives of cairn 9, 270 m north-east of Kraps Ring, merely the single side slab of a cist surrounded by slight traces of a cairn. Cairn 10 lies outside the plantation

MAP 27

below the road, 550 m east of Kraps Ring. It was first recorded in 1891 and even then was a very ragged mound with much of the material thrown out into a second pile downhill. A solitary hut circle (c. 7.0 m) lies 70 m to the north.

Worth records yet another stone row on the south-west side of Lakehead Hill, 14, but this area has been overplanted and nothing can now be seen of it. The row was about 123 m long orientated to the north-west and without any associated cairn. The number of rows on the hill before the plantation is uncertain as the records are confusing but all seem to have been single and some at least descend from a cairn and cist at the higher end.

20 Bellever Tor cairns (fig. 27.14)

The distribution of the surviving cairns on Bellever Tor is limited to the western and south-western slopes. This part of the hillside is noticeably free of surface stone and most of the cairns have been regarded as a useful source of material by the newtake wall builders. The best preserved is cairn 1 on the edge of the plantation west of Bellever Tor. When first recorded in 1890 it had already been dug into with the up-cast thrown out to the north side, giving it an egg-shaped outline, and the cover slab shifted sideways exposing three sides of a cist. The retaining circle was said to be in fair condition at that date but only 3 of its members now stand clear of the turf, with another perhaps of an inner ring surrounding the cist. The debris remaining in the cist was examined by the Dartmoor Exploration Committee in 1901 but 'nothing was found'.

Cairn 2 is possibly not an artificial mound at all but merely some heather-covered rocks which abound on the hillside here. Its artifical nature is suggested by the two stones at its base which could be part of a retaining circle and an unnatural looking slab 6 m uphill, orientated slightly off-centre. Cairn 3 lies beyond the wall in the enclosure known as Black Newtake. Of its retaining circle only two pairs of stones on opposite sides of the cist show above the turf, though very likely others are buried in place. The cist is complete apart from the lack of a cover slab. Cairn 4 is a ring cairn, a circular rubble bank about 11 m across and 0.5 m high surrounding an interior raised slightly above the outside ground surface. A single slab faces the circle 4.5 m away to the south-east. Cairn 5 is a substantial mound still a metre high, trenched at ground level from the north edge into the centre but with no sign of a cist.

Only 7 slabs remain around the north-east edge of cairn 6 though others seem to be under the turf on the opposite side. One side and end slab of the cist are also missing. Cairn 7 is a doubtful site but similar to ring cairn 4, with an outer diameter of 13 m. A trench cuts through the bank on the south side and the interior seems to have been scooped out, presumably as a source of stone. A surprising feature is the shallow ditch outside the bank which must be of comparatively recent date. The cist of cairn 8 was described as an imperfect ruin even in 1890 and only a few scattered stones mark its approximate site today.

Cairn 9 is a very slight mound with a small central cist, all four stones in place but with the cover slab missing. There is no trace of a retaining circle but the two stones outside the long sides of the cist probably form part of an inner ring. All that remains of cairn 10 is a single side slab of a cist separated by a trench from the backing stones which once supported the opposite side-stone.

21-23 Tinning in the Postbridge district

In contrast to the enormous workings in the neighbouring valleys to the east, the Walla Brook and the West Webburn, the East Dart and its tributaries were remarkably unproductive of tin between its junction with Lade Hill Brook and the small Brimpts mine near Dartmeet. Rather oddly there is some evidence that this rather barren stretch of river was the site of one or perhaps two blowing houses for smelting the tin ore.

MAP 27

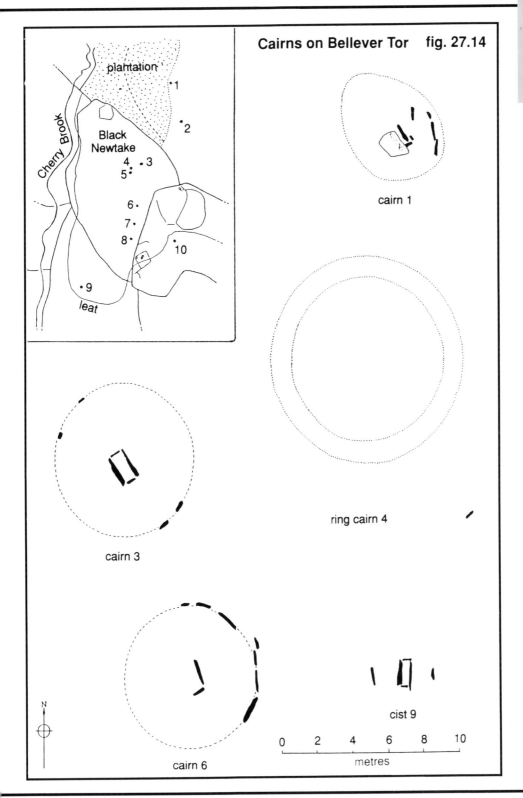

Cairns on Bellever Tor   fig. 27.14

plantation

Cherry Brook

Black
Newtake

4 . 3
5 .

6 .

7 .

8 .

. 10

. 9
leat

cairn 1

cairn 3

ring cairn 4

cist 9

cairn 6

N

0   2   4   6   8   10

metres

MAP 28

Just west of the bridge at Postbridge the track to Bellever passes a small quarry at little more than 100 m from the road, **21**. The building foundations here, known as the Barracks, were constructed in the nineteenth century to house the miners employed in the eastern valleys and were reputed to stand on the site of a blowing house. A leat to the site and a single mould stone for casting ingots are all that remain, the latter embedded in the turf beside the track about 6 m from the wall. A second mould stone of similar size used to lie a few metres away but has disappeared within the last few years.

Burnard reported the ruins of another blowing house alongside the Stannon Brook, a little way above the bridge connecting Hartyland and Ringhill with Merrypit. The foundations here are no longer recognizable but an up-ended mould stone can still be seen built into the field wall 80 m from the bridge, **22**.

In 1901 the Dartmoor Exploration Committee excavated a rectangular sunken hut (4 x 2.2 m) dug into the side of a bank about 50 m from the East Dart, **23**. The site lies 300 m from the road in Greyhound Marsh. Flints and some lumps of corroded iron were found on the original floor level, together with some shards of a cooking vessel which the excavators dated to perhaps the thirteenth or fourteenth century. The size and style are not those of a longhouse of the period and they suggested it was built by tin streamers as a summer shelter. The rectangular pit and entrance passage are still visible, though perhaps not for long as it is being used as a rubbish dump.

The main road continues westwards from Postbridge to Higher Cherrybrook bridge, the position of the latter determined by the streamworks which commence immediately above it. Apart from the low-lying area near Powder Mills Farm the streamworks are confined to a narrow band alongside the river and, higher up, its feeder from Rowtor bog.

MAP 28 The Dunnabridge Area

1 Dunnabridge Pound

The present pound is a celebrated antiquity in its own right and was in existence long before its first mention in 1342 when the bailiff paid 3d. for a new lock to the gate[31]. In the four annual drifts it was to here that horses and cattle pastured illegally on the east, south and west quarters of the moor were brought, those on the north quarter being taken to Creaber pound below Buttern Hill. Owners were fined before the livestock could be reclaimed and both lock and pound keeper were necessary to discourage irate farmers from breaking into the pound to reclaim their property, as happened in a court case presented in 1512 when John Cole and his men 'riotously took and drove away 16 steers'[31]. The stocks for the intransigent, recorded as needing repair in 1660, were probably sited on the green outside, but the holed stone which Crossing found nearby and suggested might have been for securing their legs seems to have disappeared. Immediately to the left of the gate within the enclosure is the covered pound-keeper's bench known as the 'Judges Chair', said to have been brought from Crockern Tor. More probably the slabs originated much closer on the slopes of Laughter Tor, from which the gradient is all downhill and where similar slabs can still be found.

The present wall closely follows that of its prehistoric predecessor, which forms its foundation below the downhill section but is visible as a low bank inside the wall around the rest of the perimeter. Centuries of use and probably deliberate clearance have left few traces of the settlement within. Some scattered stony mounds are perhaps the remains of interior walls or dwellings, two of which are still recognisable. A short length of ancient

MAP 28

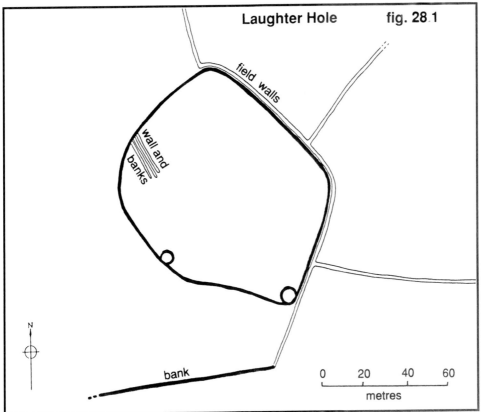

Laughter Hole   fig. 28.1

field walls

wall and banks

N

bank

0   20   40   60

metres

walling descends the slope from the edge of a hut lying a few metres from the eastern perimeter and the circular outline of the second can be distinguished against the north bank.

Dunnabridge is the largest of a group of five similar enclosures (**1-5**) all within 2 kilometres, each surrounded by a massive wall with an undivided interior and containing very few huts.

2 Laughter Hole (fig. 28.1)

Shallow grooves of ridge and furrow show that the prehistoric pound south of Winford Brook has, like its large neighbour Dunnabridge, been re-used in more recent times. A newtake wall closely follows the eastern perimeter but diverges away from the pound on the south side to continue in a straight line for about 40 m. Here it alters course westwards on the back of an ancient reave in the direction of the prehistoric enclosure south of Laughter Tor, but this section was never completed and has itself been robbed.

The ancient pound wall has been reduced to a very low bank alongside the newtake, but it was obviously substantial and is now spread to 3.5 m wide and stands up to 0.5 m high. For no obvious reason a short length of later walling is built inwards at an acute angle from the northern edge. Only two huts have been found within the pound. The smaller (c. 3.0 m) lies midway along the uphill edge but only a few slabs on end remain of the other, tucked into the south-east corner. There was probably never more than a small number of huts for it seems unlikely that many would have been cleared without trace when so much of the bank has survived.

MAP 28

3. Brimpts North

South-east of Laughter Hole enclosure the corner of the adjacent newtake wall follows part of the circumference of another prehistoric pound. The gradient is particularly steep and the ancient bank has slipped down the slope to spread over 5 m of the hillside with only the largest slabs clinging to their original position. The foundations of a pair of adjoining huts are just visible against the uphill wall. Shallow furrows 3 m apart score the interior, continuing over the lower boundary and probably associated with the bank and ditch added onto the south side of the pound.

4. Huccaby Ring

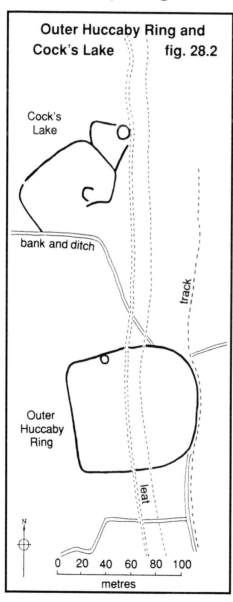

Outer Huccaby Ring and Cock's Lake   fig. 28.2

Cock's Lake

bank and ditch

track

Outer Huccaby Ring

leat

N

0 20 40 60 80 100

metres

About halfway along the track from the road near Huccaby Cottage leading to the Tor the path mounts a slight step in the hillside, the perimeter wall of Huccaby Ring. This prehistoric enclosure has sadly deteriorated since it warranted an individual name and now is probably not often noticed by those using the track which crosses its southern edge. Apart from a few massive slabs the wall stones have been removed and the rubble core allowed to collapse into a low turf-covered bank, surrounding an almost circular interior about 46 x 47 m across. Some stony mounds within may be the remains of huts but none are identifiable now.

5. Outer Huccaby Ring (fig. 28.2)

Three medieval banks with ditches butt onto this prehistoric enclosure incorporating its uphill boundary, which seems to have been reinforced as part of the later enclosure walls. Apart from the Brimpts mine leats which were cut through the centre of the pound in the mid-nineteenth century it remains otherwise undamaged. The original wall width of the prehistoric enclosure was 1.8 m between the outer faces but it has spread to 2.5 m in places and stands to almost a metre above ground level on the downhill side. The only building to be seen is a small hut (c. 4.0 m) against the north wall, though the considerable build-up of soil to the top of the lower wall may perhaps hide further structures here.

About a kilometre to the north the standing stone at the west end of Laughter Tor stone row is a prominent object on the skyline.

MAP 28

6. Cock's Lake enclosure and cairn (fig. 28.2)

A hundred metres north of Outer Huccaby Ring the double enclosure of Cock's Lake, though smaller in area, contains two medium-sized huts. The circuit wall is more irregular and less substantial, about 0.3 m high and spread to a metre across with a section of the southern boundary missing, probably robbed when the later bank-with-ditch was constructed across the south edge. A third of the circumference of the hut (7.2 m) in the larger enclosure is also missing but the other hut (6.7 m), on the edge of the leat, is in exceptionally good condition with its wall still standing over a metre high.

Banks project the walls beyond the enclosures to form the boundaries of outer fields, one of them continuing over the ridge in the direction of Laughter Hole. 300 m to the south-east another reave, barely visible on the ground, runs up the north slope on precisely the same orientation as the major reaves across Riddon Ridge (**map 18**), continuing the field system between the two Darts. Over the crest it alters course towards Huccaby Tor before regaining the alignment down to the West Dart.

A stony mound on the edge of the leat 150 m to the north is probably a prehistoric cairn. It has been dug into and the stones scattered outwards from a central pit, but there is no sign of a cist. Possibly this is the ruined cairn that Burnard 'examined in Brimpts newtake but without result'.

7 Laughter Tor South

The low bank of a small single enclosure lies just south of the excavations around Brimpts mine. Not surprisingly little remains here but a circular pit across the boundary wall is probably the site of a hut. A reave connects the outer, roughly square, enclosure to Laughter Hole pound 700 m to the east.

8 Laughter Tor South-west (fig.28.3)

An extensive settlement once covered the south-west slopes of Laughter Tor but the walls have been quarried for stone and are now reduced to banks no more than 0.2 m high. No trace of any hut dwellings can be found.

9, 10 Brownberry

Prehistoric settlements also existed south of the road alongside the West Dart but the fields here have been almost entirely cleared. Their extent is unknown but reaves east and west of Huccaby Ring continue as the present field walls on this side and suggest it was considerable. On the riverside below the field boundaries the public footpath from Dunnabridge passes through a curved line of slabs forming part of a double enclosure, **9**, around a single hut (c. 5.0 m). Further east a second hut (c. 9.0 m) lies in the angle between two field walls, **10**, but its associated enclosures have been completely swept away.

11 Lower Cherrybrook Bridge

On the hillside 350 m north-east of the bridge is a damaged hut circle (c. 6.0 m), barely 0.3 m high and with about a third of the circumference missing. The slopes are noticeably clear of surface stone and there are no traces of associated fields in the vicinity.

MAP 28

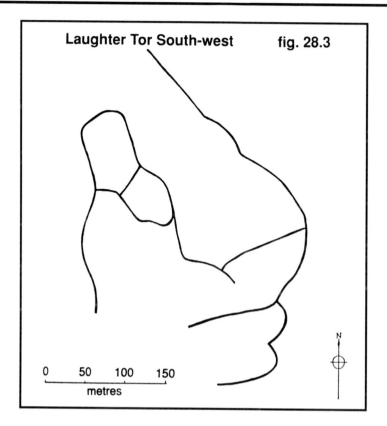

Laughter Tor South-west   fig. 28.3

0   50   100   150
metres

N

12 Laughter Tor stone rows and cairns (fig. 28.4)

Two double stone rows once descended the slope south of Laughter Tor, one originating at the longstone the other a short distance to the south orientated roughly parallel but now almost completely buried. The former is split into two sections with the central portion almost entirely missing. Grooves and pits mark the site of many of the missing stones, their fate clearly being the newtake wall which crosses the alignment, though some damage must have been caused by an earlier ditch associated with the medieval enclosures to the north-east. The longstone, 2.4m high, sited below the crest and visible at a considerable distance from south and east, was re-erected slightly out of alignment to the axis of the rows. It stands at the centre of a small cairn (c. 7.0 x 0.3 m) excavated by Burnard in 1903, who found 'a great quantity of charcoal and peat ashes, or what appeared to be peat ashes, underneath'.

An interval of 17 m separates the longstone from the first group of 8 small stones the largest only 45 cm high, set in two rows 1.7 m apart. There is then a long gap of 120 m in which only three stones have escaped removal. The final group of 14 stones increase in size towards a large slab 1.27 m high at the lower end, probably the original termination or very close to it. The present length of the rows at 164 m is therefore likely to be the original one. Downhill a few more slabs on a different alignment may possibly have been part of another structure, too close to the track to have survived intact.

The second double row is merely a fragment starting about 12 m west of the longstone, the stones just visible level with the turf. Five pairs spaced about 1.4 m apart, with gaps for

MAP 28

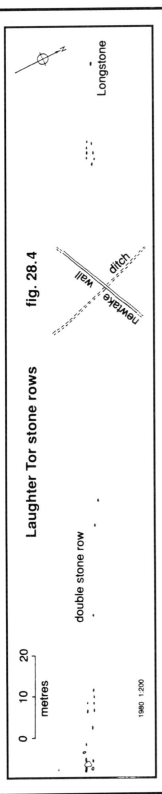

fig. 28.4

Laughter Tor stone rows

Longstone

newtake wall

ditch

double stone row

20

10

metres

0

1980 1:200

2 more pairs, can be traced for about 10 m towards the crest of the ridge on a similar orientation to the first double row, but too far out of alignment to be a continuation. No doubt it continues under the turf but there are no obvious terminals indicating its original extent in either direction,the overgrowth being such that even a small cairn could have become completely buried.

Unlocated in the vicinity are the eight small cairns without retaining circles recorded by Burnard south of Laughter Tor but within the same newtake. He excavated three of these in 1903, all of them covering pits containing charcoal 'nearly a wheelbarrowful' in one of them. The mouths of the pits were protected by little pyramids of small stones angled inwards.

13, 7, 14 Brimpts Mine

Already by 1800 Joseph Sanders was producing a small amount of tin on the Brimpts estate, though he terminated the enterprise after a few years following a disagreement with the miners.[30] Interest in the sett reawakened in 1849 when the shaft and adit were extended and a water-wheel constructed on the hillside above the farm. The wheel was fed from a leat 6 kilometres long taken off the Cherry Brook at a point west of Bellever Tor and can still be followed from here to the edge of the plantation. A small holding-reservoir was constructed along the leat north-east of Dunnabridge Pound and a slight error in the gradient east of Cock's Lake necessitated a 500 m length having to be re-cut a few metres uphill. The leat divides about 100 m before entering the plantation where it is lost amidst the trees, a few stones at the junction remaining at the site of the hatch for controlling the flow of water through the channel. The course of the leat can be picked up again some distance within the plantation, leading towards the wheel pit **13** which is still well preserved and wired off for safety.

The sett extended far beyond the Brimpts enclosures and included the ground from the East Dart to the Cherry Brook and northwards from the West Dart to Bellever Tor. Within two or three years the adventurers opened a second shaft 1800 m to the north-west on the southern slope of Laughter Tor which was eventually sunk to 26 fathoms. Now water-filled, it lies near the end of a line of pits close to the Dunnabridge to Laughter Hole track and has also been wired off, **7**. South of the shaft can be seen the slight ditch and bank for the flat rods which connected the pumps draining the mine with the water wheel 340 m directly downhill, **14**. The wheel, supplied from the leat a few metres away, has of course gone and the sides of the pit are beginning to collapse. Dressing floors lie nearby and, lower down, the foundations of a building.

Though reasonably productive, ownership of the mine changed hands several times before the workings were abandoned in 1855 after only 6 years of operation.

MAP 29

MAP 29 West Dart north of Two Bridges

1-8, 17, 18 West Dart settlements and cairns

Above Two Bridges Bronze Age colonization proceeded up the valley as far north as Rough Tor, with a remarkable concentration on the east side below Littaford and Longaford Tors, **1** (fig. 29.1). Here no less than 18 small enclosures and 80 huts can be found within 1.5 kilometres sandwiched between two belts of clitter, the easy availability of surface stone of appropriate size probably contributing to the attractions of the site. About half the huts are free-standing, the rest being built around the edge of the enclosures which in some cases is simply a clitter barrier. Apart from hut 1 all of them are very similar, ranging in size from 2.5 to 5.0 m in diameter, the great majority being under 4.0 m. Many have gaps in the south wall at the site of the entrance, occasionally with jambs in place, and a few incorporate natural boulders in their perimeter.

Immediately downhill from the centre of the settlement is the ancient grove of oak trees, Wistman's Wood, a curious survival of the forests that once spread up the valleys and which must have been a familiar environment to the early Dartmoor farmers. That oak was once widespread on the high moorland is shown by the trunks occasionally unearthed by peat cutters and by the oak charcoal recovered by archaeologists from the hearths of the hut dwellers. Its survival here is due to the support and protection against the elements and browsing animals provided by the massive granite boulders on the hillside, and also not a little to the absence of tin streaming in the valley below. The stunted and distorted growth of the trees was extraordinary enough for Risdon in the early seventeenth century to have included them as one of the 'three remarkable things' on Dartmoor, the other two being Crockern Tor and Childe's Tomb. Recently the wood has markedly increased in area and the trees in height.

The position of hut 1 (6.8 m) right at the southern end of the settlement emphasises its importance. It is much larger and more substantially built than the others and opens into its own private enclosure, a jamb stone still standing at the entrance. About 120 m uphill to the south-east is a badly damaged cairn with much of the interior scooped out revealing an earthfast slab near the centre. A larger triangular slab lies rejected on the mound but the rest of the missing material has been carted away. Immediately downhill a rectangular platform of small longhouse proportions (9.5 x 4.2 m) has been levelled into the hillside but very little of the superstructure survives.

None of the huts has been excavated and, apart from the local damage caused by a newtake wall crossing the southern end of the site, the settlement has suffered comparatively little interference. A rabbit warren was established here in 1895 by the tenant of Powder Mills Farm but was operational for only a few years. At least twenty-six buries are interspersed amidst the huts and on the hillside above. Most of them are long mounds orientated down the slope but a few near the centre are round, similar to cairns but distinguished from them by an encircling ditch. The foundations of the warren house and garden can be seen at the north end of the settlement. A much smaller warren lies downstream on the hillside above Crockern farm. The five long buries here are very solidly constructed, the one cut through by the track being a gigantic 90 m long. A third warren lies across the valley within the grounds of Beardown Farm.

Beardown Farm takes up the triangle of land north of the junction of Cowsic and West Dart rivers and was enclosed in about 1780 by Edward Bray, the father of Rev. E. Bray, vicar of Tavistock. The latter is best remembered for the selections from his diaries

Littaford Tors West   fig. 29.1

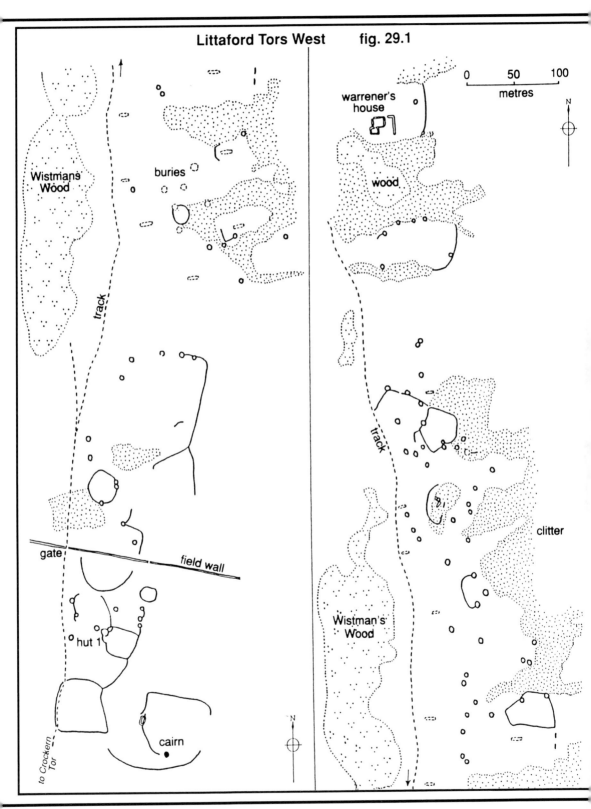

0   50   100
metres

N

warrener's
house

wood

Wistmans
Wood

buries

track

gate

field wall

hut 1

to Crockern Tor

cairn

N

track

clitter

Wistman's
Wood

61

MAP 29

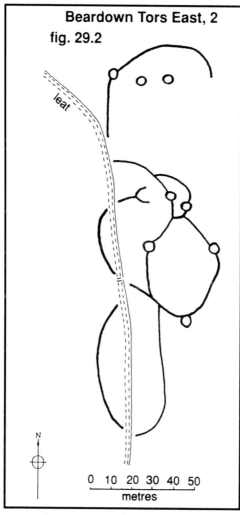

Beardown Tors East, 2

fig. 29.2

leat

N

0 10 20 30 40 50

metres

published by his wife in her letters to Robert Southey, recording contemporary events on Dartmoor and his druidical theories.[22] A more eccentric whim was to 'people the desert' of the Cowsic valley by having his poetry inscribed on the boulders in and around the stream and to 'consecrate particular rocks to particular persons', To Cicero, To Shakespeare, etc. Some of the inscribed boulders beside the bridge, dotted on the map, can still be read though most of the inscriptions are hidden below a covering of moss. His diaries record a number of antiquities that have disappeared including one or more settlements on the site of the farm itself 'destroyed when my father erected his ring-fence'.

The settlements on this, west, side of the valley are more widely dispersed with upwards of a kilometre separating most of them. The main exceptions are the two single unconnected enclosures set high above the river east of the plantation, of similar size and only about 70 m apart. The south enclosure, **2**, with five huts (2.5-4.0 m) on an exceptionally steep slope facing south-east is partly covered by the plantation. The other, **3**, contains only two huts (3.0, 4.0 m) but a third larger dwelling (5.0 m), a few metres outside the south wall, has been dug into at some time. Settlement **4** once consisted of at least two enclosures but only occasional slabs in line on a very slight bank reveal their outline, the upper boundary having been destroyed during construction of the Devonport leat. The five huts (2.5-5.0 m) that remain are all outside the circuit wall nearer the river. Settlement **5** (fig. 29.2), also cut through by the leat but rather better preserved, consists of eight huts (3-4.0 m) within at least four small enclosures.

The perimeter wall surrrounding settlement **6** is still more or less continuous. Banks sub-divide the interior into three unequal parts but the expected hut foundations have so far not been discovered. Settlement **7**, sheltered from the westerlies at the bottom of a steep hillside, is very overgrown. Most of the uphill walls have disappeared under the turf and only two huts (2.5, 4.0 m) remain visible, though almost certainly others here are hidden from view. Settlement, **8**, at 500 m above sea level one of the highest on the moor, is in a similar situation and condition, on rising ground less than 50 m from the river. A tinners' leat on the way to a hillside gert 700 m downstream cuts across the uphill edge close to four of the five huts (2.5-4.3 m). Four of these were 'explored' by the Dartmoor Exploration Committee in 1898 but only one produced any artefacts and rather more prolifically than usual; fragments of pottery, cooking stones, much charcoal and some flints, including two scrapers and a tanged and barbed arrowhead. The others show comparatively little sign of disturbance and may not have been very thoroughly excavated, which may explain the lack of finds.

MAP 29

East of Lydford Tor a cairn, **17**, with a cist empty and exposed lies 20 m from the edge of a tinners' gully. Both side and an end slab are in place and about half the retaining circle, 4.5 m across, shows above the turf. A much better preserved cairn, **18**, with a noticeably off-centred cist lies on the south-west side of Crow Tor. The cist is almost square with all four sides in place and the cover slab levered to one side. The small retaining circle, 4.0 m across, is complete and most unusually many of the cairn stones remain to the height of the capstone. Baring-Gould in about 1900 found it in much the same condition as at present but was able to recover a flint scraper from the remaining debris.

9-12 Cherry Brook west bank settlements and cairns

The valley of the Cherry Brook was never as densely populated as the neighbouring valleys of East and West Dart and the few settlements that exist have not survived in good condition. The largest, **9** (fig. 29.3) lies on the west bank just north of Lower Cherry Brook

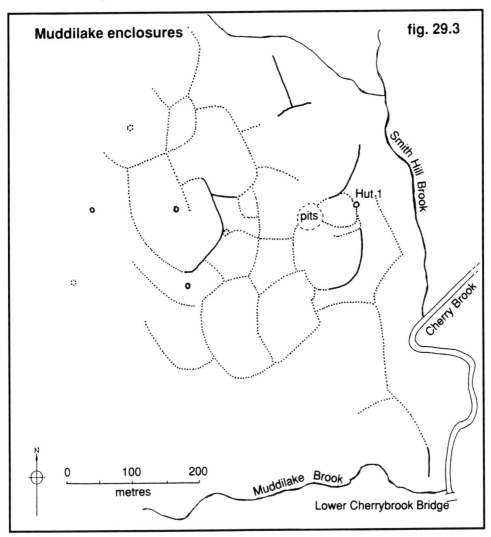

Muddilake enclosures

fig. 29.3

Smith Hill Brook

Hut 1

pits

Cherry Brook

N

0   100   200

metres

Muddilake Brook

Lower Cherrybrook Bridge

MAP 29

bridge and once covered the summit and eastern flank of Muddilake, the low rounded hill sandwiched between the brook and its first two tributaries. Some shallow trenches and a few disconnected lines of stones, mostly too large to have been of use elsewhere, are all that can be seen of the enclosures on the ground, but the pattern shows up clearly on aerial photographs and even from the opposite hillside when the light is favourable. Only hut 1 (6.9 m) of large stones and sited nearest the river is in reasonable condition. Three more higher up the hillside have had the wall stones removed and are reduced to low circular banks 9.0-11.0 m across. The sites of at least three others are visible from the air but the original total was probably higher.

Before its final rapid descent down to the Cherry Brook, the Muddilake flows through a wide boggy plain from its source in Crockern newtakes. South of the spring a circular bank of earth and small stones, **10** (c. 9.0 m), occupies the high ground facing down the valley, perhaps a ring cairn but more likely the sole remnant of a homestead whose field walls have been entirely cleared away.

North of Powder Mills Farm lie the Stennen Hill settlements, **11**, apparently two unconnected enclosures with huts and now separated by a newtake wall. In the lower settlement the foundations of six huts can be detected a few metres below the wall but its circuit boundary has all but disappeared, the missing stones no doubt doing duty in the modern replacement. The shell of a deserted farmhouse and byre straddles the wall of the upper enclosure, a feeble structure of mainly a single line of slabs set in a low bank. Three huts are attached to the wall with another standing free near the centre (3.0–4.0m). A hundred metres to the east is the first of a pair of slightly larger huts (c. 5.0 m) with entrances downhill, the nearest having a peculiarly pointed jamb stone.

Only 8 m north-east of the second hut a kerb circle surrounds a well-preserved cairn and cist with all four side slabs in place and cover slab tilted to one side. A second cairn and cist about 70 m downhill has not survived so well, only one side slab remaining next to a pit in the centre of the mound. It may have been one of these cairns in which, according to the Rev. Bray, who did not seem to entirely believe the story, a 'pot of money' was discovered by two labourers engaged in removing the stones.[22] The pot may well have been one of the Bronze Age cremation urns commonly found in cairns but the money is more difficult to explain. The cairn on Yar Tor known as The Money Pit suggests a similar find and the Rev. Bray records that some time before 1827 the uncle of one of his tenants, Hanniford, had found some silver coins 'about the size of a sixpence' in several cairns including one on White Tor to the north that has not been relocated. That 'money' was to be found in cairns seems to have been a common belief founded on fact and may well explain why so many were dug into before the early nineteenth century. Also on the same tor and at about the same date an even more curious find of some human hair was made in a cist that was being demolished, a find that was repeated when Soussons Down cairn was excavated in 1903 (**24.2**.6) and a probable example of witchcraft. Coins were unlikely to be confused with Bronze Age grave goods such as were presumably found in the Crock of Gold cairn on Royal Hill or the gold-studded dagger from Hamel Down, and the silver in particular must be a later deposit, perhaps another manifestation of the same belief.

About 700 m to the north a single hut settlement, **12**, (c. 4.0 m) with triple enclosures occupies a shelf on the hillside above the Cherry Brook.

13-15,a Settlements along the Cowsic and Beardown Man

The four or five settlements in the underpopulated Cowsic valley are small affairs, grouped closely together alongside the upper reaches of the river. The northernmost, **13**, is a double

MAP 29

enclosure with five huts (2.5-4.0 m) and includes much dead ground in the form of a rock pile. The course of the river here is confined within steep banks and can have barely altered over the millenia since the two huts perched on its edge were constructed. An outlying hut (3.0 m) lies 250 m upstream associated with very slight traces of walling and probably belongs to a separate settlement.

A short distance downstream at Broad Hole the valley opens out as the steep slopes of Lydford Tor recede to the east and the river begins to meander across the flat boggy plain below Beardown Tors. Here, set on a knoll on either side of the river, two minute homesteads guard the defile. Each is a single oval enclosure less than 25 m across at most with a tiny hut (2.5 m) built across the line of the circuit wall, too feeble to have been more than a token barrier. Much of the interior of the one on the eastern bank is taken up by a large mound which does not appear to be entirely natural and at some period has been trenched. The uphill boundary has disappeared from a larger enclosure, **14**, occupying a similar position on the west bank less than 100 m downstream. Three huts (3.0–4.0 m) are built across its perimeter wall but more unusually it includes a cairn within the walls, still substantial despite having been dug into.

Apart from these comparatively trivial relics the Cowsic valley can claim one major antiquity, Beardown Man, **15**, a massive granite slab high above the river on the edge of a featureless plateau below Devils Tor. The depth of peat here has reduced its original height by at least a metre to its present 3.5 m. Another stone of prehistoric interest has been built into Long Plantation wall about 300 m north of the road, **a**. This block, obviously brought here from somewhere in the vicinity and painted for some reason with the number 81, has been identified by Greeves as a cup-marked boulder, one of only three so far recognised on the moor. Fourteen circular or oval 'cups' can be identified on its exposed face, four of them particularly well formed.

16 Higher White Tor stone rows (fig. 29.4)

Only twelve stones of this double row remain in place, rather less than the twenty-one recorded by the Dartmoor Exploration Committee in 1898. Some have fallen since then and twenty-four can now be found lying flat, many of them covered by turf. It was probably of the Hurston Ridge type with a cairn at the upper end but no trace of this remains, though it is likely to have been close to the present end of the rows as a short distance uphill some large earth-fast blocks interrupt the alignment. The lower terminus is also indeterminate and the present length of

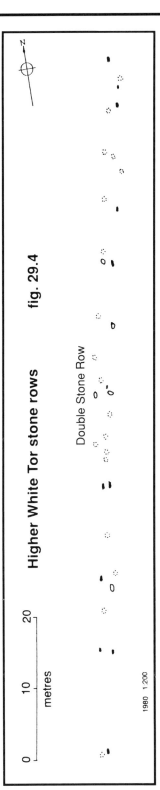

fig. 29.4

Higher White Tor stone rows

Double Stone Row

metres

0 10 20

1980 1 200

MAP 29

95.4 m must be only a fraction of the original. The surrounding hillside seems to have been swept clear of small surface stones and the damage to the monument may well have been caused by the builders of the nearby newtake wall. The rows are set about 1.4 m apart but too few stones remain standing to estimate the intervals along the rows.

TH1-4 Tinning in the Cowsic and upper West Dart Valleys and Crockern Tor

Both these upland valleys were a disappointment to the tin prospectors. Isolated pockets of alluvial tin alongside the Cowsic were soon worked out yielding little profit, though the substantial pebble mounds at Holming Beam show that at least this small side valley was productive. The West Dart was almost as barren. North-east of Two Bridges a shallow trench follows the back of a lode over the ridge separating the West Dart from Muddilake Brook, and three kilometres upstream a wider cut was excavated into the hillside north of Beardown Tors. The adjacent tributary below Crow Tor was also streamed.

A tinner's hut **TH1** lies near the junction of this brook with the main stream, very similar in plan to the one excavated by the Dartmoor Exploration Committee at Greyhound Marsh near Postbridge (**map 27**) except that the entrance here is on the opposite side. Its single rectangular room (c. 4.5 x 2.0 m) was dug lengthways into the bank and then roofed over at ground level. The Committee suggested that their building was for seasonal occupation and dated from the thirteenth or fourteenth centuries, a conclusion which probably applies to this one also. A single-roomed dwelling, **TH2** (4.5 x 2.5 m), of a slightly different pattern was built sideways into a bank at the northern end of the streamworks with the entrance through one of the long sides. Another building of this type, **TH3** (4.5 x 2.0 m), with several courses of stone still standing to over a metre high can be found built into a pebble mound near the end of some streamworks south of Brown's House. According to Baring-Gould, Brown's House was built, occupied and ruined within a single lifetime in the early nineteenth century, with only a fraction of the surrounding wall of the ambitiously sized newtake completed north of the house.[18] Its eastern wall ends close to the source of the Cherry Brook which after a sluggish start descends rapidly down to Hollowcombe Bottom. Just below the falls a few stones around the edge of a rectangular platform levelled into the hillside are all that remains of a small building, **TH4** (c. 3.5 x 2.4 m). Slight undulations between it and the river probably cover some tinners pebble mounds and several hundred metres downstream a leat emerges from the boggy ground higher up on the west bank.

At Crockern Tor, north of Two Bridges, were held the Stannary Parliaments and it was to here that the Lord Warden of the Stannaries summoned the tinners of Devon to 'consult, enquire and take deliberation ... for the redressing and amending of any inconveniences or abuses within the Stannaries', or more succinctly 'to put down vice and extoll virtue'.[31] Up to the thirteenth century the tinners of Devon combined with those of Cornwall in an assembly on Hingston Hill, in Cornwall. From about 1305 the Devon men attended a separate parliament here on Crockern Tor. This rather unimpressive tor in the centre of the moor seems to have been chosen as equidistant between the three stannary towns of Ashburton, Chagford and Tavistock and close to the junction where tracks from these towns met. It was also equally inconvenient and remote, for the farms and newtake walls which now surround it were not to be built for centuries and the nearest habitations were the ancient tenements strung along the East and West Darts.

When summoned by the Lord Warden the four Stannary Towns, Plympton having been added to their number in 1328, each elected 24 stannators to attend the parliament, and thus about a hundred officials along with a much larger number of interested parties assembled on the slopes of the tor. No details are recorded of sittings prior to 1494 but twelve are now known to have been held on the tor at irregular intervals up to 1703,[43] the

MAP 30

session in 1600 being presided over by Sir Walter Raleigh, the Lord Warden at that date. Tin production on Dartmoor was in steady decline after the peak years in the first half of the sixteenth century, and by the middle of the eighteenth century very little was being produced. Mrs. Bray[22] refers to a later parliament than the one recorded on Crockern Tor in 1703 but certainly no more took place here after the middle of that century. The last assemblies on the tor were no more than a formal opening of the session after which the stannators retired to complete their business in the greater comfort of one of the stannary towns. The tin industry made a vigorous recovery in the nineteenth century but the different conditions of mining company enterprises did not lead to a revival of the ancient parliament.

Surprisingly little remains on the tor to record the four centuries of considerable power and authority exercised by the Stannary Parliament, particularly in its earlier years, over the land and inhabitants of the county. Risdon, writing sometime before 1630 describes the tor, though perhaps he never visited it, as remarkable for the 'table and seats of moorstone, hewn out of the rocks, lying in the face of all weather ...'.[44] None of these are now to be found, though the curiously shaped stack south-west of the tor known as Parliament Rock, with probably natural steps up one side, may have served the 'Cryer of the Court' or some other function. Certainly by the late eighteenth century the tor was as bereft of Risdon's furniture as it is now and visitors at the time were told conflicting rumours of their fate, all more or less unlikely. The 'Judge's Chair' at Dunnabridge pound was said to have been brought from the tor, as was the roof of a shelter near the entrance to Dunnabridge Farm, or alternatively that Judge Buller's men broke up the stones for use at Prince Hall. Probably nothing more than a moorstone table for the clerk ever existed on the tor with nature providing the seating, anything more formal being contrary to the free spirit of the tinners.

MAP 30 Blackbrook and the Upper Walkham

1 Dead Lake Foot settlement (fig. 30.1)

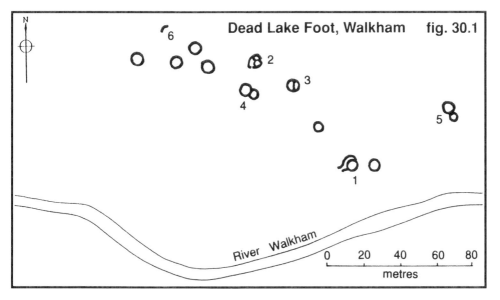

Dead Lake Foot, Walkham   fig. 30.1

MAP 30

Prehistoric settlement along the Walkham starts about 5 kilometres from its source with a small group of huts beside Dead Lake. The fourteen huts here are confined by a steep hillside to a narrow plain on the north bank of the river, without any obvious remains of surrounding enclosures. Several huts have unusual features. Hut 1 seems to have been rebuilt in antiquity, in order to halve its size to 2.5 m, the original outer wall remaining as a corridor around the outside and still retaining both entrance jambs. Hut 2, never very large (4.1 m), has been partly built up and divided into three, though it is difficult to see for what purpose. Hut 3 (3.8 m) is probably a more recent rebuild, a straight wall having been built across the centre using the stones of one half of the hut, converting it into a smaller rectangular building. Huts 4 (3.4 m) and 5 (3.5 m) both have annexes added to one side in the usual manner, and an arc of stones at 6 is probably the dismantled remains of another building uphill. The rest are equally small, 2 to 4 m in diameter, the walls of most of them having collapsed into the interior.

2 Langstone Moor settlement (fig. 30.2)

In 1894 the Dartmoor Exploration Committee followed up their first excavation at Grimspound with a rather less successful one at the prehistoric settlement on Langstone Moor. A combination of bad weather and an untrained workforce allowed them to carry out only a superficial excavation of 11 out of the 51 huts, which from a later perspective was probably to the good. The huts were only roughly cleared down to floor level and few artefacts were spotted; some worked flints including a 'scraper-knife', a whetstone and a polished red pebble. Several huts had a raised sleeping platform along one side.

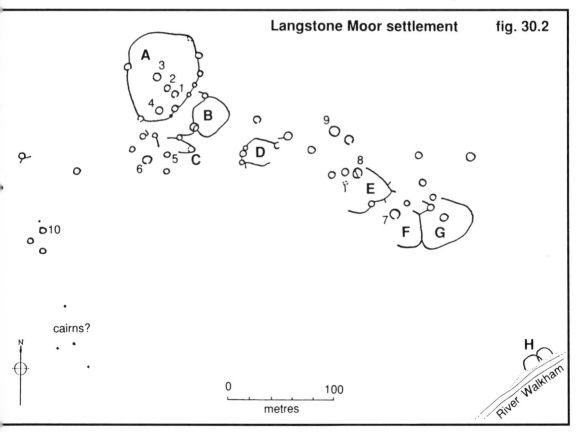

Langstone Moor settlement   fig. 30.2

MAP 30

An excellent plan of the site was published in 1901 to which some extra enclosure walls can reasonbably be added, as can three probable huts on the circuit wall of enclosure A. Some of the buildings are more clearly defined on the ground than their plan shows but there was no indication of which had been excavated. These would probably have included the four free-standing huts within this enclosure; 1 (4.2 m), which retains its door posts, 2 (4.0 m), 3 (5.1 m) and 4 (5.2 m), all good examples. Enclosure A is the best preserved of the seven (A-G), most of the others being incomplete. Stray lengths of walling, some originating on the huts, show that the network of fields was once more extensive than now appears. There are considerable gaps in the remaining walls but the site is too remote to have been robbed and probably the missing slabs have fallen in place and lie buried beneath the turf.

Both huts 5 (3.7 m) and 6 (4.6 m) were also probably among those excavated, as was one of the largest, 7 (6.8 m). The latter is still an impressive building, constructed of large stones with one doorpost in place and the other lying at its foot. Rivalling it in size is hut 8 (6.8 m), divided by an interior cross-wall, but by far the largest in the settlement appears to have been hut 9 (approx. 8.5 m). Two-thirds of its circumference has been dismantled but its outline survives as a circular platform levelled into the hillside. The rest of the huts in various stages of decay range in size from 2 to 5.7 m across.

At the bottom of the slope and probably associated with the settlement is a pair of intertwined enclosures, without any associated huts, opening on to the river. Perhaps also contemporary are the five or six small piles of stones on the hillside within sight of the huts to the south-west which may prove to be burial cairns like those higher up the hill to the north. These appear to be entirely structureless, 3-4 m across and less than 0.3 m high. The best preserved (3 x 0.3 m) lies only a few metres from hut 10 (4.9 m), a building with a curved interior dividing wall.

The site is dominated by the huge cone of Great Mis Tor across the river from which a good view of the whole settlement can be obtained, laid out as if for inspection on ground clear of both bracken and surface stone. Out of sight from the huts but only 200 m away on the crest of the hill is the Langstone Moor stone circle, built most likely by earlier generations. The hut dwellers must have been well aware of it and understood its significance, something which yet eludes the archaeologist.

3 Great Mis Tor West

A group of five huts are to be found on the lower slopes west of Great Mis Tor 200 m from the river, on a patch of open ground surrounded by a large area of clitter. The site was partially enclosed by a single line of slabs between two such areas forming an uphill boundary, though this could never have been more than a token barrier by itself and the rest of the site was left open towards the river. This is likely to have been the original arrangement as its remoteness and the amount of surrounding stone are excellent protection against later depredation. The huts, 3 to 4.5 m in diameter and only one retaining a definite entrance to the south, are all of slight construction with walls 0.2 m at most above ground level.

4, 5 Little Mis Tor West (figs. 30.3,4)

Downstream the valley becomes much more densely populated with over a hundred huts to be found within 1.5 kilometres along the east valley side, most of them grouped into three settlements. By contrast the west bank seems to have been unoccupied apart from a few huts north of Shillapark Farm (**map 31**) though possibly the latter may overlie an early site. The three main settlements **4**, **5** and **9** were deliberately laid out within the clitter for clearer

MAP 30

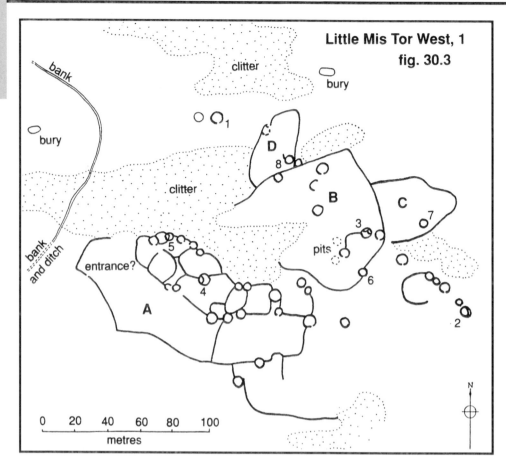

Little Mis Tor West, 1

fig. 30.3

ground in their immediate vicinity is noticeably free of huts and enclosures. Stones for the walls needed to be dragged only a minimum distance into position and the clitter itself provided part of the barrier without requiring reinforcement. As usual there was little, if any, attempt to clear the interiors of the fields.

The extent of the surrounding clitter has ensured that the settlements west of Little Mis Tor are extraordinarily well preserved, with little sign of later interference. The north settlement, **4**, is made up of 40 huts, 2.5 to 8.5 m in diameter, most of them enclosed within five fields (fig. 30.3). The largest hut, 1, exceeding the next in size by 1.5 m, lies outside the fields to the north of the settlement. A tall jamb stone still stands at the entrance and a bury has been built a few metres from its wall. Several other huts retain one or more door posts in position at south facing entrances, and three of the larger ones have curved interior walls: 2, 3 and 4.

Nineteen huts are enclosed within field A, crammed closely together in the northern half and joined by numerous short walls forming paddocks between them. One of the smaller structures in the north-west corner is almost filled with stones, 5. The perimeter is broken in several places but a gap on the downhill side bounded by a pair of slabs set across the wall may be an original entrance. Pits within field B and a partly demolished hut show that the site has not entirely escaped attention. One hut, 3, is partitioned into three by a pair of interior walls and another, 6, apparently predates the circuit wall which meets assymetrically on either side.

The well-constructed wall of field C surrounds a single small hut 7 (3.8 m). Field D, its

MAP 30

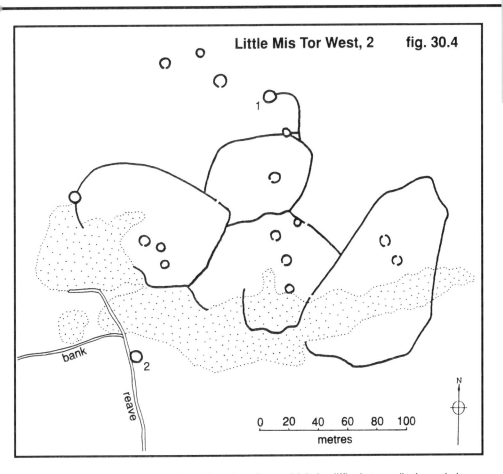

Little Mis Tor West, 2   fig. 30.4

west wall rather unnecessarily bounding the clitter which is difficult to walk through here, also encloses a small hut (3.5 m) and perhaps a second on the opposite side. The wall seems to be inturned here as part of an elaborate entrance though it is more likely to be the result of later disturbance. The small enclosure E associated with up to five huts is incomplete but the gap was probably closed originally by some form of less durable fencing. Downhill a bank apparently of contemporary origin, winds around the hillside separating settlement from river. Its south end is accompanied by a ditch acting as a leat for the middle blowing house.

Unconnected with these fields and separated by a patch of open ground is another group of 17 huts to the south, **5** (fig. 30.4). The similarity of the walls and irregular shape of the fields confirm that they must have been in use at the same time. One to four huts occupy each of the four fields, with an extension to the north connecting the largest hut 1 (6.9 m) to the group and three particularly well preserved free-standing huts to the west of it. Hut 1 has been rebuilt in more recent times, stones having been placed across the entrance and added to the wall. The huts, some retaining jambs at the entrance, are on average smaller than the northern group, ranging from 2.8 to 6.9 m across. Several are reduced to their foundations and perhaps had been dismantled to provide material for new buildings nearby.

Hut 2 (6.2 m) is built against a reave which runs into the clitter on the west side of the settlement. The reave reappears orientated downhill towards the Walkham though interrupted by the longhouses before reaching the river. The alignment may well have continued on the opposite bank as the lower end of the Roos Tor reave but this section has

MAP 30

been lost within the Shillapark enclosures. South of hut 2 the reave is substantial enough to suggest it has been added to and certainly the bank and ditch returning to the river 150 m away is the boundary of a later enclosure probably associated with the longhouses.

The reave builders did not trouble to build up the next section with imported stone across the clear ground to the south, now a low bank, but it once again becomes substantial within the clitter beyond the tinners' gully before being overbuilt by the present newtake wall. The reave does not reappear on the far side and may have returned to the river on the line of the present wall beside the road.

6 Little Mis Tor West 3

A pair of huts (both c. 6.5 m) independent of the large settlement uphill survive within a bank and ditched enclosure, probably associated with the longhouses and cut through by a later tinners' gully. The area is very disturbed and there is no trace of a circuit wall, though some of the hut slabs are still in place.

7 Merrivale Bridge North 1

An almost circular enclosure about 55 m in diameter surrounds a pair of huts at the centre, one of them 5 m in diameter and clearly visible, the other represented by a short arc of stones. The circuit wall was rather casually built between naturally placed rocks, with some slabs set on edge and others simply pushed into position.

8 Merrivale Bridge North 2

More regular sided prehistoric fields enclose the area along the river bank just north of the bridge. The foundation of three huts (3.5-5.0 m) can be found built on to the inside of the wall of the first field, but part of the area enclosed is particularly stony and more may exist here. The mound of stones 5 m across within the adjacent field is more likely to be a kerbed circle surrounding a cairn, with much of the interior thrown outside to the south.

Below the bridge the present fields increase on both banks of the river and all traces of prehistoric settlement have been lost from a gradually widening band downstream.

9 Merrivale Bridge East (fig. 30.5)

The prehistoric remains on the hillside east of Merrivale Bridge are amongst the most interesting as well as the best known on the moor. Stone rows, circle, huts and enclosures are visible on both sides of the Tavistock to Princetown road which cuts through the centre of the village on the long descent down to the bridge. Luckily the site has proved an exception to the rule that the proximity of a road inevitably leads to its destruction. Some of the huts still stand very close to the verge indeed, one of them even neatly bisected and half of it allowed to remain. No doubt this is partly because of the unhandy size of many of the remaining stones but there must always have been an element of restraint on the part of the newtake wall builders and others. Its survival is all the more surprising because of the long tradition of granite working on the neighbouring Peter Tavy and Whitchurch Commons, culminating in the enormous expansion of quarrying during the last century around the tors to the south. In the eighteenth century Donn's map (1765) shows that a well used track branched off the present road at the corner of the enclosures downhill and passed right

Merrivale Bridge East   fig. 30.5

E

field wall

ditch

Tavistock to Princetown road

house

A

B

C

D

1
2
3
4
5
6
7

N

0 20 40 60 80 100
metres

MAP 30

through the site, though a traveller, Andrews, using his map a few years later complained that 'it was so inconsiderable that we did not notice it'.[52]

Not that the village has escaped considerable damage. The road must itself overlie some huts, and others no doubt contributed to the material used in consructing the present road when it was turnpiked soon after 1772. The Rev. Bray[22] counted 'about' 34 huts south of the road in 1802, of which there are now 27 remaining. In a further visit he made here thirty years later he found a man building a house nearby, probably the one attached to enclosure D. The latter admitted damaging some of the huts and digging into others but the Reverend neatly persuaded him that there would be more profit in acting as a guide for tourists if the site was left as it was. Bray also notes that the prehistoric village was known locally as the Potato Market where provisions used to be exchanged between the moorland folk and those of Tavistock during plague years, a more likely site perhaps than that shown on Donn's map at Two Bridges.

The six huts excavated by the Dartmoor Exploration Committee in 1895 were all found to have been previously dug into, by the road menders they suggested, and Burnard attributed the total loss of another hut shortly before 1902 to the same agency. More immediately obvious are the many stone pits, some of them within the enclosures, and the numerous holed and fractured blocks of surface stone scattered over the hillside. An almost completed edge runner for a cider press still remains where it was worked, incongruously propped up next to the wall of enclosure B from where it was extracted.

Though the number of huts is comparable to the settlements west of Little Mis Tor, **4** and **5**, this village was organised rather differently. The five very small enclosures are separate and include only 8 of the 41 huts within or on the perimeter, the majority being free-standing nearby. All the enclosures are sited on the edge of the clitter despite the ample area of stone-free hillside in the vicinity, while the interiors are remarkably encumbered with surface blocks. The mainly double-slabbed circuit walls seem to have been constructed after the huts, their extraordinarily irregular outline resulting from including many of the larger earthfast boulders in the perimeter.

The interior of enclosure A is exceptionally stony and is in poor condition having lost its north wall and a section of the south corner. The double-slabbed west side survives best, built quite unnecessarily through a particularly stony patch of clitter. The peculiar outline of B seems to have been designed to include one hut and exclude another. None of the gaps in the wall have original features and are probably of recent origin to facilitate the removal of stones, many of those remaining showing the usual signs of having been worked on. The edge runner lies next to the south wall. The smallest enclosure C seems to have been of slighter construction. Part of the boundary connecting it with hut 7 (6.8 m), which is still substantial, is now a disorganised scatter and the other side is missing altogether. The south west corner of enclosure D was chosen for the site of a small two-roomed dwelling and garden plot abutting the road, built here in 1832. The building has been dismantled and only its lower courses remain. The circuit wall around enclosure E, its inner and outer faces less than a metre apart, connects 3 huts, though the south side is almost obliterated.

The huts vary in size from 2.7 to 9.5 m, the great majority being between 6 and 7 m across, and where visible the entrances face south or south west. Those dug into by the Dartmoor Exploration Committee can still be identified by the pits and hollows within but judging by the small size of some of the trenches the excavations were hardly thorough. They seem to have chosen those nearest the rows 1 (6.3 m), 2 (5.3 m), 3 (4.4 m) 4 (5.0 m); the largest hut 5 (9.3 m) sited at the centre of the settlement which was built of massive slabs and still retains a pair of jambs at the entrance; and 6 (5.6 m) next to the road. Their results were summed up in a few lines. Charcoal was found within all the huts and two were apparently paved but the only artefact found was a flint flake.

The settlement approaches to within 50 m of the important ceremonial centre uphill but they are probably far from contemporary and many centuries may have passed since the

MAP 30

stone rows and circle were laid out facing the sunset on the slopes above. How the villagers viewed these monuments has yet to be determined but the close association of their dwellings here and at similar sites on the moor suggest it was with respect rather than awe.

10 Langstone Moor stone circle and cairns (fig. 30.6)

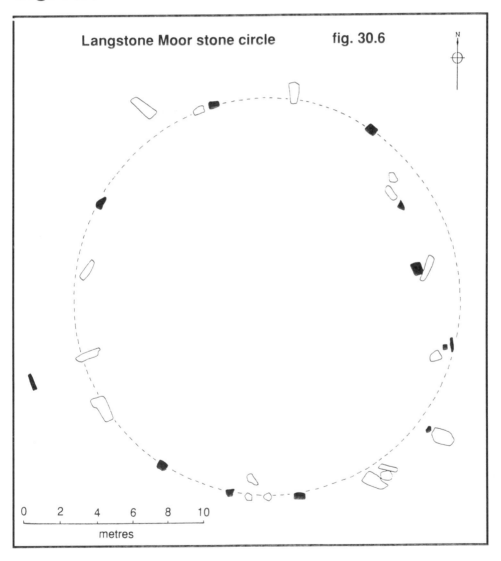

Langstone Moor stone circle   fig. 30.6

On a clear day the view from the circle sited just below the summit is exceptionally fine to the south and west but the monument itself has been sadly disfigured. All the stones were lying flat and undamaged prior to 1894 when the Dartmoor Exploration Committee re-erected them in pits still then visible in the peat. The circle became a casualty of World War

MAP 30

Two when troops stationed nearby used the stones for target practice, fracturing 10 and overturning others so that only three now remain in position. Many of the shattered fragments lie around the site but it would be a considerable task to restore the monument to anything like its previous appearance.

Before its destruction there were sixteen stones in a 20.9 m circle through their centres. Two on the eastern side are set well inside the circumference, either an original feature as D-shaped circles are fairly common elsewhere, or possibly an error of restoration. The Exploration Committee suggested the outlying slab 3 m west of the circle and facing towards the centre was the remnant of an outer ring of stones. Apart from a few shallow pits the interior appears to be untouched, the only find by the Committee during the restoration being a possible 'cooking stone' in one of the socket holes.

Out of sight a little over 100 m south-east of the circle is a line of three small cairns, none more than 0.3 m high. Their insignificant size ensured they escaped detection by casual diggers prior to the excavation of all three by the Exploration Committee in about 1898. Several loose blocks lie on the uneven surface of the north cairn and two slabs of the retaining circle remain around its edge. As usual a central pit had been dug into the subsoil but it contained no trace of an interment or charcoal. About 10 m to the south-west the second cairn covered a central cist which, exceptionally, had not been disturbed. It had a paved floor and contained wood charcoal and bone ash mixed with earth. A pit now marks its site, for the Committee members were so taken with its 'beauty' that they had it transported to Plymouth Museum for display. The third cairn 14 m to the south is even more inconspicuous than the others but like the first a central pit contained nothing but soil.

11 Conies Down stone rows (fig. 30.7) and Conies Down cairn

Remote from the present road and beyond the reach of the Cowsic newtakes the double stone row on Conies Down might be expected to have survived the centuries in fair condition, but this is not the case. A few pits nearby show that tinners worked the hillside but the most likely cause of damage, apart from time itself, was probably the curiosity of travellers on the Lich Way to whom the rows must have been a well known landmark. This ancient track to Lydford church and court from the farms on the eastern side of the Forest was in frequent use in medieval times and its course is still faintly visible as it crosses the lower end of the rows.

Only twenty-one stones remain in place, the majority being either fallen or missing, perhaps buried under the turf, and neither end of the rows appear to be complete. The original length was probably not much more than at present, 172 m, for a small group of boulders which seem to be in their natural position are in line about 20 m beyond the last stone at the lower end. The stones

fig. 30.7 Conies Down stone rows

double stone row

metres

1980 1:200

MAP 30

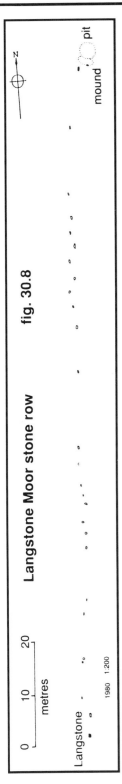

Langstone Moor stone row

fig. 30.8

increase slightly in height towards the upper end where the final slabs stand next to a very low mound about 3 m across. If this is the remains of a cairn it must always have been of slight construction as there would seem to be little point in carting away its material when there is an ample supply lower down the hillside. The monument was never impressive, the average height of the stones being only 26 cm, and there is a gradual change in direction of 3° between its ends.

Four hundred metres to the north-east the summit of the hill is occupied by a large turf-covered cairn which has been dug into from its southern edge. No stones are visible in the saucer-shape depression in the centre but a setting of three slabs near the northern edge may be the sides of a cist which contained a secondary burial inserted at a later date into the side of the mound.

12 Langstone Moor stone row (fig. 30.8)

The standing stone at the lower end of the row is visible from a considerable distance and has given its name to the surrounding Langstone Moor. It was lying flat until 1893 when it was re-erected in its original socket hole to stand 2.76 m high. The stone already had its peculiarly lopsided profile but its pitted surface is the result of being used for target practice during the last war, like the nearby stone circle.

North of the Langstone a single row of twenty-six small stones, but with many gaps, is aligned uphill. The majority have fallen and the twelve that remain in place are on average only 19 cms high with no obvious increase in height towards either end. In 1895 the Dartmoor Exploration Committee examined some of the socket holes but nothing was found beyond establishing that the missing stones could not have been of any great size either. A flat circular area a short distance beyond the last surviving stone uphill is probably the site of a cairn which has been entirely removed.

The Committee suggested that the substantial bank of stones running parallel about 70 m to the west and ending in the soft ground at the head of the Colly Brook covered a second stone row which also started at a cairn at the higher end. A line of slabs is indeed visible along one side of it but the cairn appears to be merely a pile of stones displaced from the bank to allow the passage of the Peter Tavy branch of the Lich Way. Rectangular foundations are built against the west side of the wall but it appears to be older than this, perhaps a Bronze Age reave as it has much the same alignment as the White Tor reave to the west, or even an outwork of the 'fort' on the summit.

MAP 30

13-15 Cairns north and west of Cocks Hill

The Lich Way is well defined as it crosses the saddle north of Cocks Hill, perhaps as a result of the extra pack horse traffic it once carried from the streamworks on the Walkham. At the crest of the ridge the track passes the base of White Barrow cairn, **13**, a Forest bound since the eighteenth century, which has a central pit but is still substantial (21 m across by 1.7 m high) despite its vulnerable position.

The cairn on the summit 700 m just south of west has not fared so well, with much of its structure having been carted away, **14**. Masses of small stones are exposed around its north edge and the opposite side has almost gone. A deep saucer shaped depression at the centre is nearly down to ground level. A much smaller cairn, **15**, lies just below the summit 550 m to the north of White Barrow. A few stones show through its rather uneven surface but its inconspicuous size, only 9.0 m across, has probably preserved it from serious digging.

16 Greena Ball Barrows

Crossing recorded three burial mounds in a line on the north slope of Greena Ball to which can be added a fourth mound of similar dimensions a short distance uphill. No stones are visible within the mounds nor on the surrounding hillside and the turf is more likely to cover barrows rather than cairns. All are substantial, up to 1.5 m high, with smooth surfaces apart from some shallow pitting which suggests they are undamaged, an unusual state probably due to their remote situation.

17 Little Mis Tor south-east Cairn

Sited on the summit this large but low cairn has suffered some trenching around the eastern side, perhaps the work of peat cutters, but otherwise appears to be undamaged. An outer bank 22 m across surrounds a level interior rising to a slight mound at the centre on which are lying several small stones. The few slabs visible within the bank show that it was built with inner and outer faces around a rubble core.

18-21 Tin working, blowing houses and longhouses along the Walkham (fig. 30.9)

Though by no means one of the major sources of tin on the moor, the upper Walkham valley contains some of the most interesting remains from all periods of the industry. The highest deposits were encountered along Spriddle Lake, once the first large tributary of the Walkham but now donating its entire flow into the prison leat which also takes a contribution from the main river. About 200 m above the original confluence is a small streamwork, the waste mounds mainly on the west bank opposite the collapsing walls of a small tinners hut (1.8 x 2.5 m).

Below the junction are the remains of Wheal Prosper tin mine at the lower end of an older openwork excavated up the west valley side **18**. A leat taken off the Walkham several hundred metres upstream forks before the workings, its lower branch carrying water to a wheel pit now filled in, and the settling pits. Within the gert is the North Lode shaft, whilst beyond it near the valley floor is a nineteenth century tinners building (c. 7 x 8 m), its walls still standing to a metre and more high. The Lich Way crosses the Walkham immediately below the mine on its long journey from the eastern side of the Forest to Lydford. Here it becomes well marked and is joined by a deeply worn track along which the tin from the workings was once transported.

For 350 m downstream mounds of discarded pebbles line the banks as far as the shaft

MAP 30

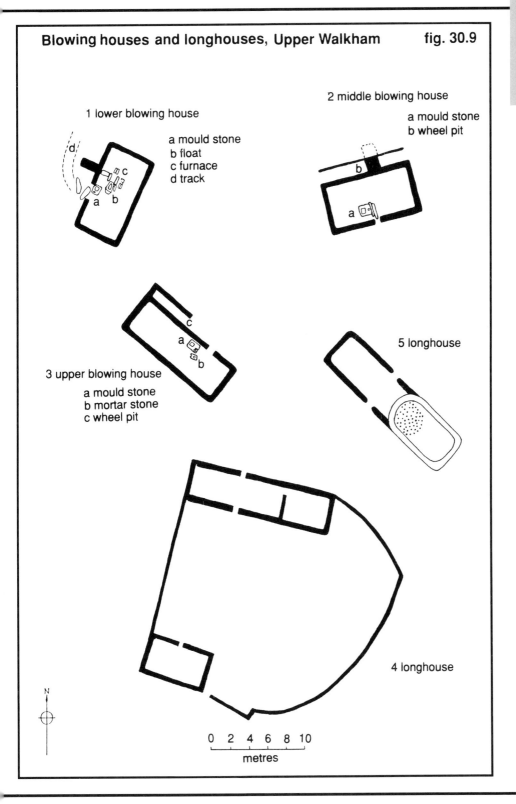

Blowing houses and longhouses, Upper Walkham   fig. 30.9

1 lower blowing house

a mould stone
b float
c furnace
d track

2 middle blowing house

a mould stone
b wheel pit

3 upper blowing house

a mould stone
b mortar stone
c wheel pit

5 longhouse

4 longhouse

0 2 4 6 8 10
metres

N

MAP 30

and adit on the South Lode, visble up the west side of the valley. A stream still trickles from the mouth of the adit but both it and the shaft are now blocked. The mine was opened probably in 1806[48] and worked intermittently to 1854, always promising good returns but never producing the hoped-for results.

Only occasional patches of tinners' mounds accompany the river downstream, the main deposits being along the few short tributaries. The largest excavation, up to 5 m in depth, is around the head of a very minor stream which joins the Walkham at the angle where the great bulk of Greena Ball forces the river to alter course to the west. Significant deposits were also extracted from Dead Lake.

The quantity of ore obtained was enough to warrant no less than three blowing houses in the valley. The first of these, the upper blowing house*, **19**, is encountered on the right bank north of Shillapark Farm enclosures (fig. 30.9.3). A silted up leat taken off the Walkham 400 m further upriver carried water to the wheel pit alongside the building. The walls have collapsed inwards hiding the site of the furnace but the bulky mould stone, with two sample moulds below the main cavity, is still in place beside the entrance. Next to it is a small part of a fractured mortar stone with a pair of holes in its surface, one of them broken at the edge of the block. That this building accommodated stamps as well as the furnace is suggested both by its unusual length and by the heaps of sand piled outside, the waste product of the crushing process.

The middle blowing house, **20**, lies on the opposite bank 500 m downstream (fig. 30.9.2). One jamb still stands at the entrance, the other with the lintel resting on the edge of a mould stone, also with a sample mould. The wheel pit on the opposite side of the house is well defined and could accommodate a small wheel with a breast of about 0.3 m and diameter of 3.5 m. Immediately uphill are the foundations of a medieval farmstead, (fig. 30.9.4), which was probably long abandoned by the time the blowing house was constructed. The longhouse (15 x 3.5 m) shares its enclosure with another small building. About 40 m further in the same direction are the foundations of a second longhouse (18 x 3.5 m), much of its wall having been demolished in order to reconstruct the upper room, probably by the tinners themselves (fig. 30.9.5). The rebuilding, curiously curved at its lower end, has itself crumbled, choking the interior with a pile of rubble.

The lower blowing house, **21**, 300 m above Merrivale Bridge, preserves more interesting features than most, but curiously no definite signs of a wheel pit or leat which would have had an ample supply from the first tributary upriver (fig. 30.9.1). The upper end of this little brook has been thoroughly streamed 600 m down from its source, its bed widened into a gully 50 m across and deepened by over 3 m. A huge granite doorpost of the blowing house remains standing at the entrance but the other has toppled over taking the lintel with it. Near the centre of the room the sides of the furnace are still in place with room for the bellows behind, and the float for receiving the molten metal, originally horizontal, is upended in front of it. From here the tin was ladled into the mould stone lying close to the door which has a sample mould in front of the main cavity and a groove to accommodate a lifting bar for removing the solidified metal. Sandy waste is absent and the building probably functioned solely as a blowing house.

On the opposite bank a little way upstream a line of pits can be seen ascending the hillside, the site of Wheal Fortune tin mine – begun in 1806 and worked on and off until about 1860.[49] A leat, fed from a rectangular reservoir at the lower end of these workings, winds around the slope below the Merrivale enclosures to a wheel pit (c.5.0 x 1.0 m) a short distance downstream from the blowing house. The water-wheel probably worked a head of stamps.[49] A second wheel pit now filled with masonry can be seen below a well-preserved leat embankment at the upper end of the workings. The outflow from here was carried to yet another water-wheel which worked a stamping mill and buddles on the other side of the

* At present (1991) being excavated by the Dartmoor Tin Working Research Group.

MAP 30

quarry embankment immediately to the south. This embankment was part of an astonishing scheme for constructing a railway bridge across the Walkham at this point, to connect Merrivale quarry with the Princetown line near King Tor. The proposal was actually approved in 1908 but nothing more came of it.[50]

The Merrivale sett included Beckamoor Combe to the west (**map 31**) which has been streamed for a kilometre below its source. A small tinners' hut (3.0 x 2.2 m), with a fireplace taking up the whole of one end, is built into the upper end of the gully.

a-c Boundary Stones

From Rundlestone Cottages to Great Mis Tor a line of six roughly shaped pillars, **a-b** all unlettered, marks the boundary between the Forest and the parish of Walkhampton. North of the tor the boundary continues undefined to Dead Lake and then on to the White Barrow. Great Mis Tor was one of the original stations in the 1240 Perambulation of the Forest but it was only in 1702 that the Rundle Stone was included as a boundary point, though this did not preserve it from destruction at the end of the last century. The stone was probably originally erected as a waymark on the north side of the road to Tavistock, a short distance east of the present Forest boundary. Ogilbys map[36] of 1675 depicts it as 'a great stone called Roundle' standing on a mound on the summit of the hill, where it must have been a conspicuous object from a considerable distance in both directions, and a useful guide before the surrounding moorland was enclosed. It had the letter R cut into one face and measured over 2 m high above the mound on which it stood when Crossing examined it in about 1881, a few years before it was removed.

Around and within the prison lands a second set of stones mingles with those marking the Forest border, inscribed with the letters *DCP* standing for Directors of Convict Prisons.[13] A 500 m gap in the circuit of newtake walls north of Langstone Moor stone row is filled by a bank and ditch. Three boundary stones, **c**, one at each end and at the centre, have the letter *H* cut into their moorside faces, no doubt the initial of a former landowner.

Fices Well

The original circumstance which led to the building of the little structure of granite which covers the spring has long been lost to legend but according to Mrs Bray[22] the slabs were erected in gratitude by a lost and thirsty traveller, an unlikely tale considering the Blackbrook flows not 20 m away. Certainly by the nineteenth century it was attributed to John Fice, identified by the Rev. Bray with John Fitz of Fitzford, astrologer, whose strange history and that of his descendants is recounted by Baring-Gould[35]. Some support for either spelling of the name is given by the inscription cut into the face of the granite cover, 'IF 1568', which still appears remarkably fresh. In Bray's time the surrounding area was marshy but since then the ground has been drained by an underground conduit from the well-head and the outer circular wall built around it for protection.

In 1906 an exceptionally interesting find, now in Plymouth Museum, was made nearby when a track was being constructed within the prison enclosures. One of the prisoners unearthed a bronze rapier, of Middle Bronze Age date, about half a metre below the surface where it had lain undisturbed since being lost by its original owner.[42]

Blackabrook Peat Tramway

A short distance uphill from Fices Well a track continues the public footpath northwards through the prison enclosure, ending at a walled platform about 200 m beyond the wire fence. This was the collecting and loading point for the tramway which carried peat from the

MAP 31

turf ties on the slopes around the Blackbrook to the naphtha works at Princetown. Southwards the track takes the course of the tramway as far as the main road, continuing towards the prison on the far side as a levelled embankment through the fields. The peat was converted into naphtha primarily as a fuel for gas lighting but with side products such as candles and mothballs.[47] The tramway was constructed by the British Patent Naphtha Company which started production in 1844, originally at Bachelor's Hall outside the town. Two years later the company took over part of the prison building which had stood empty since the last prisoners of the Napoleonic War had been repatriated thirty years previously, but the timing was unfortunate. Most of the Australian Colonies were now refusing to accept any more convicts and the shortage of accommodation for them at home led to the reopening of the prison in 1850. Not surprisingly the company relinquished possession with very bad grace but it had not been a financial success and the entire operation was discontinued after only six years.

Merrivale Warren

Some thirty buries are widely dispersed amongst the prehistoric settlements on the west slope of Mis Tor. All are turf covered with a shallow surrounding ditch and most are small, typically 10 x 4 m and well under a metre high. The warren covers an area of 73 hectares, spreading uphill beyond the newtake wall and bounded only by the River Walkham to the west.

The warren was already long disused by 1832 when visited by the Rev. Bray, normally well informed about local affairs, who interpreted them as tumuli in 'the sacred cemetery of the Druids'.

MAP 31 Merrivale to Cudlipptown Down

1 Cox Tor higher settlements and summit cairns (fig. 31.1)

In contrast to the hillside almost clear of surface stone facing Great Staple Tor and Roos Tor, the west side of Cox Tor is cluttered with rocks and boulders. The upper slopes here were nevertheless chosen for the site of two small homesteads. Site 1, perched on a narrow shelf on the hillside, has a central hut (5.5 m) enclosed by a rather structureless boundary wall composed mainly of stones simply rolled into position. A break in the downhill corner is approached by a track through the clitter which may well be original and a water supply was provided by a spring a short distance away.

Enclosure 2 in clearer ground is easier to approach from uphill where there is also a convenient spring. The wall is better constructed except on the lower side where a wide patch of surface rock forms the boundary, but strangely there is no sign of the expected hut. On the exceptionally steep slope to the north some light stony banks delineate long narrow fields associated with the enclosure, abutting onto the end of a contour reave. The latter threads its way for 300 m through the rock fields to the north where it alters course downhill in the direction of Great Combe Tor. It seems to have followed the construction of the narrow fields at the south end which it meets at an angle, and beyond continues after a short gap to terminate at a rock pile.

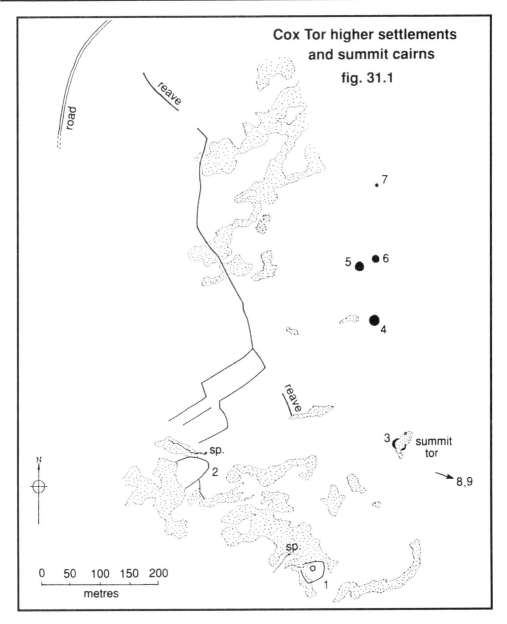

MAP 31

Cox Tor higher settlements
and summit cairns

fig. 31.1

Cairns dominate the summit ridge, though perhaps not as many now as formerly. In 1893 R.N. Worth recorded traces of four circled cairns on the plateau of the tor, one of them with a stone row orientated north and south, but none of his descriptions correspond with the cairns now visible here and the row has not been relocated. The tor rocks support a triangulation pillar on top and an enormous mass of small stones over 2 m high piled around the base, 3. Some of these were reorganized into a smaller cairn on the summit as one of the many commemorations on the moor celebrating the 1887 jubilee, but the original labour may well have been of Bronze Age date. The foundations of a small oval building less than 2 m across tucked into the rocks a few metres away was excavated by the Dartmoor Exploration Committee but nothing was found to indicate when it was built.

MAP 31

A more typical cairn, 4, about 18 m in diameter and with a deep central pit stands prominently on the ridge about 150 m to the north, also overlying an outcrop of rock, as do the two smaller cairns 60 m further on in the same direction, 5 and 6. The latter were excavated by the Dartmoor Exploration Committee in their 1898 season and each was found to consist of an outer circular bank infilled with loose stones and earth at the centre, but with no trace of a burial or indeed of any finds at all. The small cairn 7, only 5 m across was not mentioned in their report but this also has been trenched. The Committee then dug into two small cairns 60 m south of the tor, in neither of which was anything found. These were part of a small cairnfield with five to seven members but only two are easily identifiable south-east of the tor, 8 and 9. A final target of the Committee was a hut circle about 185 m to the south-east of the tor, with walls 'exceptionally high' and fallen doorposts. Nothing is now to be seen of this and the hut circles shown here on the Ordnance Survey map are more likely to be upcast surrounding a series of pits.

2-5 Cox Tor reaves and lower settlements

Boulder-strewn ground separates the tor rocks from the crags immediately to the south where the foundations of a semi-circular wall about 10 m long run between two rock piles. Too large for a hut, its position on the highest point with a magnificent view down the Walkham valley to the south gives the impression of being a look-out. At the foot of the rocks a reave descends eastwards in the direction of the saddle between Great Staple and Roos Tors, gradually diminishing in size and robbed in places before finally fading out opposite the head of Beckamoor Combe. In the other direction the alignment is continued further down the west slope of Cox Tor towards a homestead **2** built against its north side. An outer enclosure wall, bisected by a track, contains a hut (c. 5.0 m) at the centre closely surrounded by an outer ring of slabs. Another hut (8.5 m) lies about 400 m to the north-west, **3**, on the edge of the moorland just above Coxtor Farm. Only the base course remains without associated enclosures, but there is little surface stone in the vicinity and the ground may have been cleared to provide material for nearby field walls.

A second reave running parallel to the upper one but 750 m to the south also ends on Beckamoor Brook. The bank supports a line of slabs from the edge of the gully to end abruptly on level ground 190 m to the west. Half the circumference of a hut (c. 7.0 m) is all that remains of a homestead on the opposite bank, **4**, where leat, track and road converge, resulting in very disturbed ground. Slight remains also survive of a settlement, **5**, below the road 450 m to the south-west where a few slabs remain in position on the low banks that once were the walls of three huts (5 to 7 m). Some of the rebuilt walls of the abandoned fields downhill may have had a prehistoric ancestry.

The barely visible bank of a third parallel reave can be detected just above the road north of the tor.

6 Cox Tor North-east (fig. 31.2)

The largest settlement on Cox Tor was laid out on its stone-free north-eastern slopes facing the Roos Tor settlement and with a splendid view up the Wedlake valley. The twenty-four huts and five enclosures (A-E) are well spread out along the hillside making it impossible to see one end of the village from the other. The settlement though has suffered grievously from stone robbing, with many huts reduced to low circular banks and large sections of the perimeter walls entirely missing, those nearest the edge of open ground faring the worst. Ridge and furrow within the ancient field which cuts across the lower pair of enclosures has further damaged the structures within. Tinners also worked the hillside, their numerous pits

MAP 31

infiltrating the settlement and, being of similar size to the huts are difficult in some cases to distinguish from them. Three-quarters of the measurable huts are from 5 to 6.5 m in diameter, the rest being slightly smaller, but none of their entrances have survived.

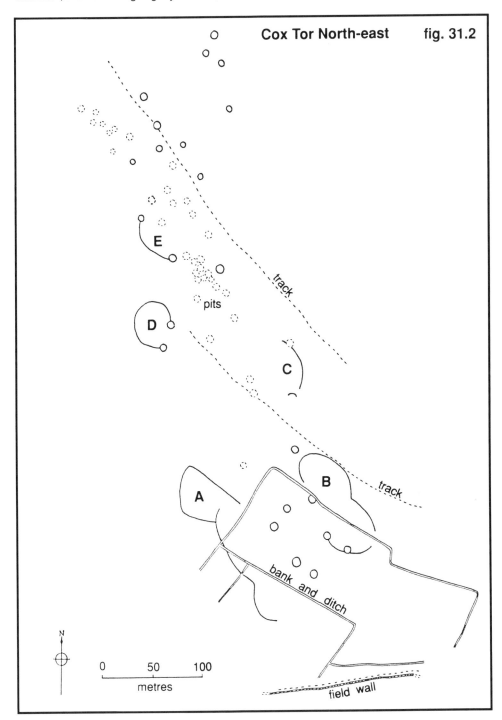

Cox Tor North-east   fig. 31.2

MAP 31

7 Roos Tor North-west (fig. 31.3)

This important settlement of seventy-three huts is one of the largest on the moor and remains unexcavated despite the Dartmoor Exploration Committee's threat to 'take it in hand'. Protected by its remoteness and the abundance of surface stone nearby, much of it is remarkably well preserved, particularly the larger huts below the drain which cuts through the site. Even the group of huts engulfed by the Wedlake enclosures appear to be more overgrown than damaged.

The settlement is bounded on the south-west by a reave which meanders uphill to the rocks below the foot of the tor, substantial but adding little to the barrier naturally provided by the mass of surface stone. The huts and their tiny fields are strictly confined to the east of the reave, facing the neighbouring settlement on the opposite slope on Cox Tor. Downhill the reave becomes exceptionally massive where the present tracks cut through it and continues, not to the river as expected, but curves around below the settlement where it is lost within the present fields.

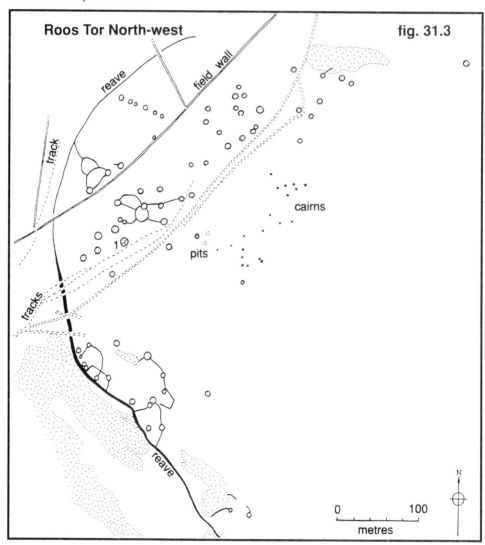

Roos Tor North-west   fig. 31.3

reave · field wall · track · cairns · pits · tracks · reave

0   100

metres

MAP 31

The huts are grouped closely together, many of the neighbouring ones joined by short lengths of walling to form small enclosures against the reave. In some places bands of clitter were found to be adequate without the labour of erecting a wall. Huts vary from 2 to 9 m in diameter, the majority being comparatively small, from 3 to 5 m across, with only six exceeding 7 m. The largest hut, 1 (9.0 m) near the centre of the settlement, is subdivided by a pair of interior curved walls.

A series of small turf-covered mounds are laid out on the shallower slopes immediately uphill from the lower huts. A group of seven cairns 4 to 6 m in diameter are particularly striking but there are at least thirteen smaller ones intermixed with tinners' pits nearby and this may well prove to be the cemetery of the settlement.

The foundations of a single hut (c. 3.0 m) can be detected beside the track on the river side of the reave and a neatly shaped cairn of stones 4 m across a little further along. Despite its similarity to a burial mound the position of the latter suggests it is more likely to be the result of field clearance.

8 Roos Tor South-east

The southern continuation of the reave recommences at the foot of the tor rocks, picking a winding course through the clitter before straightening out on the clearer ground as it descends towards the Walkham. This section, like many on the eastern side of the moor, has been adopted as a parish boundary. Visible sign of the reave is lost at a small area of clitter on the corner of Shillapark north field. The direct course would have taken it through the field aligned with the Little Mis Tor reave on the opposite bank of the Walkham but of this there is no sign.

A few huts can be found near Shillapark corner. An isolated one (c. 7.5 m) reduced to its foundations lies about 15 m north of the reave some distance uphill, three more (c. 3.5-6.0 m) within the clitter itself, and another (6.3 m) just downhill from the leat. Nearer the river a sixth hut (3.0 m) is closely surrounded by an outer bank 3 m outside it from which all the sizeable stones have been removed for use elsewhere.

9 Wedlake (fig. 31.4)

South of White Tor a winding reave descends to the Colly Brook terminating a secondary reave orientated to the south-west, parallel with the river. The free end of the latter is lost to view a little beyond a small rock pile but probably continues buried under the turf for an unknown distance. Reaves and river thus surround the Wedlake settlement of sixteen huts on at least three sides.

The huts share four enclosures A-D the walls of which are fragmentary and, apart from field A, seem to have been poorly built, merely small stones piled against a single line of slabs. Tinners' excavations take up part of the interior of the riverside enclosure, D. The remains of the huts are far more substantial, nearly a metre of soil having been removed from the interiors during the 1905 excavations by the Dartmoor Exploration Committee who 'thoroughly explored' all of them. The biggest hut, 1, (9.2 m), considerably larger than the rest (2.5-6.5 m), is free-standing near the centre of the settlement and has a smaller annexe built on to one side. Its south-east entrance was paved and it produced the greatest variety of finds including pottery, cooking stones, flint and possibly a sling stone. Charcoal and a possible cooking stone were found within the annexe (3.8 m) which was entered on the north side, though the doorway is no longer visible. The most impressive building at present is the oval-shaped hut, 2, (4.8-5.7 m) which has two enormous jamb stones at the entrance, one of them fallen, which must have greatly impressed the neighbours. A number of huts

MAP 31

were found to have been paved, at least at the entrance which was generally orientated to the south, although two were thought to have faced north and west. Hut 4 (4.9 m) had two steps down into the interior. Several produced the usual finds associated with a dwelling including pottery, flints and cooking stones, and charcoal was found within half of them. More interesting finds, but not commented on by the excavators, were what was thought to be lumps of copper ore from hut 5 (4.6 m), iron ore from hut 7 (2.5 m) and an iron horseshoe about halfway above the original floor level of hut 6 (5.2 m).

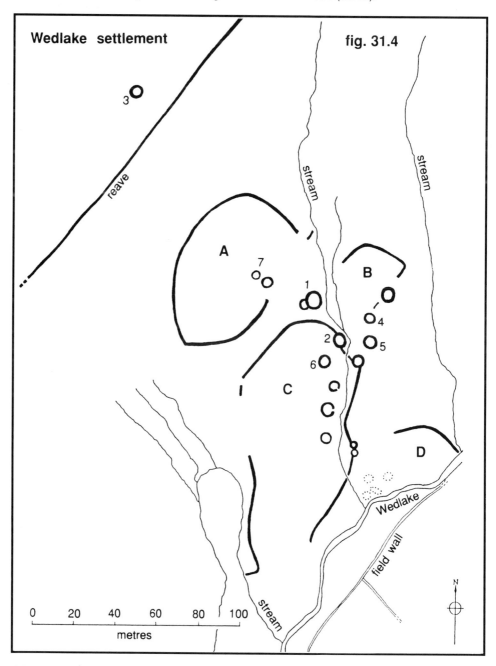

Wedlake settlement   fig. 31.4

MAP 31

10 Lower Godsworthy (fig. 31.5)

Closely surrounded on three sides by the present enclosures the remains of what was once a large settlement across the summit of the ridge above Lower Godsworthy Farm are very slight. All stones of useful size have been carted away leaving the remaining banks nowhere more than 0.2 m high, and even these disappear around the edge of the settlement. Traces of a circular bank presumably of a hut, can be detected at 1 and three more circles of similar size corresponding with slight curves in the perimeter walls show on aerial photographs at 2, 3 and 4.

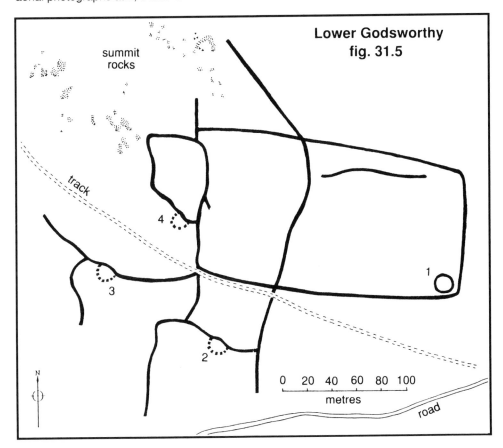

11 Smeardon Down

A rock ridge forms the backbone of Smeardon Down and the shelter of its southern side was selected for the site of a prehistoric homestead. A single line of slabs connectng the various piles forms the boundary around what seems to be a large oval-shaped hut (8 x 10 m), with rubble wall and uneven interior, approached by a passageway about 2 m wide. An embanked pit on the summit east of the enclosure connected to the nearest stack by a bank and ditch may be the remains of a second hut, or more likely a cairn which has been thoroughly dug into. Also on the summit further east is a semi-circular enclosure probably associated with the homestead, its rubble bank no more than 0.3 m high and cut through by a newtake wall on the north side.

MAP 31

12 White Tor West (fig. 31.6)

An exceptionally well-preserved settlement, considering how close it lies to the present field boundaries, no doubt partly due to the large size of stone used in both perimeter and hut walls. A 10 m section of the west wall has been lost but elsewhere it is in remarkably good condition with inner and outer slab faces a fairly constant 1.8 m apart infilled with smaller stones. It seems to have been constructed after the huts had been built, expanding to include huts 1 and 2 and butting onto the wall of hut 7. Three of the seven huts, probably 2, 3 and 5, were excavated by the Dartmoor Exploration Committee in 1898 or the following year with 'poor results'. There was some evidence of fire but all that was found were some flint chippings and a piece of pottery of a type similar to that from Smallacombe Rocks (**map 2.1**). The huts are similar in size, (4.7 to 6.2 m across), with entrances where present towards the south and south-west. Both huts 1 and 7 have interior divisions.

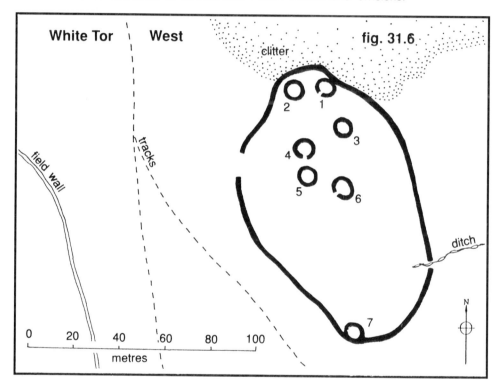

13 White Tor Fort and nearby huts (fig. 31.7)

White Tor is conspicuous from afar on the edge of the high moorland, the ground falling away on all sides though less steeply to the east. A pair of massive concentric walls connect up the largest rock outcrops on the summit, fortifying a level area some 0.8 hectares in extent, supplemented by the natural clitter of the upper slopes. Reaves originating on the Youldon and Colly Brooks are aligned on the summit from north and south ending at the clitter below the fort, a short continuation of the latter crossing the summit to the west of it. Another section running into the clitter from the north-east corner of the fort, which must already have been built, is probably the higher end of the Youldon Brook reave. The settlements between the rivers are obviously confined to the area west of the reaves, whereas the cairns, many in groups, have an unrestricted distribution. The

MAP 31

Dartmoor Exploration Committee carried out some excavations here in 1898 and 1899 but with disappointing results, the period of its construction among other questions remaining as uncertain as before.

Both inner and outer walls have collapsed downhill and are now a tumbled mass of stones, but they were originally of solid construction 3.0 to 3.5 m wide at the base. The exterior wall was about 1.5 m high, slightly lower than the inner wall which judging by the amount of stone was about 2 m high. The distance varies between the walls, narrow on the north side where they have collapsed together but up to 12 m apart on the east where the lower wall diverges to include some of the lower rock stacks in the perimeter. Offset entrances were found on this side, a little more than a metre wide and protected by spur walls, though perhaps these were not original features. Traces of one or two cross-banks between the walls here are probably associated with hut 2.

Cairns, hut circles and rock shelters exist on the summit both outside and within the walls but none of them are necessarily contemporary with the fortifications. Most of those within the fort were excavated by the Exploration Committee (1-9) though their report is not always easy to understand. They described structure 1 as a double hut circle with an inner chamber entered through the other, its floor strewn with charcoal and so perhaps the

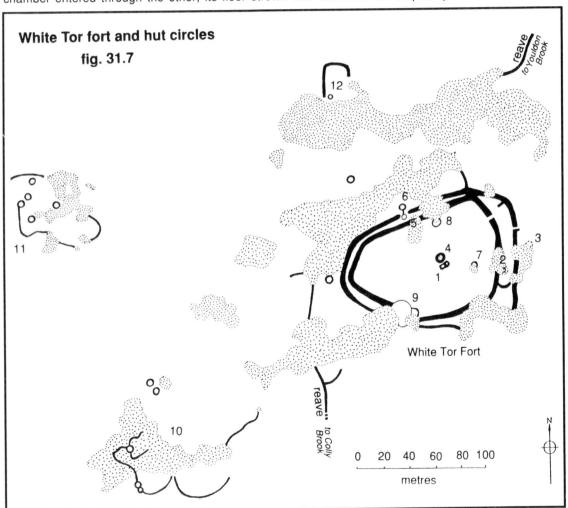

White Tor fort and hut circles

fig. 31.7

reave
to Youldon Brook

12

11

6
5 8
3
4
7
1 2
9

White Tor Fort

reave
to Colly Brook

10

0   20   40   60   80   100

metres

N

MAP 31

cooking-place. The outer chamber produced pottery and numerous flint flakes and chippings, enough to identify it as a knapper's workshop. Structures 2, 3, 7, and 8 are rock shelters, curved walls built against the base of some of the larger natural rocks and perhaps un-roofed. Structure 2 also had an inner chamber in which was found an unidentified piece of slag, and all revealed some evidence of occupancy such as pottery, flint or the cooking pits which were found within two of them. Huts 5 (3.0 m) and 6 (2.5 m) on the north side of the fort are connected by a short bank across the line of the outer wall which must have been demolished here to make way for them, demonstrating that the fort had passed out of use by the time these huts were constructed.

Structure 4 in the centre of the fort puzzled the members of the Committee, unable to decide whether it had originally been a hut circle or merely a heap of stones like 9, though from the quantity of material the latter seems more likely. The present hollow surrounding the central rock pillar is a product of the excavation as initially the mass of small stones was piled up around it like a cairn: some flints were found together with a few shards of prehistoric and medieval dates. The enormous cairn of stones piled up around the rocks at 9, as around many of the smaller Dartmoor tors, was equally puzzling. The Exploration Committee removed sixty-five cubic metres of stone next to the rocks and trenched down to the underlying calm expecting any deposit to be in this area, but apart from two small flint flakes nothing was found to indicate its purpose. The base course of a rock shelter is built on to its east side.

Below the fort to north and west several groups of huts with connecting walls are sited on the edge of the clitter, five huts each at 10 and 11, and one within a rectangular enclosure at 12. None of these are more than 3 m in diameter.

A neolithic polished stone axehead 0.25 m long, now in Plymouth Museum, was found at Wedlake Farm in 1964, and a polished greenstone axe, apparently damaged during manufacture, in the Bagga Brook upstream. Numerous flints of mesolithic and later types have been collected from the area south and east of the tor. The latter were found scattered alongside the track from near the south-south-east cairns **20** to beyond Langstone Moor stone row where there was a large cache of 441 flints heaped together.

14 White Tor North (fig. 31.8)

Below the clitter north of White Tor a densely-packed enclosure has been built at the junction of the Youldon to White Tor and the Cudlipptown Down upper reaves, which have been considerably reinforced as part of the boundary. Fifteen of the twenty-five huts are crammed together in the upper part of the main enclosure and others have been built within extensions against the outside of the boundary wall. The huts are small, all but four of them being less than 3.5 m across. The largest, 1 (5.7 m), on the edge of its own small plot in the north-east corner, has a curved interior wall the same height as the outer one. The interior of the enclosure is particularly stony and many of the huts utilize the natural rocks as part of their walls.

Cudlipptown Down upper reave continues north-westwards along the flank of White Tor before sharply altering course over the summit towards Broadmoor Brook. It fades out at some distance before a newtake but the south wall of the latter continues the alignment downhill. Two more reaves cross the Down to the north which also originate on the Youldon Brook reave but these are neither as straight nor as neatly aligned as the parallel reaves on the east side of the moor. How far downhill to the west the land was colonized is at present impossible to say but a prehistoric settlement reappears on the next piece of open ground, Smeardon Down **11** and a hut circle, or possibly a barrow, was discovered well below the moorland edge near the Rectory in Peter Tavy.

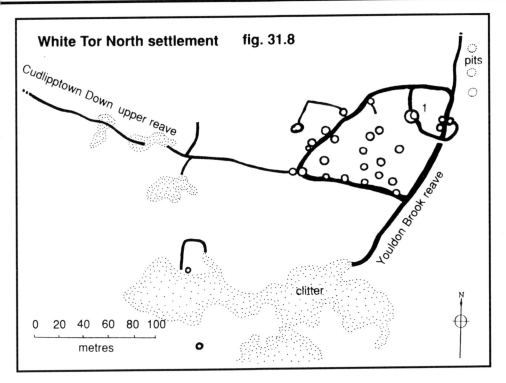

White Tor North settlement   fig. 31.8

MAP 31

15 Cudlipptown Down East (fig. 31.9)

Only a small section of the settlement lies on the Down, the major part being within the newtake to the east. Its fields are attached to the east end of the Cudlipptown lower reave but they may well have been laid out first as the reave makes a significant re-alignment just before the junction. Four huts 4-7 m in diameter remain in the upper rectangular enclosure, bisected by the present field wall, from which a number of parallel strips descend downhill towards a branch of the White Tor reave. The latter continues below the strips, by-passing a small building (7 x 4 m) in the centre of the newtake, to end on a tributary of the Youldon Brook, the other branch apparently forming the upper margin of later fields on the opposite slope. The original plan has been confused by the number of worn-down parallel banks which sub-divide the newtake but some at least are likely to have had a prehistoric ancestry.

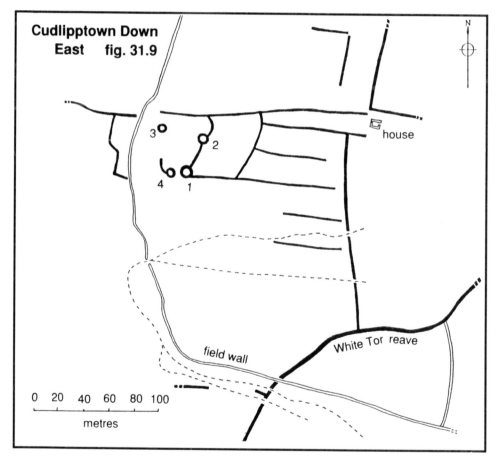

16 Cudlipptown Down Central

The east end of Cudlipptown Down middle reave leaves the Youldon reave at right angles but soon curves away to the west along the flank of the hill, and at about 550 m alters course by 30° to the south-west. A triangular enclosure at the corner enfolds four small huts (2.2-3.8 m) against the uphill side of the reave. Immediately downhill at least two more huts

MAP 31

and part of an enclosure wall are similarly associated with the lower reave. Westwards the middle reave continues over the ridge towards a pair of cairns in line, 0.2 m high by 3.0 and 4.5 m in diameter. A short distance beyond are the possible remains of another but the course of the bank here becomes uncertain and difficult to follow.

17 Cudlipptown Down West

A quite substantial group of fields existed on the west side of the Down built on to both sides of Cudlipptown lower reave, but an unknown area has been engulfed within the present enclosures. What remains has been further damaged by the mine buildings and workings on the north slope and only very slight banks and a single hut circle (c. 6.2 m) remain of the prehistoric settlement here. The reave continues across the field boundary and becomes over-built by the present wall. Downhill to the north-east an isolated stony mound is probably a burial cairn.

Eastwards the lower reave, like the other two, alters course over the north side of the Down but in a more irregular fashion apparently to avoid areas of soft ground, whilst a central section of about 200 m is missing altogether.

18, 19 Cairns north of Roos Tor

Four dispersed cairns can be found on the rise about a kilometre north of the tor. The outer Wedlake enclosure wall has been driven across a cairn, **18**, on the hillside next to a spring, causing severe damage. Most of the structure within the field has been demolished but the moorside section has been allowed to remain, albeit with a deep central pit. The fine cairn 200 m uphill is in much better condition, its surface uneven but with no deep pitting and possibly substantially intact. A circular bank, about 20 m outside diameter, surrounds a lower interior composed of small stones.

Two more cairns, **19**, lie on the summit of the hill, both of them trenched from the south-west edge towards the centre by members of the Dartmoor Exploration Committee in 1898 or the following year. The excavated stones, not yet covered by turf, were roughly tipped back into the pits but the neat coursing of the interior stonework of the larger cairn can still be seen along the sides of the trench. The uneven surface and oval outline of the latter, spread to 15 m across, shows that there had been considerable earlier disturbance but the cremation at the centre was untouched. A flat stone covered a central pit full of ashes and charcoal. The excavators, discouraged by a rainstorm and disappointed by this result, retired after only an 'imperfect' examination of the smaller cairn to the north-east.

20 Cairns south-south-east of White Tor

The trenches are still plainly visible across the four cairns on the hillside 250 m south-south-east of the tor, dug into by the Dartmoor Exploration Committee during their excavations of the summit fort. They did not consider the cairns merited individual description but all apparently covered central pits containing ashes and charcoal, and a few flint flakes were found. The two mounds with central hollows 100 m below the track were excavated a few years later, marked X and Z on the map accompanying their tenth report, together with another nearby. The eastern cairn Z covered nothing more than a flat stone at the centre but a flint was found in each of the other two which were considered to be 'primitive habitations'. Yet another small cairn accompanied by some rubble banks lies closer to the river to the south-east.

MAP 32

21 Cairns south-south-west of White Tor

The Committee also trenched another group of three cairns south-south-west of the tor lying approximately where a short, surfaced track branches off the Lich Way. An elongated cairn (13 x 5.7 m) is easy to identify but the other two are doubtful, one of them perhaps being the low mound surrounding a natural rock a few metres to the east. The other may be the semi-circular bank opposite a mound on the other side of the long cairn, bisected by the track. As before the cairns covered central pits containing ashes and charcoal.

22 Cairns east of White Tor

Three cairns are close together on the summit of the ridge and a fourth, containing a cist, is conspicuous a short distance further to the east. The north cairn is a flat-topped grass-covered mound with the tops of a ring of stones showing through the turf around the outer edge. It was probably from this cairn that the Exploration Committee obtained the perforated stone illustrated in their report. The pair of cairns to the south are no more than slight mounds covered by a scattering of small stones. About 100 m eastwards three sides of a cist supported on one side by a natural rock stand above the remains of its cairn. The Committee cleared out the cist but someone had preceded them and nothing was found.

23 Cairns north-west of White Tor

The flat-topped cairn between the middle and upper Cudlipptown reaves north-west of the tor was dug into by the Dartmoor Exploration Committee during their White Tor Fort excavations, described merely as 'giving no results'. They replaced the stones, as yet not covered by turf, in the T-shaped trench through the centre leaving most of the cairn undisturbed.

About 60 m to the south is an unusual type of ring cairn. A bank now spread up to 3.5 m wide but with traces of an inner and outer kerb surrounds a flat interior 11.4 m across. Six stones are placed symmetrically on the bank, two pairs each about a metre apart on the north-west and south-east sides and two single stones an equal distance between them. Two of the paired stones have slipped sideways but these four seem to be set with the longer faces across the bank.

The prominent position on a knoll only 3 m from Cudlipptown upper reave of a small pile of stones 2.5 m across suggests it may well prove to be a burial cairn.

a-e Boundary and inscribed stones

The small parish boundary stone **a** (*P/W*) on the saddle midway between Roos and Great Staple Tors was the scene of a violent dispute recorded by Crossing[s], between the men of Peter Tavy and those of Whitchurch over the stone's precise position. Stone **b** (*PTG 1*) at the corner of the Wedlake enclosures on Peter Tavy Great Common was one of a pair, the other on the west bank of the Walkham, defining the northern boundary of a sett for quarrying granite granted by the Duchy in 1847 to Edgcombe and White of Tavistock.[46]

The ring of pillars, **c** (*B*), surrounding Roos Tor were set up by the Duke of Bedford in about 1880 to prevent damage to the tor rocks by the granite workers. Many of the pillars are accompanied by flat slabs incised with a dashed circle, similar to those around Pew Tor and serving the same purpose. Granite was being worked in the vicinity well before Merrivale Quarry was opened in 1875 and the production of paving slabs here has been well described by Helen Harris[47]. Numerous sett-makers' 'bankers' or stone benches on

MAP 32

which the work was carried out can be found on the south-eastern slopes of Staple Tors, a particularly good example, protected by a shelter of stone chippings, being within the clitter on the east side of Great Staple Tor. This one is approached by a well constructed track on which the cart ruts are still visible, its lower edge built up with fractured slabs and levelled into the hillside.

The line of stones lettered *RB* set up along the bank and ditch ringing the Dennithorne enclosures **d** were probably an attempt of many years ago to reclaim the abandoned upland fields now cut through by the Tavistock to Princetown road. Mrs Bray[22] pieced together the story of George (?) Stevens who poisoned himself after an unsuccessful love affair and was buried in Stevens Grave, **e**. The site is marked by a triangular pillar (*S*) at a cross-tracks, like Jay's Grave (**map 21**), beside the Peter Tavy branch of the Lich Way.

MAP 32 The Lower Tavy

1 Standon Down North-west settlement and cairns (fig. 32.1)

The north-west slopes of Standon Hill support one of the largest Bronze Age villages on the moor. Seventy huts, many of them in excellent condition, are sited on a gentle slope above the Tavy with a spendid view down the valley to the south-west. The huts are built closely together, some of them almost in contact, and the majority are joined to their neighbours by a network of up to four walls forming a maze of small paddocks between them. Probably most of the huts were originally connected in this way for the walls are of slight construction and are probably simply buried where there are obvious gaps on the plan. One exception may have been the largest building, hut 1 (7.8 m) which occupies a typically prominent position on the upper edge of the settlement overlooking the rest. Its nearest neighbour 2 (6.4 m) is also a substantial building but with a crosswall dividing the interior, as has hut 3 (6.0 m). A hollow way between hut 4 (4.3 m) and one of the boundary walls may be the original track into the settlement from the direction of the river.

The Dartmoor Exploration Committee excavated forty-three huts in 1901. They noticed that quite a number had been rebuilt, by shepherds they suggested, but the newer work of stones loosely piled on the ancient foundations is easy to recognize. The huts vary in size from 2 to 7.8 m across, though the great majority are no more than 5 m. Where still visible the entrances face southwards, hut 5 (6.0 m) retaining both jambs and having a large slab as a natural sill outside the doorway. Most were found to be at least partly paved which accounted for the comparatively few finds made by the excavators, the large hut 1 for instance producing only a single piece of flint. Nearly all showed some evidence of occupation such as wood and peat charcoal, cooking stones and pebbles of various sizes. The excavators suggested the larger pebbles could have been anvils and pounders, the others perhaps being sling stones or even counters in some Bronze Age game. Also found were flints in 12% of the huts, pottery (16%) and rubbing stones (12%).

The excavated huts, marked with a central dot in fig. 32.1, can be recognized by their sunken uneven floors but otherwise the settlement remains much as it was in the 1901 plan accompanying the excavation report. A few more walls that are clearly visible have been added in the present survey and the three huts shown as broken circles are no longer identifiable. Huts 45, 67 and 70 are missing from the excavator's plan and their 15 and 52 seem to refer to the same building, but one of their huts, 6 (2.0 m), is unnumbered and two more, 7 (4.0 m) and 8 (damaged), which were no doubt intended to be included, have been added.

MAP 32

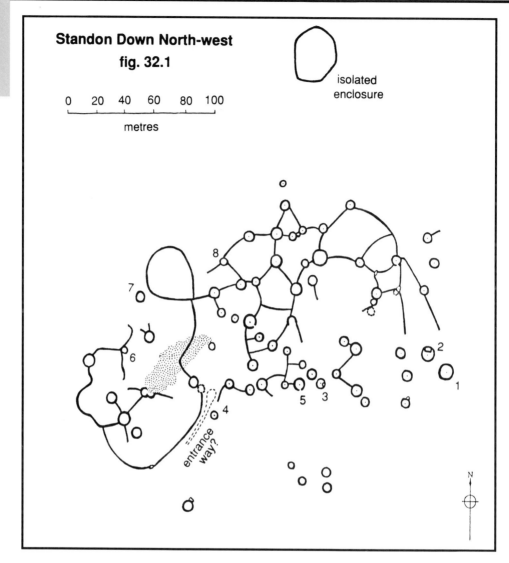

Standon Down North-west

fig. 32.1

0   20   40   60   80   100

metres

isolated
enclosure

8

7

6

5   3

4

2

1

entrance
way?

N

North of the settlement a low rubble bank surrounds a separate enclosure about 30 m across, with no associated huts but probably contemporary with the settlement. More huts are shown on the Ordnance Survey map about 350 m to the east, out of sight of the settlement, but the pair of mounds here on the bank of a stream are more likely to be well-robbed cairns. The south mound 4.8 m across has a deep central hollow and is surrounded by an outer ring of stones. The other, 5 m away, also has a well-defined rim around a raised but dished interior.

2 Nattor Down settlement and cairns (fig. 32.2)

Prehistoric settlement covered a considerable area of the hillside west of Ger Tor, the upper limit defined by a reave running between the Tavy and Willsworthy Brook, cutting off a triangle of land between the two rivers. The southern half of the reave, on the steep slope

MAP 32

down to the Tavy, has been completely rebuilt though for some reason the new work was never carried across the ridge. How far the prehistoric settlement extended into the present fields downhill to the west is unknown but only a pair of medium sized but much damaged cairns, 1 and 2, spread to 13 and 10 m across, survive below Wheal Jewell leat. This section of the leat, which still carries water and must be crossed via the clapper bridges has at some period been redug at a higher level. There has also been some loss of the prehistoric enclosures north of Hamlyn's Newtake wall. Another reave, peculiarly irresolute in direction, bounds the settlement a short distance away to the south-east.

Three incomplete enclosures remain, A-C, surrounding a curious mixture of cairns and huts. The lower enclosure A which can be partly traced as a line of slabs set in a low bank north of the newtake wall, includes a damaged cairn within the circuit, 3. A weighty flat slab, partly turf covered, appears to overlie a hollow in its centre and may perhaps be the cover of a cist. The much more substantial boundary of paired slabs around the middle enclosure includes three huts (5.8-6.8 m) along the north-west wall, a smaller one (4.1 m) in poor shape attached to it by an extension wall from the boundary, and a free-standing pair (5.7, 6.0 m) near the centre. A hollowed cairn, 4, 4.6 m in diameter, is also included within the circuit.

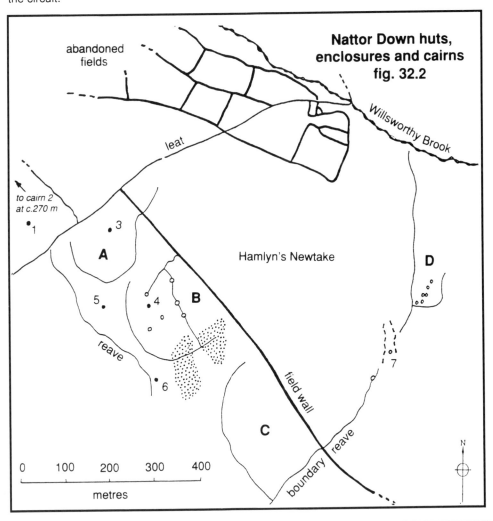

Nattor Down huts, enclosures and cairns fig. 32.2

abandoned fields

Willsworthy Brook

leat

to cairn 2 at c.270 m

1

3

A

Hamlyn's Newtake

D

5.

4

B

reave

6

field wall

7

C

reave

boundary

0   100   200   300   400

metres

N

MAP 32

A more interesting cairn with cist, 5, lies between these enclosures immediately to the south-east. One side and end slab of the cist remain in place and a ground-level trench has been cut to the back of the latter from the edge of the mound. The flat slab on the side of the mound is probably the cover slab. Yet another likely cairn, 6, lies uphill to the north-east, a circle of slabs surrounding a raised interior.

A range bunker lies between the middle and upper enclosure C, the wall of which is mostly an insignificant arc of slabs attached to the Willsworthy Brook boundary reave, not traceable within the newtake. Several small circular areas levelled into the hillside can be found within the boundary but no definite remains of huts.

3 Hamlyn's Newtake huts (fig. 32.2)

The west end of the Nattor Down boundary reave starts at Willsworthy Brook and ascends directly uphill as a substantial bank before changing direction towards Ger Tor. There are many minor alterations of course for no apparent reason and a gap midway where later pits and gullies cut across it. The hut circle 7 (5.8 m) at this point has been rebuilt, probably as an animal pen, and the foundations of another lie against the reave to the south. Just downhill a group of six small and overgrown huts all of similar size (3-4 m) have been built north of the reave, on the opposite side to the Nattor Down enclosures. A circuit wall D, now open downhill but probably buried here, encloses them against the reave.

4 Ger Tor North-east settlement and cairn (fig. 32.3)

A well-preserved settlement of rather different character to the other prehistoric villages along the Tavy is laid out in the sheltered dip north-east of Ger Tor. The widely dispersed huts are larger and more solidly built, without the tiny paddocks associated with the Watern Oke and Standon Hill settlements. A 'hasty examination' was made of four of these, 'only one exhaustively' by Baring-Gould in 1893. The site on the upper hillside, fully 90 m above the river, has a splendid view down the Tavy valley to the south-west.

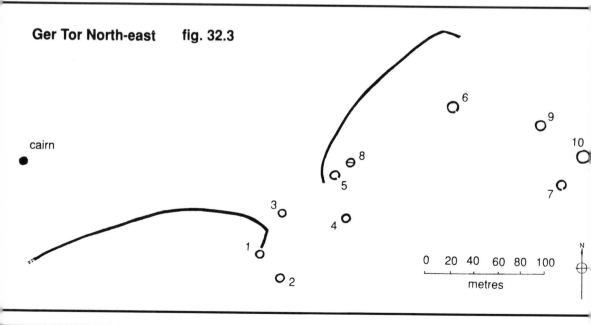

Ger Tor North-east   fig. 32.3

cairn

0 20 40 60 80 100

metres

MAP 32

Two curved reaves form the northern boundary of the settlement separated by a gap of about 50 m midway where there is a cluster of huts. The west boundary bank starts from hut 1 (4.0 m) and curves around the base of Ger Tor before altering course in the direction of the summit rocks. Three more huts of similar size, 2 (3.7 m), 3 (3.7 m) and 4 (4.4 m), occupy the gap before the next section continues eastwards, stopping well short of a minor tributary of the Tavy which presumably bounded the settlement on this side. The remainder of the group are larger and huts 5 (5.9 m), 6 (7.6 m) and 7 (4.9 m) retain both jamb stones at the entrances which face downhill to the south. Hut 8 (5.8 m) has a straight interior wall and excavation showed that it had been at least partly paved. Huts 9 (6.3 m) and 10 (7.6 m) are both good specimens, the latter, along with hut 6, being the largest in the settlement. The only finds made were a piece of flint in one of the huts, numerous cooking stones, and some pebbles which the excavator suggested may have been sling stones.

The west reave approaches to within about 80 m of a cairn near the summit of the hill, the highest in the line of cairns on the south-western slopes (fig. 32.2). There is no sign of a cist but stones from a central pit have been thrown out on the downhill side.

5 Watern Oke West (fig. 32.4)

The most ambitious single project undertaken by the Dartmoor Exploration Committee was the excavation in 1905 of ninety-four huts at Watern Oke, on the north side of the Tavy, when eight men were employed as diggers for nearly two months during the summer. A good plan accompanied the report to which can be added; a few more walls that are clearly visible, hut 1 (2.3 m), hut 2 (c. 2.0 m) and the slight remains of two others at 3 and 4. The walls connecting the huts were not excavated and probably much of the network remains buried under the turf. The floors of the huts are well below ground level outside and, except for a covering of turf, the site is much as it was left by the excavators. Apparently no restoration was carried out and apart from the loss of the roofs the site gives a good impression of how a large Bronze Age village must have looked soon after it was abandoned.

Although the Committee described the excavations as one site there are actually three unconnected groups of huts here separated by open ground, though perhaps all occupied at the same time. By far the largest group of seventy-eight huts is confined to a thick belt of clitter to the west, laid out around the margins of the stony ground and in any clearer spaces within. There are numerous small paddocks but the total area enclosed is only about 0.4 Ha. Apart from a group on the eastern edge of the clitter, 5-8, all the huts are small, 2 to 4.3 m in diameter, and many are markedly oval in shape. The usual collection of cooking stones and flints were recovered from hut 5 (5.0 m), but hut 6 (5.8 m) produced a most uncommon object, a blue glass bead with a hole bored through the centre. Hut 7 (5.4 x 4.5 m) and its companion 8 (4.6 x 2.8 m) stand somewhat apart from the rest, the site of the former chosen to take advantage of a large natural rock as a jamb stone. The most desirable site though must belong to hut 12 (3.4 m) on a knoll overlooking the river.

One other hut slightly larger than the rest, 9 (4.6 m), lies on the edge of an open plateau within the clitter alongside a rectangular structure (7.8 x 3.0 m) which has an entrance in one of the long sides. The latter is possibly of a later period, but unfortunately nothing apart from a fireplace was found within to determine its date.

Certainly of more recent date is the 'sentry box', 10, on the eastern edge of the clitter, a drystone walled cache rather more than a metre high and still roofed with a large flat slab. It remains undisturbed as it was left by the Committee 'to the inquisitive destruction of the coming archaeologist'. Hut 11 (4.0 m) is one that has obviously been partly rebuilt as a shelter.

MAP 32

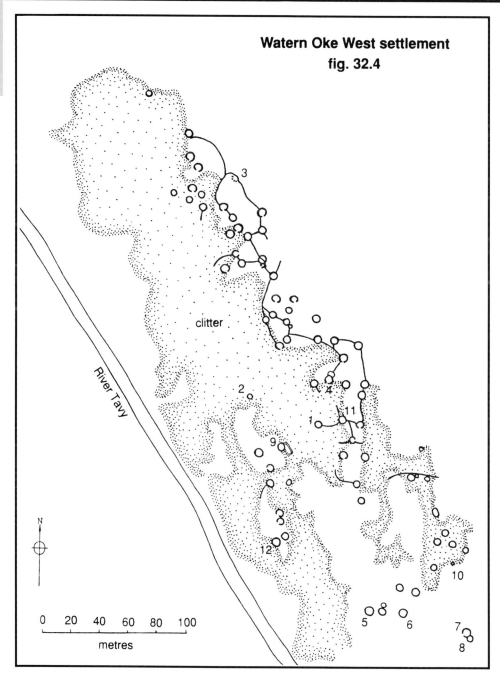

Watern Oke West settlement
fig. 32.4

The excavation results showed that practically all huts contained some evidence of occupation, such as fireplaces (47%), cooking stones (38%), flints (23%) including a few arrow heads, and other stones apparently used for a variety of purposes, such as whetstones, pounders and possibly sling shots. Some huts were paved though the majority seem to have had earthern floors, and a few were subdivided by interior walls. Entrances faced approximately southwards, on the opposite side to the fireplace.

MAP 32

6 Tavy Cleave East

Midway between Watern Oke and Standon Hill north-west settlements is a small prehistoric village amidst a patch of clitter overlooking Tavy Cleave. The huts are more widely dispersed here and without their network of tiny enclosures, though linear contour banks above and below them probably acted as an outer boundary to the settlement. The site has not been excavated but the twelve huts to be found here are in good condition and one of them has been partly rebuilt. The largest hut (c. 7.5 m) is surrounded by a roughly circular enclosure 35 m across, the only one with this refinement. Its nearest neighbour 20 m away (c. 7.0 m) has a smaller hut (c. 2.0 m) built on just outside its entrance, the jambs still in place. Another hut to the north only about 4 m in diameter has an exceptionally long entrance passage, over 2.5 m long. The rest of the huts vary from 2 to 5.5 m across and, where visible, the entrances open along the contour to the south.

7 Lower Rattle Brook, east bank settlement

Settlement intensifies on both sides of the brook as it nears its confluence with the Tavy, that on the east bank being slightly upstream from its opposite number at Dead Lake Foot. The poor remains of this settlement occupy about 150 m of river frontage but natural overgrowth makes the huts and walls exceptionally difficult to identify. Tin streaming, boggy ground next to the river, a leat supplying the nearby water-wheel and a number of ditches and tracks have combined to obscure the plan of the site. Many huts seem to have been joined by walling like the large settlement at Watern Oke, but most can only be seen on aerial photographs and the visible remains are very fragmentary. Some fifteen huts are clear enough but odd piles and arcs of stones are probably remnants of others. The huts are all small, varying in size from 1.5 m to 4.5 m in diameter.

8 Dead Lake Foot (fig. 32.5)

The boundaries of this settlement cut off a corner of the west bank of the Rattle Brook as it alters course around a small promontory of higher ground just north of its junction with Dead Lake. Heather covers much of the site and both huts and enclosure walls are overgrown and difficult to follow in places. The deeply worn peat track from Amicombe Hill fording the brook below the settlement cuts through the site, altering course around the prehistoric obstructions before continuing uphill over the southern flank of Hare Tor.

The tops of sixteen huts can be found here though there may well be others no longer visible. All are small, the largest, 1, being only 5.1 m in

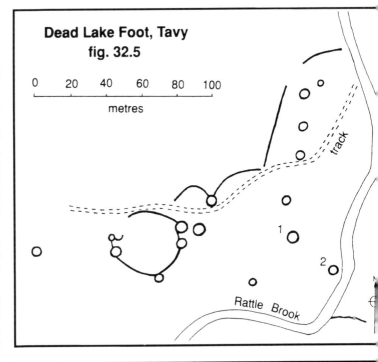

Dead Lake Foot, Tavy
fig. 32.5

0   20   40   60   80   100

metres

track

1

2

Rattle Brook

MAP 32

diameter. Hut 2 (4.1 m), built right on the river bank, shows that the course of the stream has changed little over the millenia since it was built. Five or six huts are on the margin of a roughly circular enclosure 34 m across and the arcs of banks above the track suggest that these too once formed part of complete enclosures.

9 Rattlebrook Foot

Yet another settlement occupied the western promontory above the junction of the Rattle Brook and Tavy but the site is exceptionally overgrown and little remains visible above the engulfing turf. The tops of at least four huts (4-5 m) can still be detected, as can slight traces of banks between them that once were surrounding enclosures. Much obviously remains hidden and the size of the settlement is quite unknown. A short distance uphill a low mound, larger and more regular than the natural hummocks, may be an associated cairn.

10 Sharp Tor settlement

The large egg-shaped enclosure on the lower slopes of Sharp Tor surrounds ten huts, the site facing Doe Tor across a shallow valley. The double-slabbed circuit wall of medium-sized slabs is mostly a metre in width, outside faces, though wider along the south side. Most of the huts, 2.5 to 5.0 m in diameter, are built close to or against the perimeter wall as are the foundations of a rectangular structure (c. 8.5 x 5.0 m) near the lower boundary. One hut nearer the centre has an entrance facing south-east and an annexe on the downhill side. From the amount of surrounding clitter the interior may have been partly cleared to provide material for the wall and huts, but the number of small slabs remaining show that there was no serious attempt to remove all the surface stone.

11 Hare Tor West

Five huts lie close together facing White Hill at the foot of the long western slope descending from Hare Tor. With the well used Rattlebrook track passing close by and newtakes encroaching on either side the site was too accessible to have escaped considerable damage. The hillside is noticeably clear of surface stone and what was available was no doubt eagerly requisitioned to provide material for the nearby field walls. Few slabs remain around the huts (5.0-7.5 m) and none at all in the largest, and here and there a few stones in line are all that survive of surrounding enclosure walls.

12 Standon Farm

Some of the walls of the strangely shaped fields on the hillside above Standon Farm are very likely to overlie the boundaries of a prehistoric settlement here, but only a few of the ancient slab walls can be found unaltered. The northern newtake wall adopts part of the course of a rubble reave originating on the Tavy and orientated on the summit though the latter can only be traced a short distance uphill from the field corner. The poor remains of a single hut (c. 7.0 m) built onto the reave is now included within the field. A much better example (7.5 m) with massive double-slabbed walls 1.3 m thick lies on the opposite side of the reave a short distance downhill, accompanied by a small companion building (3.0 m) nearby and the disturbed foundations of another close to the field wall.

MAP 32

13-15 Baggator Brook

The slight prehistoric remains along the banks of Baggator Brook give no indication of the original size of settlement in the valley. Upstream a short, curved reave on the north side of the river runs towards the lower end of a more recent bank and ditch orientated on the summit cairn. The latter descends on the other side through the clitter towards Baggator Farm and encloses a particularly stony patch of hillside. Below the reave a single small hut circle (c. 4.0 m) lies about 40 m from the river, **13**. Part of a rubble enclosure wall barely 0.2 m high is still visible uphill but most of the circuit is buried beneath the turf.

A second reave winds uphill from the southern tip of Standon Hill, also orientated on the summit but ending in the clitter after some 200 m. At least three huts (5-6 m), all in poor condition, can be found close to its east side, **14**, the lowest merely a circular platform levelled into the hillside with all wall stones removed.

Facing these on the opposite side of the river South Common Plantation overlies a settlement of unknown extent, **15**. The tops of one or possibly two huts show above the turf close to where the lower end of a contemporary enclosure bank disappears under the plantation wall.

16, 17 Cairns on Standon Hill

Like so many hilltops the summit of Standon Down is crowned by a large cairn 18.5 m across and still 2 m high, which it shares with some wooden huts and shelters, **16**. It was sited not quite on the highest point and includes the summit rocks in the periphery. Stones removed from several deep pits at the centre have been thrown outside concealing much of its outer face which here and there can be seen to have been constructed of neatly coarsed blocks, with a slight batter inwards towards the top. This is one of the few large cairns where the original diameter can be accurately measured.

A small cairn about 5 m across lies on the moorland side of the Standon Farm enclosures, **17**, but its elaborate structure has been severely damaged. The tall slabs of a kerb retaining circle remain standing around the eastern quadrant, the rest having fallen flat or been robbed. A single stone on end is probably the last of an inner ring of tiny diameter surrounding a central cist. The latter was in poor condition when first noticed by Crossing[10] and is now no longer visible.

18 Limsboro cairn

Limsboro or Lunts Barrow, one of the few cairns to have a personal name, is a boundary point of the Forest, first included in the 1608 Perambulation. It was visited by the Rev. Bray in 1802 who described it as 'an immense heap of stones with a little cavity in the top; in the centre is a large stone'. Much of its material must have been removed since then, perhaps to the buildings at the peat works in the valley below (**map 33**) and the 'large stone' now rests on the tor rocks well above the remaining stones. These are loosely piled around the base of the little tor in a completely structureless fashion, sharing the summit with a firing range flagpole.

19-21 Cairns on Hare Tor and Doe Tor

A solitary cairn (7.5 x 0.6 m) lies prominently on the hillside well down the south-east flank of Hare Tor, **19**. A ground-level trench has been neatly cut across it from edge to edge in a

MAP 32

purposeful fashion rather than the usual casual pit at the centre which suggests it was an unrecorded archaeological investigation, perhaps undertaken during the Watern Oke excavations in 1905. In that year the Rev. Anderson did indeed excavate a cairn on the hillside some 270 m to the west but this one was much smaller, 3.4 m across by 0.5 m high, and has yet to be relocated. It had a retaining circle around the outside and covered a pit at the centre containing charcoal, ash and 'human cinder dust'. The month before he had opened an even smaller one (1.2 x 0.6 m) on the other side of the Tavy opposite the Watern Oke settlement. This contained burnt earth, charcoal, ash and a flint blade, though he does not record whether these also had been placed in a pit. Anderson then 'cleared the surface of the deads' which presumably only means that he scattered what was left of the tiny structure. Not surprisingly it has not been recorded since.

Far more substantial is the flat-topped cairn (10.0 x 1.3 m) sited 50 m below the crest of the ridge connecting Hare Tor with Sharp Tor to the north, **20**. Although the centre has been completely disorganized and is now a mass of loose stone, the outer rim and sides appear to be intact. It is presumably the one excavated by Baring-Gould and Anderson in 1905, though their map co-ordinates do not agree. Few archaeological excavation reports are as succinct as the one given in the Barrow Report for that year; '... the result may be summarised as nil'. The additional detail promised never appeared. Boundary stone WD19 stands close by.

Multiple tracks have been worn deep into the hillside between this cairn and a heather-covered companion 120 m downhill to the south-west. About a third of the material has been removed from its eastern side but it is still a substantial monument, 10 m across and a metre high.

Another cairn with a boundary stone close by, WD16 lies near the bottom of the incline east of Doe Tor, **21.** At its centre is a cist with both end stones and a side slab remaining, the latter having been replaced in position when the cist was excavated in 1905.

Another slab lying below the cairn was probably either the missing side or the cist cover. The excavators cleared out the cist but it had been rifled long before and only a minute fragment of charcoal was recovered. The tops of two small stones show above the turf within the mound which are probably part of an inner ring surrounding the cist.

22 Cairns on White Hill (fig. 32.6)

White Hill appears rather unimpressive when approached from the west viewed against the backdrop of higher and more rugged ground behind, but once it was one of the most sacred places on the moor. No known settlements or enclosures of prehistoric date encroach upon its flanks which were entirely given over to the burial of the dead. Well over sixty cairns, large and small, can still be found here grouped into four separate cemeteries, but the hill is too close to the edge of the moor, and incidentally included within Willsworthy firing range, for the monuments to have escaped undamaged. The slopes are now remarkably stone free, much of it having been collected by the cairn builders themselves, so providing a convenient source for nearby newtake walls. Range bunkers and stone pits confuse the site and all are to some extent overgrown, some of the smallest cairns having no doubt been completely buried beneath the surface.

The south-west cemetery is more spread out than the others and includes the largest cairns laid out in a line. Three of these, probably numbers 3, 4 and 5, were untouched before they were excavated by Baring-Gould in about 1888. Despite their comparatively large size he found only a shallow pit dug into the subsoil at the centre of each containing charcoal and ashes. At about the same date a 'small but perfect knife' was found in the vicinity.

Cairn 1 is a ring cairn, a low circular bank with an outer diameter of 19 m originally surrounding a flat interior. It has been disfigured by a long trench cut through the centre with

MAP 32

the upcast tossed out on one side. The central trench of cairn 2 (c. 13.0 x 1.0 m) is shallow but much of the north side has been carted away, and 5 m away a pit and mound is probably all that remains of another, 3 (c. 9.0 x 0.2 m). Cairn 4 (c. 9.0 x 1.2 m) has a massive central pit and much of the structure of 5 (c. 10.0 x 0.7 m) has been removed. Cairns 6 (c. 7.5 x 0.5 m) and 7 (c. 5.0 x 0.2 m), 4 m apart, have also been much damaged, but 8 (5.0 x 0.2 m) on a slight knoll overlooking the rest has escaped lightly with only a shallow central depression. Cairn 9, isolated from the rest on the opposite side of the summit, is another ring cairn. The circular bank, externally 16 m across but only 0.1 m high, surrounds a flat interior only marred by a small trench on one side. The mound on the summit next to the flagpole appears to be an entirely modern erection, but the remains of another cairn 14 m across which was reported nearby in 1950 has not been relocated.

Well downhill to the north-east is cairn 10 (8.0 x 0.6 m), with a hollow at the centre exposing a side and two end slabs of a cist. The structure is very overgrown but the tops of an outer ring of stones can just be seen a metre from its base. The outlying slab set at right angles 25 m downhill appears to have been deliberately placed in this position.

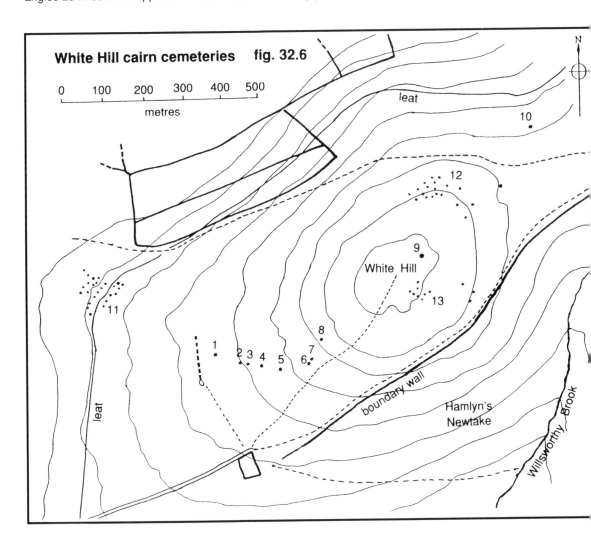

White Hill cairn cemeteries   fig. 32.6

0   100   200   300   400   500

metres

MAP 32

The cairns in the other cemeteries are smaller, rarely exceeding 4.5 m across by 0.3 m high, a few being oval rather than circular. The Wheal Jewell Mine leat cuts through the west cemetery 11, which contains about two dozen cairns, all of them interfered with and mishapen. One was dug into by Baring-Gould during his excavation of the cairns uphill but he found it to be entirely structureless with no trace of a deposit and he doubted that they were burial sites at all. The north-east cemetery, 12, contains about the same number of cairns, of similar size but rather more spread out and many of them apparently undamaged. The south-east cemetery, 13, is centred just below the summit where there are eight cairns 3.0 to 6.5 m in diameter, the largest having been thoroughly trenched. Another three members of this group lie closer to the newtake wall about 100 m downhill.

Which community chose to bury their dead here is uncertain, the nearest known settlement being the five huts on the lower slopes of Hare Tor to the east, but this site was hardly populous enough. A possibility could be the settlements with their numerous dwellings along the Tavy and Rattle Brook, such as Watern Oke, which are ill-provided with burial mounds. Alternatively large settlement sites now destroyed may once have existed along the Willsworthy or Walla Brooks, though there is no evidence for this.

Tinning along the lower Rattle Brook and Baggator Brook

The Rattle Brook and its Dead Lake tributary were the only major source of tin in the Tavy valley. Streamworks are continuous for 2.5 kilometres upriver from a little above Dead Lake junction to beyond Bleak House (**map 43**). A short distance above Rattle Brook Foot the lowest courses of a tiny tinners' hut (c. 2.5 m square) are set well back from the west bank into the base of the steep hillside here. That this choice of site, fairly common, had its dangers is shown by the massive blocks that have crashed down into the interior from the slopes above.

The Dead Lake tributary has been subject to intensive streamworking almost from its source down to the confluence with the main river, its bed having been expanded to 80 m across and 3 m deep in places. 150 m upstream is the first of several gullies which have been driven into the banks on both sides of the Rattle Brook. This one has a well-preserved wheel-pit (7.0 x 1.8 m) with some walling on the north side, apparently fed from a leat taken off 400 m upstream, though it no longer reaches this far.

An even larger openwork 8 m below the surface has been dug into the opposite bank 200 m further upriver. The tinners who excavated this huge pit probably lived in the two-roomed building below it, built into the pebble mounds discarded at an earlier date beside the river. A leat into the openwork for washing out the ore leaves the main river some distance above its junction with the Scad and Green Tor Water (**map 43**).

Baggator Brook was much less heavily streamed than the Rattle Brook, with some shallow workings near its source ending at a small openwork on the left bank. Further down though, on the south-west flank of Standon Hill just above the newtake wall, is the open adit of a tin mine which was worked as recently as 1925.[66] Decaying wooden props are visible within the neatly revetted entrance and a leat, taken off next to boundary stone WD28 upstream, continues past a short distance uphill.

a-h Boundary stones

Two groups of lettered stones are to be found in the vicinity of the lower Tavy, both based on Willsworthy Army Camp. The older set of stones, **a-b**, are spaced around the crumbling walls of Hamlyn's Newtake, each a few metres outside the boundary and with the letter H crudely cut on one face.

MAP 32

The other group of forty-six stones was erected soon after 1900 when Willsworthy was purchased by the War Office for use as a firing range.[11] These squared pillars are all labelled *WD* and numbered from *1* to *46*, though stone *17* seems to have been missed out. It should have stood in the short gap between Doe Tor, **21**, (*WD16*), and Walla Brook Head, **d** (*WD18*), and it is probably not unconnected that an extra stone simply inscribed *WD* lies near the base of **e** (*WD20*) at the head of Dead Lake. The series, dotted on map, starts west of the camp buildings and continues clockwise to Doe Tor Brook **c** (*WD15*), Walla Brook **d**, Dead Lake **e**, Western Red Lake **f** (*WD22*) Baggator Brook **g** (*WD27*), Tavy **h** (*WD33*), and so back to Willsworthy.

MAP 33 The Upper Tavy

1 Watern Oke Central and East huts (fig. 33.1)

Watern Oke Central and East huts   fig. 33.1

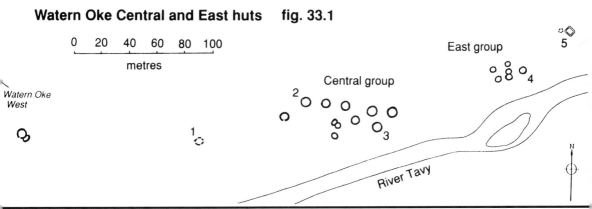

The three groups of huts at Watern Oke excavated by the Dartmoor Exploration Committee in 1905 appear to be independent of each other, though they may well have been in use at the same time. The central group of eleven huts lies on the other side of clear ground 170 m east of the village (**map 32.5**) close to the riverbank. The circular depression, 1, now visible as an isolated pit between them, was thought at first to be a hut but proved not to be so.

The huts of the central group were more solidly built than those to the west and are consequently better preserved. The finds were of similar type but in considerably greater quantity, hut 3 (3.9 m), for instance, containing over a hundred stones that had been put to various uses, and about half the huts produced pottery fragments and flints. The largest hut, 2 (5.2 m), is slightly uphill from the rest (2.8-4.0 m). By contrast the eastern group of six small huts (2.5-4.6 m) were all crudely built and produced very few finds. The only unusual artefact recovered was a 'piece of glass' from hut 4 (4.6 m) but this did not receive any further description except for a query as to its antiquity.

The Exploration Committee then excavated the roughly rectangular building, 5, assuming it to be a rebuilt hut. Finds of prehistoric date were made within it including a whetstone, pottery and a fine flint arrowhead, but these may have been intrusions as the structure is probably a tinners' hut built opposite the first of the streamworks along the Tavy. A piece of corroded iron which was also found, perhaps the remains of a knife, probably belonged to this later period. The hollow in the hillside immediately uphill to the west was interpreted as the cook house.

MAP 33

The excavators suggested that there were signs of even more huts to the north of this building which they were unable to investigate but the surface stones here do not seem to form any coherent pattern.

Also slightly puzzling was the last building described in the report, numbered 82, in an isolated position on the opposite side of the river west of Western Red Lake (**map 32**). It was described as a fine hut circle 6.2 m in diameter in which was found flint, charcoal and 'traces' of pottery. The excavation is roughly 3 m square and what little can be seen of the walls of the building within the pit appears to be cornered. It seems more likely to be of later construction, perhaps a shepherd's or tinners' shelter.

Tinners' huts

Apart from blowing houses and the longhouses of medieval farmers there are a considerable number of a third group of abandoned buildings, commonest in the upper valleys of the north moor, which are smaller and more crudely built.[54] Many of these are labelled tinners' huts on Ordnance Survey maps. No doubt most of them were, though there were others such as peat-cutters, shepherds and herdsmen who lived and worked on the moor for a considerable part of the year and who also built small dwellings for themselves. Generally each is likely to have erected his shelter conveniently close to his occupation, the peat-cutter near the turf ties on the hillside and the tinner on the riverbank close to his streamwork, though some of the buildings sited within the tinners' gerts, probably taking advantage of the masses of handy-sized stones, were obviously built after these had been abandoned. Many of the huts are of slight construction and some have no doubt collapsed into unrecognisable ruins whilst others, still visible, surely remain unrecorded.

A good series of tinners' huts are to be found at intervals along the banks of the Tavy and its tributaries, each closely associated with a small area of pebble waste mounds. The huts are tiny, the largest being only about 5.5 by 3.5 m across, though most are much smaller than this and could have accommodated only one or two people at most. They were probably occupied only in the warmer months by independent tinners, each working his own small patch of the river bed. Rather unexpectedly the huts are much less common along the more heavily streamed rivers such as the Lyd or North Walla Brook where dozens must have laboured over many years.

The huts were of the simplest construction, only roughly rectangular and usually single-roomed with a doorway in one side and probably roofed with turves or heather. Where there was a steep bank conveniently close they were built into the base of the hill to ease the roofing problem. Most are now little more than foundations, their similar state of decay and infilling of peat suggesting that they were in roughly contemporary occupation before the end of the seventeenth century. One of the few huts attributed to the tinners which has been excavated, at Greyhounds Marsh near Postbridge, (**map 27**), though not exactly comparable in construction to the Tavy buildings, was dated to the fourteenth century at the latest. The excavation of the hut at Watern Oke (**33**.**1**.5) was less informative as, apart from the prehistoric material, the only find from a later period was an undated piece of corroded iron.

2-8 Tinning along the Upper Tavy

No very significant amounts of tin were obtained from the upper Tavy, what deposits there were occurring in small pockets along the main river and its tributaries. From South Tavy Head almost the first streamworks are centred around a tinner's hut **2** (2.0 x 4.5 m) of which

MAP 33

only the lowest course remains. Four hundred metres downstream there is even less of a pair of huts **3** which seem to have been deliberately demolished, perhaps to provide material for the others nearby. Only the end walls are left of the first building (c. 2.0 x 4.8 m), sited on a knoll above the river, and 40 m away practically all of the other has disappeared leaving a rectangular platform of similar dimensions levelled into the hillside. Hut **4** (2.1 x 4.3 m) is a low-walled ruin about 50 m from the riverbank[54]. No tinners' dwellings have yet been located at Fir Tor Brook which has been streamed head and foot, nor along the first 600 m of Eastern Red Lake, but there are two buildings above the junction of the Tavy with Amicombe Brook **5**, (both c. 3.0 x 2.0 m).

Apart from a small area of gravel mounds at the confluence of its twin sources below Black Hill, the Black Ridge Brook is free of streamworks down to its junction with Amicombe Brook. A tinner's hut, **6** (c. 4.5 x 3.0 m), lies within the mounds at the fork, slightly larger and better built than most, its damp and sunken floor now the home for a bed of rushes. No building has yet been found along the waterlogged banks of Amicombe Brook which must have been a wet and uncomfortable place even for the tinners. The mounds, no wider than a few metres from the bank, accompany the river from a shallow excavation near the source downstream for 1.5 kilometres to its junction with Cut Combe Water. Occasional patches of pebbles can be found alongside the latter as far as its first tributary which drains the east side of the ridge between Cut and Black Hills. The foundations of a building here, **7**, a few metres from the junction, are only roughly rectangular (c. 4.2 x 2.5 m) with an entrance on the north side. A second building, **8** (c. 2.0 x 3.0 m), lies on the edge of a slightly larger area 50 m wide midway along its course downstream. Most of the wall stones have now fallen into the interior of this small building.

The Phillpotts peat passes

A thick bed of peat covers much of the northern highlands but, instead of a smooth surface, the hummocky ground is rent by deep fissures making progress both slow and troublesome for the walker as much as the horseman. Not so for the fox, who was often able to take advantage of this difficult country to elude his pursuers of the hunt. Around the turn of the century Frank Phillpotts (1837-1909), a keen huntsman, determined to lessen the odds so much in favour of the quarry by cutting the peat passes across the most difficult areas of fen between the firmer ground on either side.[53]

Nine of these passes were dug around the centre of the moor, ranging in length from over a kilometre to a mere 60 metres. Constant maintenance has kept them open and they are now marked by small cairns along their length and by a short granite post at each end. A bronze plaque commemorating Phillpotts is attached to each of the posts. Without the benefit of the rider's extra height the passes are not always easy to find and in any case are rarely of much use to the walker unless he finds himself close by and they happen to coincide with his direction.

The Little Kneeset pass connects the valleys of Black Ridge Brook and Cut Combe Water. The northern marker post is visible from the river below but the pass itself is easily lost amongst the peat hags on the summit. A much shorter cut, about 200 m, crosses the summit between the Tavy valley and Walkham head but the high ground is reasonably firm and level alongside and certainly easier to walk on than the track through the pass. The longest pass of all though, over 1 kilometre, is that over the summit of Black Ridge, from near West Okement head to the upper valley of Black Ridge Brook.

Much older than the Phillpotts passes and at least partly artificial is Cut Lane, on the route from Postbridge to Okehampton, or to Lydford as an alternative to the Lich Way. It connects the Tavy valley via Cut Combe Water with that of the East Dart, crossing the northern slope of Cut Hill to which it gives its name.

MAP 34

9 Walkham Head peatworks

A vast amount of peat has been taken from around the head of the Walkham valley, most of it before the 1840s[47] for use at the copper and lead mines near Mary Tavy. Boggy pools surround what little remains to be seen at the site on the east bank of the river, merely a few piles of stone and the foundation platforms of three or four buildings. From here a tall stone can be seen a short distance up the slope on the opposite bank, the last standing post that once supported the roof of the Turf House where the slabs of peat were stored.[55] Packhorses carried the peat to the mines along the deeply worn tracks encircling Lynch Tor, leaving the moor at Baggator gate. The track around the northern flank joins another from turf ties at the head of Eastern Red Lake.

At the end of the last century a local farmer cutting peat in the turf ties around Walkham Head found a polished flint axe of neolithic date about 2 m below the surface.

MAP 34 The Upper East Dart and North Teign valleys

1-3 Quintin's Man, Marsh Hill and Sittaford Tor cairns

Quintin's Man, **1**, now shares the southern tip of Whitehorse Hill with Observation Posts and flagpole where perhaps there was once a standing stone, as the name implies, like Beardown Man on Devil's Tor (**map 29**). There is however no record of a menhir ever having stood here, though a second cairn was reported nearby of which there is now no sign. The cairn is a fair size (17.0 x 1.8 m) and much of it is still undamaged. The stones at the centre have been disturbed and roughly replaced but the sides of the pit are exposed showing that the interior was composed of neatly-coursed slabs laid at an angle to the horizontal.

Not so far relocated are the two ruined cairns within Teignhead newtake excavated by the Dartmoor Exploration Committee in about 1901. This area comprises 125 hectares of hillside east of the nearby wall and as the cairns were probably small, and were described as ruined even then, they will not be easy to find. One cairn covered a pit containing wood charcoal but the result of the other excavation was not considered worth recording.

What remains of the cairn on the summit of Marsh Hill, **2**, shows a similar construction to Quintin's Man. It has been completely gutted at the centre, presumably to provide the walls of Statts House which shares the hilltop, leaving just the outer rim of slabs.

The little cairn with a probable cist on the south flank of Sittaford Tor, **3**, seems to have passed unnoticed by the early antiquaries except for a casual mention by Breton,[56] but it is an interesting example. An outer circle of small slabs about 5 m across surrounded a ring of much larger stones, three of which still stand close together around the east side. A flat slab at the centre may well be the cover of a cist which will certainly prove to have been robbed at some time in the past.

The sites from Map 34 continue on page 153

THE MAPS

Lynchets on south end of Challacombe Down

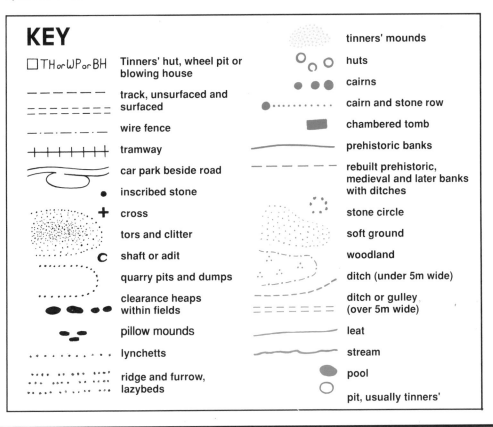

KEY

☐ TH or WP or BH	Tinners' hut, wheel pit or blowing house
‒ ‒ ‒ ‒ ‒ / = = = =	track, unsurfaced and surfaced
_._._._._	wire fence
+++++++	tramway
car park beside road	car park beside road
●	inscribed stone
+	cross
tors and clitter	tors and clitter
C	shaft or adit
quarry pits and dumps	quarry pits and dumps
clearance heaps within fields	clearance heaps within fields
pillow mounds	pillow mounds
lynchetts	lynchetts
ridge and furrow, lazybeds	ridge and furrow, lazybeds

tinners' mounds	tinners' mounds
O O O	huts
● ● ●	cairns
●··········	cairn and stone row
▬	chambered tomb
prehistoric banks	prehistoric banks
‒ ‒ ‒ ‒ ‒	rebuilt prehistoric, medieval and later banks with ditches
stone circle	stone circle
soft ground	soft ground
woodland	woodland
ditch (under 5m wide)	ditch (under 5m wide)
ditch or gulley (over 5m wide)	ditch or gulley (over 5m wide)
leat	leat
stream	stream
●	pool
○	pit, usually tinners'

MAP 24
CHALLACOMBE DOWN AND SOUTH BIRCH TOR

Above: Birch Tor and Vitifer Mines   Inset: Challacombe Stone Rows

MAP 24

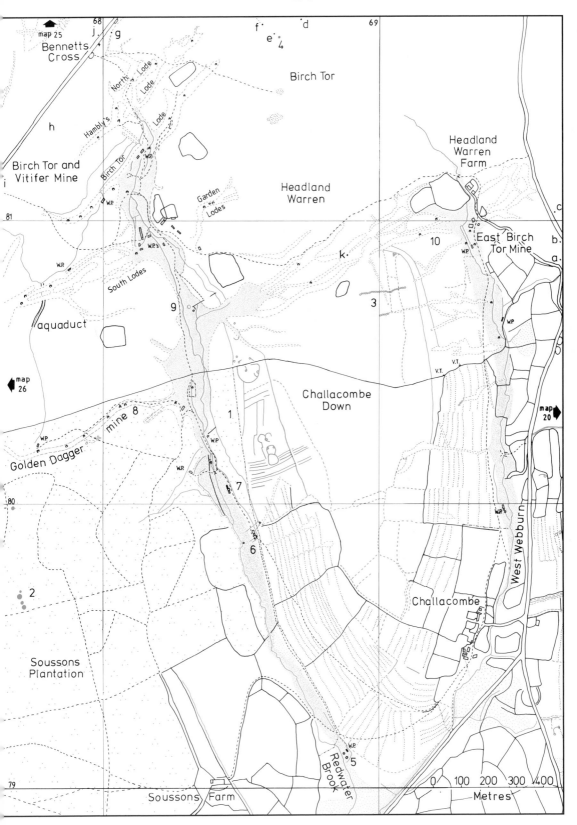

map 25

Bennetts
Cross

North - Lode

Birch Tor

Lode

Hambly's

Birch Tor

Lode

h

Birch Tor and
Vitifer Mine

i

Garden
Lodes

Headland
Warren

Birch Tor

f   d
e   4

Headland
Warren
Farm

East Birch
Tor Mine

c

b

a

10

k

W.P.

81

W.P.

W.P.

W.P.'s

W.P.

South Lodes

9

3

W.P.

aquaduct

map
26

mine 8

Challacombe
Down

V.T.

V.T.

W.P.

map
20

Golden Dagger

W.P.

W.P.

1

W.P

W.P.

W.P.

7

80

6

W.P.

West Webburn

2

Challacombe

Soussons
Plantation

W.P.

5

Redwater Brook

79

Soussons Farm

0 100 200 300 400

Metres

MAP 25
CHAGFORD COMMON AND BUSH DOWN

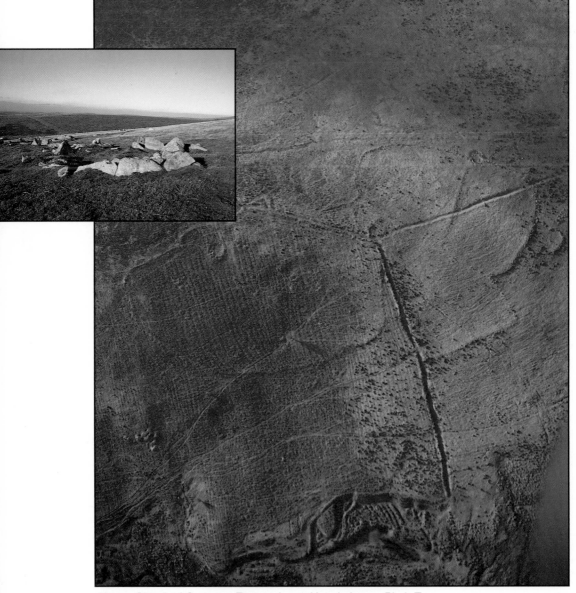

Above: Chagford Common East   Inset: Hut circles on Birch Tor

MAP 25

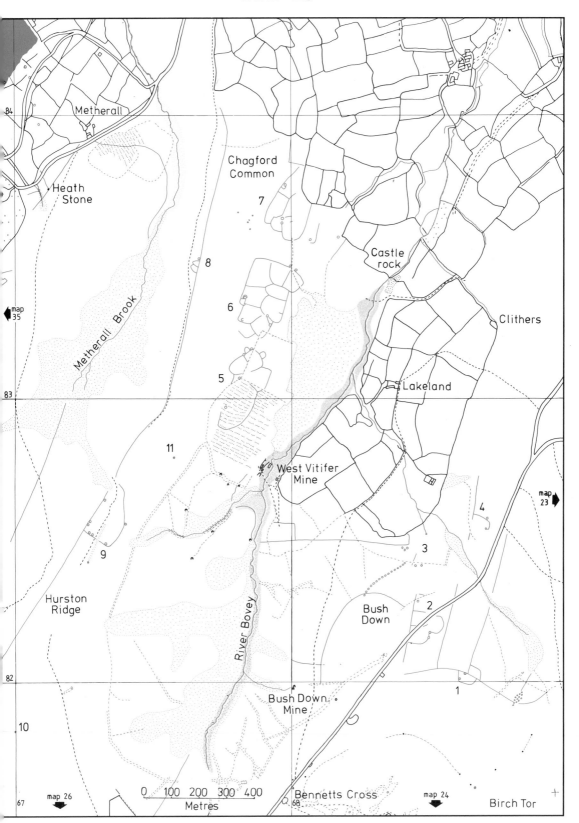

Metherall

Heath
Stone

Chagford
Common

7

8

Castle
rock

Clithers

map
35

6

Metherall Brook

5

Lakeland

83

11

West Vitifer
Mine

4

map
23

9

3

Hurston
Ridge

River Bovey

Bush
Down

2

82

1

10

Bush Down
Mine

map 26

0 100 200 300 400
Metres

Bennetts Cross

map 24

Birch Tor

67   68

MAP 26
UPPER WALLABROOK AND STATTS BROOK

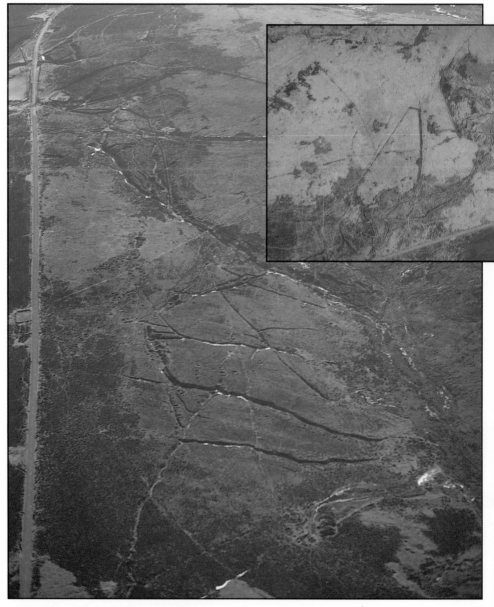

Above: Bush Down   Inset: King's Oven

MAP 26

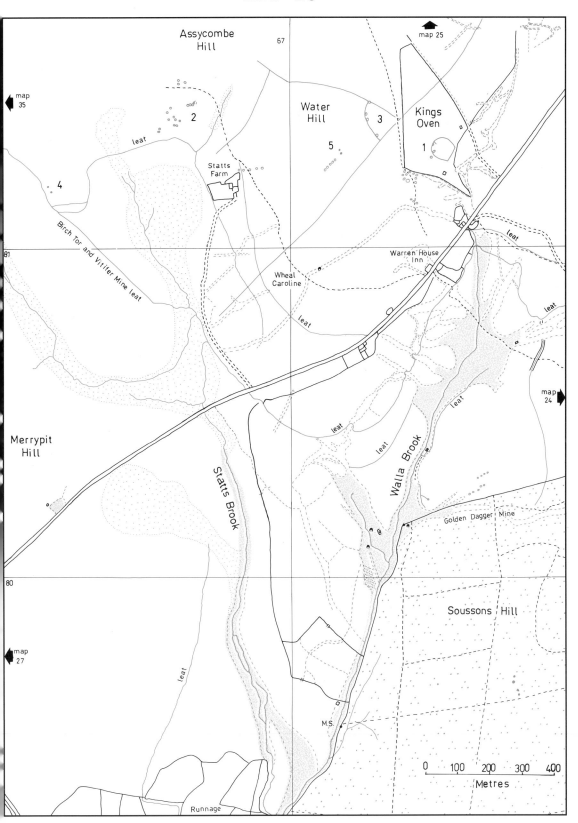

Assycombe Hill

67

Water Hill

Kings Oven

map 25

map 35

2

3

5

1

leat

Statts Farm

4

Birch Tor and Vitifer Mine leat

Warren House Inn

leat

leat

81

Wheal Caroline

leat

leat

map 24

leat

leat

Merrypit Hill

Statts Brook

Walla Brook

Golden Dagger Mine

80

Soussons Hill

map 27

leat

M.S.

Runnage

| 0 | 100 | 200 | 300 | 400 |

Metres

MAP 27
THE
POSTBRIDGE DISTRICT

Top: Kraps Ring   Above: Broadun

MAP 27

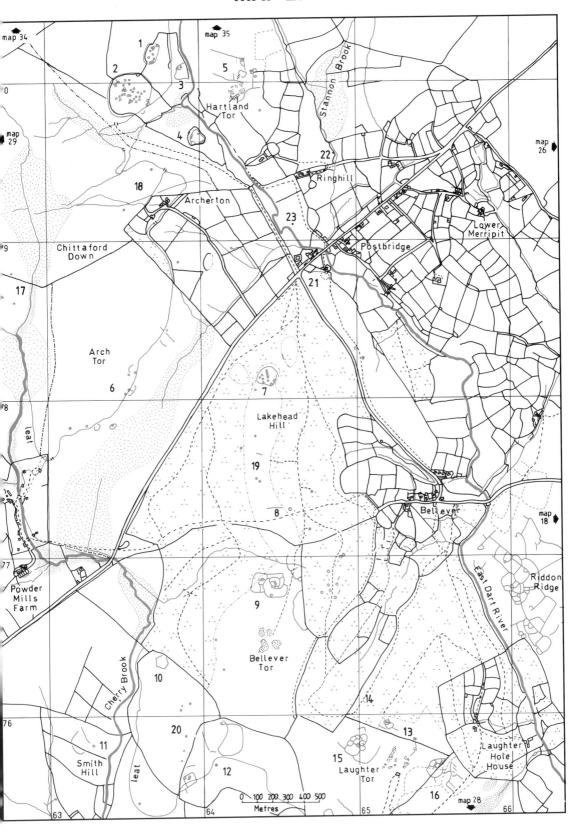

map 34

map 35

map 29

1

2

3

5

Hartland
Tor

4

22

Ringhill

map 26

18

Archerton

23

Lower
Merripit

Chittaford
Down

Postbridge

17

21

Arch
Tor

6

7

Lakehead
Hill

19

map 18

8

Bellever

leat

9

Riddon
Ridge

East Dart River

Powder
Mills
Farm

Bellever
Tor

10

Cherry Brook

14

13

Laughter
Hole
House

76

11

20

Smith
Hill

leat

12

15

Laughter
Tor

16

map 28

0 100 200 300 400 500
Metres

63

64

65

66

MAP 28
THE DUNNABRIDGE AREA

Top: Dunnabridge Pound   Above: Outer Huccaby Ring

MAP 28

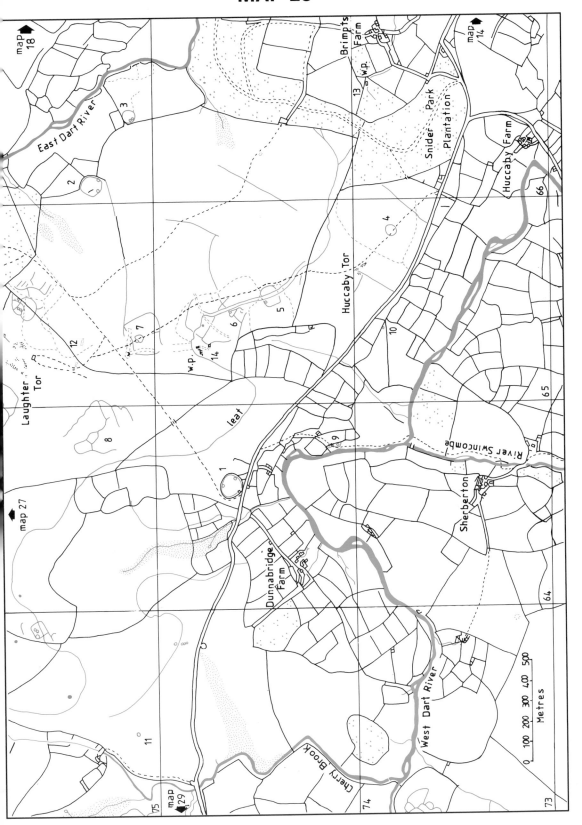

map 18

East Dart River

Brimpts Farm

w.p.

13

Snider Park Plantation

Huccaby Farm

map 14

66

3

2

4

Huccaby Tor

map 27

Laughter Tor

12

7

6

5

w.p.

14

10

65

leat

8

9

11

River Swincombe

1

Sherberton

Dunnabridge Farm

64

West Dart River

Cherry Brook

0 100 200 300 400 500
        Metres

75

map 29

74

73

MAP 29
WEST DART NORTH OF TWO BRIDGES

Above: Crockern Tor   Inset: Cairn and cist, Crow Tor

MAP 29

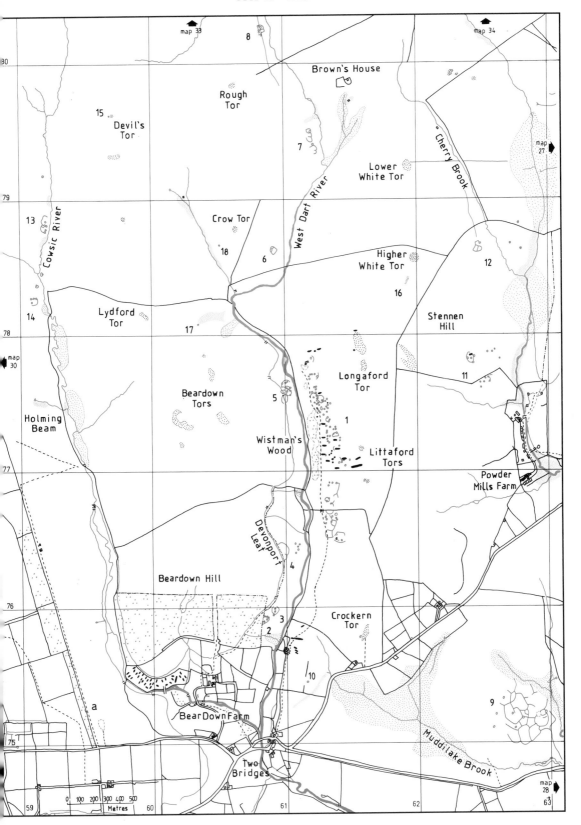

map 33
8

Brown's House

Rough
Tor

15
Devil's
Tor

7

Lower
White Tor

map 34

Cherry Brook

map 27

79

13

Cowsic River

West Dart River

Crow Tor

18

6

Higher
White Tor

16

12

14

Lydford
Tor

17

78

Stennen
Hill

map 30

Beardown
Tors

5

Longaford
Tor

11

1

Holming
Beam

Wistman's
Wood

Littaford
Tors

77

Powder
Mills Farm

Devonport Leat

4

Beardown Hill

76

3

2

Crockern
Tor

10

9

a

BearDown Farm

75

Two
Bridges

map 28

Muddilake Brook

0 100 200 300 400 500
Metres

59   60   61   62   63

MAP 30
BLACKBROOK AND THE UPPER WALKHAM

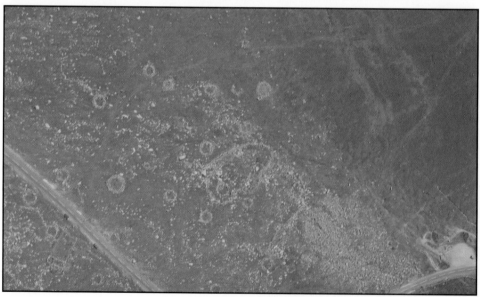

Top: Langstone Moor settlement   Above: Merrivale Bridge East huts

MAP 30

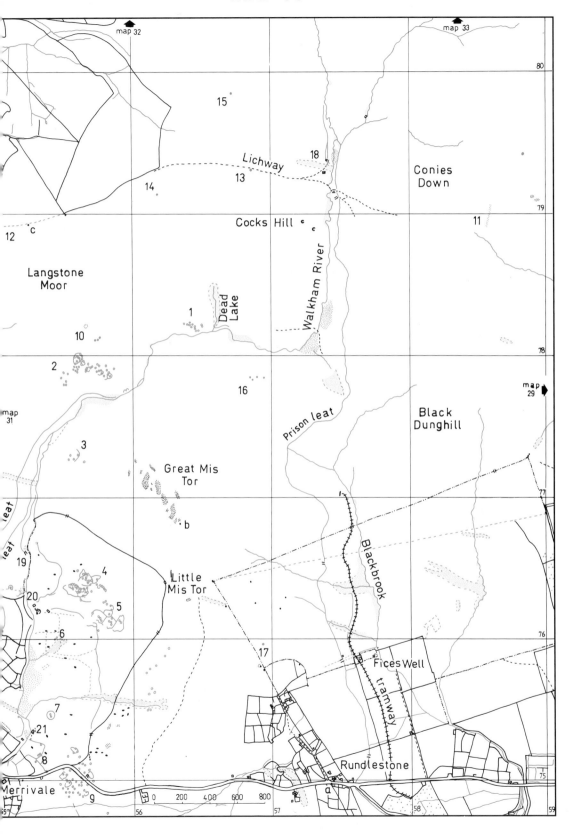

map 32

map 33

80

15

Lichway

18

Conies
Down

13

14

79

Cocks Hill

11

12   c

Langstone
Moor

Walkham River

Dead
Lake

1

10

78

2

16

map
31

Prison leat

Black
Dunghill

map
29

3

Great Mis
Tor

77

b

Blackbrook

19

Little
Mis Tor

4

20

5

76

6

17

Fices Well

tramway

7

21

Rundlestone

75

8

Merrivale

g

0   200   400   600   800

a

57   56   57   58   59

MAP 31
MERRIVALE TO CUDLIPPTOWN DOWN

Cudlipptown Down

MAP 31

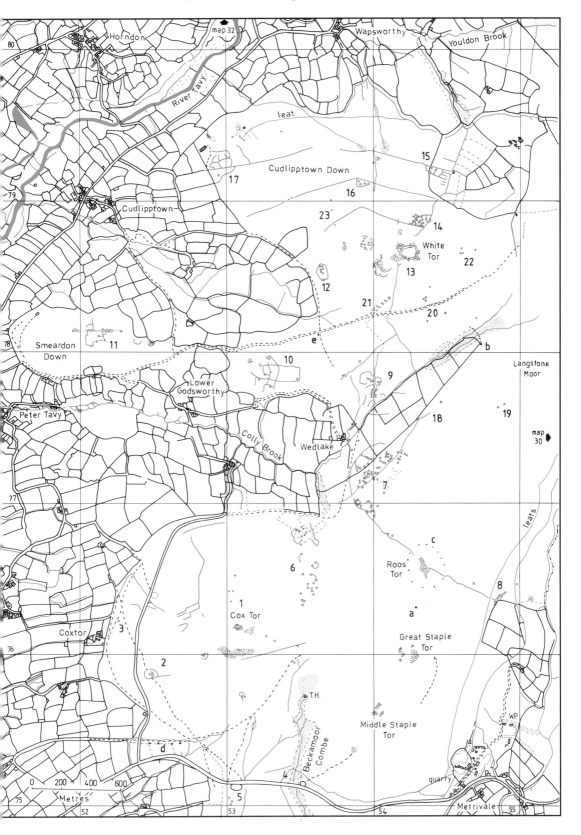

MAP 32
THE
LOWER TAVY

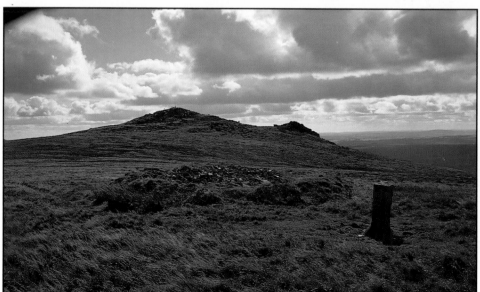

Top: Watern Oke West   Above: Sharp Tor South cairn

MAP 32

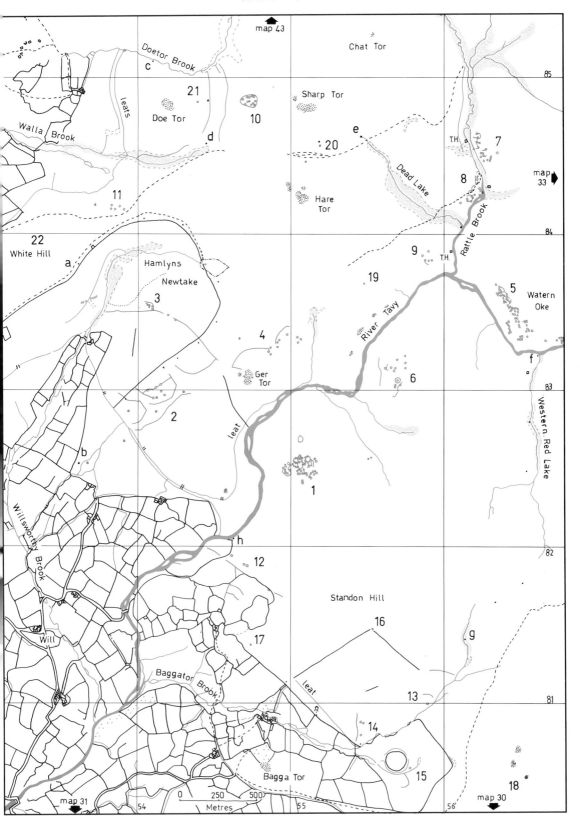

map 43

Chat Tor

Doetor Brook

c

21

Doe Tor

10

Sharp Tor

e

20

T.H.

7

Walla Brook

d

leats

Dead Lake

8

map
33

11

Rattle Brook

84

85

22

White Hill

a

Hamlyns

Newtake

3

9

T.H.

19

5

Watern
Oke

River Tavy

4

Ger
Tor

2

6

f

83

leat

b

1

Western Red Lake

Willsworthy Brook

h

12

82

Standon Hill

Will

17

16

g

Baggator Brook

leat

13

81

14

15

18

map 30

Bagga Tor

0   250   500

Metres

map 31

54   55   56

MAP 33
THE
UPPER TAVY

The Turf House

MAP 33

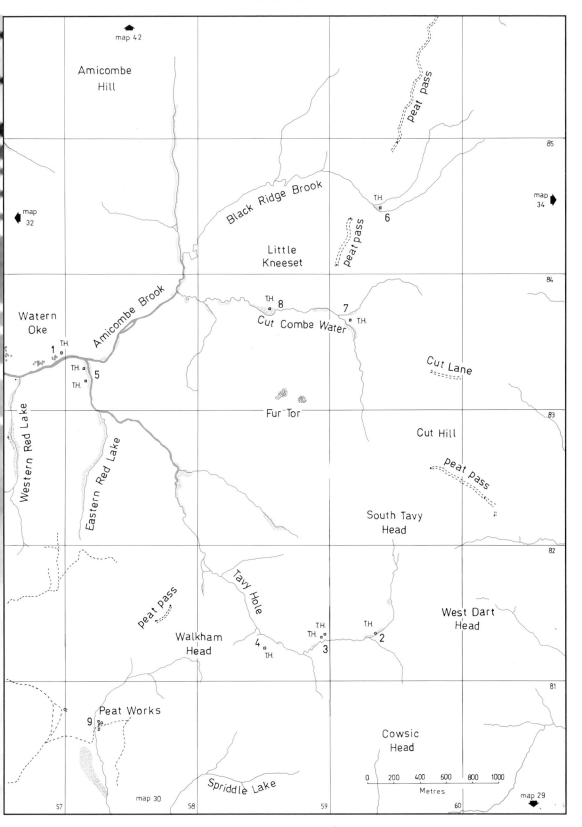

map 42

Amicombe
Hill

85

Black Ridge Brook

map
32

T.H.
6

Little
Kneeset

peat pass

map
34

84

Watern
Oke

Amicombe Brook

T.H.
8

7
T.H.

Cut Combe Water

1 T.H.

T.H.
5
T.H.

Cut Lane

Fur Tor

83

Cut Hill

peat pass

Western Red Lake

Eastern Red Lake

South Tavy
Head

82

Tavy Hole

peat pass

West Dart
Head

Walkham
Head

T.H.
T.H.
4
T.H.
3

T.H.
2

81

Peat Works

9

Cowsic
Head

Spriddle Lake

0   200   400   600   800   1000

Metres

map 30

map 29

57   58   59   60

MAP 34
THE UPPER
EAST DART AND
NORTH TEIGN VALLEYS

Top: Beehive hut, Lade Hill Brook   Above: Peat Pass, Whitehorse Hill south

MAP 34

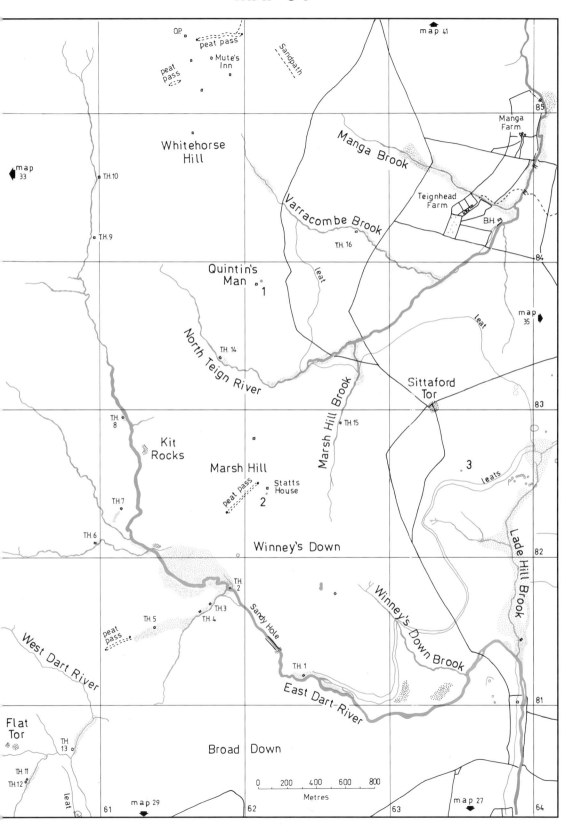

Q.P.
peat pass
peat pass
Mute's Inn
Sandpath

map 41

Manga Farm

map 33

Whitehorse Hill

Manga Brook

T.H.10

Varracombe Brook

Teignhead Farm

B.H.

85

84

T.H.9

Quintin's Man
1

T.H. 16

leat

map 35

North Teign River

T.H.14

leat

Sittaford Tor

83

T.H. 8

Kit Rocks

Marsh Hill Brook

T.H.15

3

leats

Marsh Hill

peat pass

Statts House

2

T.H.7

Winney's Down

82

T.H.6

Lade Hill Brook

T.H. 2

Winney's Down Brook

T.H.5

T.H.3

T.H.4

Sandy Hole

peat pass

West Dart River

T.H. 1

81

East Dart River

Flat Tor

T.H. 13

Broad Down

0   200   400   600   800
Metres

T.H. 11
T.H.12

leat

61

map 29

62

63

map 27

64

MAP 35
FERNWORTHY FOREST AND WHITE RIDGES

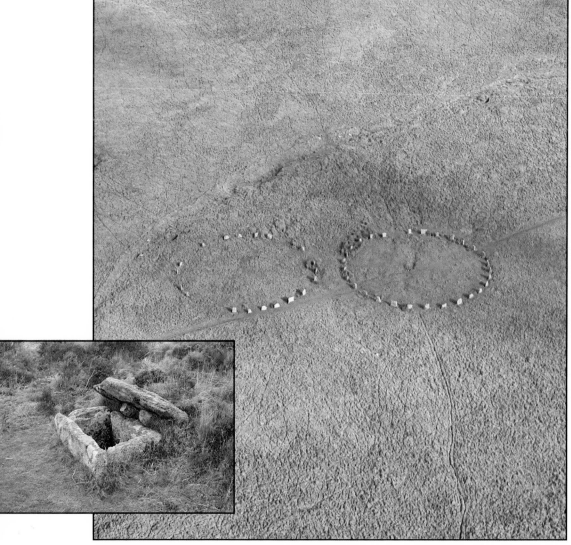

Above: Grey Wethers stone circle
Inset: Thornworthy Tor cist

MAP 35

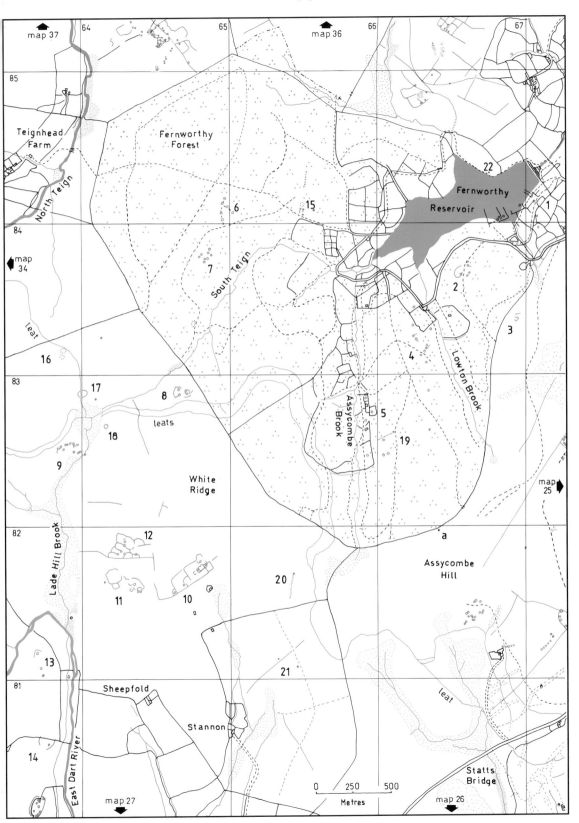

map 37
64
65
map 36
66
67

85

Teignhead
Farm

Fernworthy
Forest

22

Fernworthy
Reservoir

1

84

map 34

6

15

North Teign

South Teign

7

2

3

leat

16

Lowton Brook

4

83

17

8

18

leats

Assycombe
Brook

5

19

9

White
Ridge

map 25

82

Lade Hill Brook

12

a

Assycombe
Hill

11

10

20

13

21

leat

81

Sheepfold

Stannon

14

East Dart River

Statts
Bridge

0   250   500
Metres

map 27

map 26

MAP 36
EAST SHOVEL DOWN AND THORNWORTHY DOWN

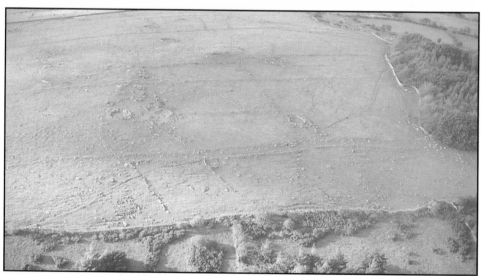

Top: Shovel Down Stone Rows 2 and Fourfold Circle
Above: Kes Tor settlement

MAP 36

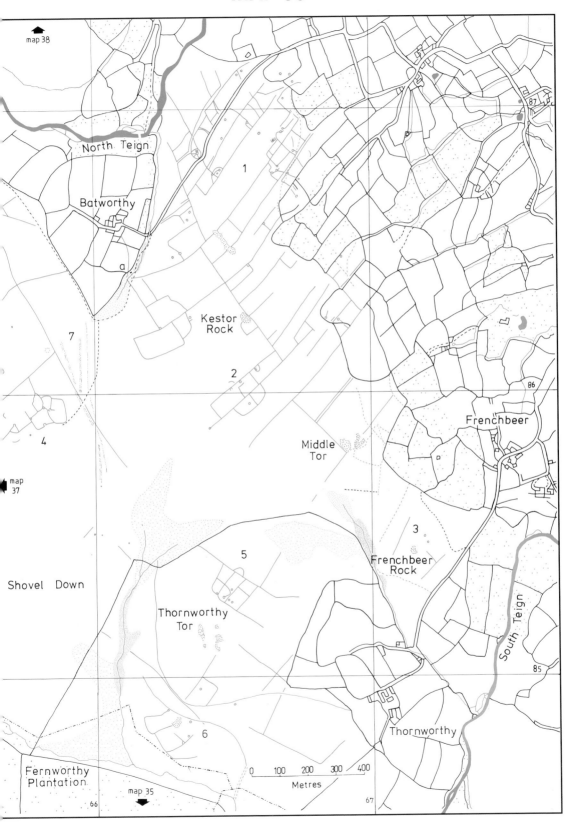

map 38

North Teign

Batworthy

a

Kestor
Rock

1

2

7

4

map
37

87

86

Frenchbeer

Middle
Tor

3

5

Frenchbeer
Rock

Shovel   Down

Thornworthy
Tor

South Teign

85

6

Thornworthy

Fernworthy
Plantation

map 35

0   100   200   300   400
Metres

66

67

MAP 37
WEST SHOVEL DOWN AND STONETOR HILL

Top: Stonetor Brook East enclosure
Above: Tinners cache, Stonetor Brook

MAP 37

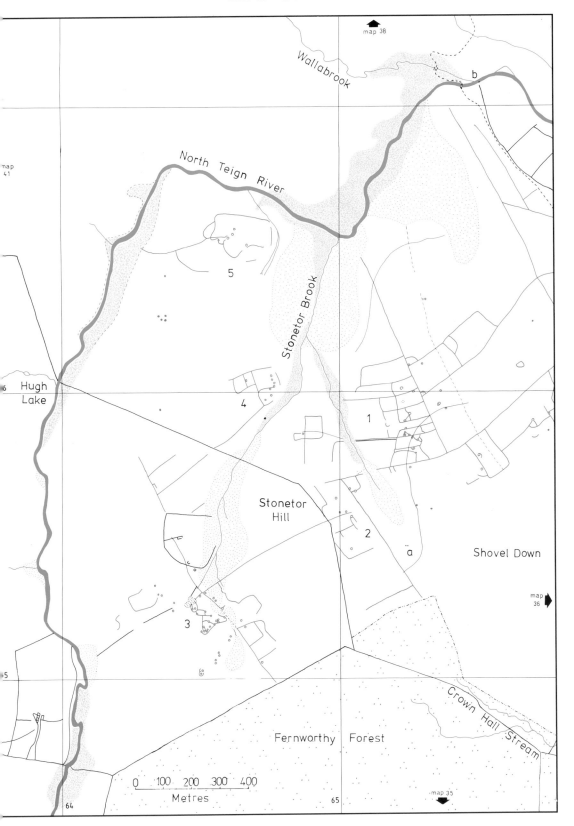

map 38

Wallabrook

b

North Teign River

map
41

Stonetor Brook

5

Hugh
Lake

4

1

Stonetor
Hill

2

a

Shovel Down

map
36

3

Crown Hall Stream

Fernworthy   Forest

0   100   200   300   400
Metres

64   65   map 35

MAP 38
BUTTERN HILL AND SCORHILL

Top: Buttern Hill north
Above: Scorhill stone circle

MAP 38

map 39

Forder Brook

7

Buttern

Moortown

89

Whitemoor
Marsh

6

Kennon
Hill

5

a

4

11

map
41

3

9

Buttern Hill

Creaber
Pound

2

88

South
Creaber

10

Bradford leat

Scorhill
Down

1

Walla Brook

8

Scorhill

North Teign

0 100 200 300 400

Metres

map 37

Teign-e-ver
Bridge

65

66

map 36

87

MAP 39
THROWLEIGH COMMON

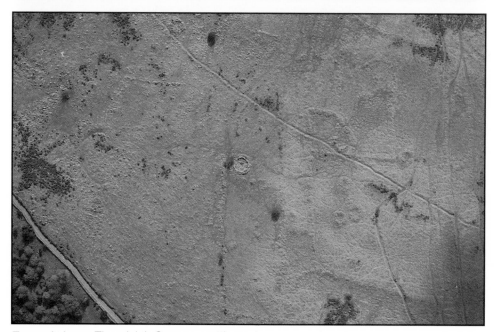

Top and above: Throwleigh Common settlement

MAP 39

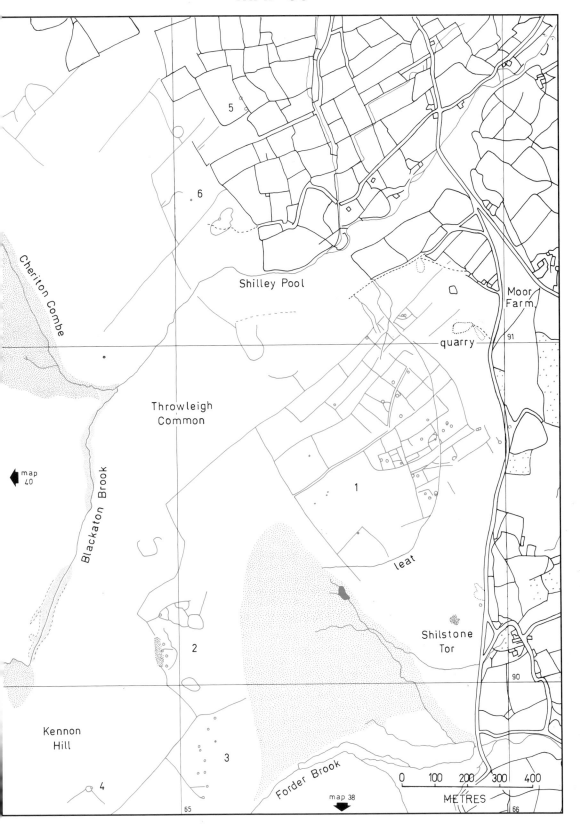

5

6

Cheriton Combe

Shilley Pool

Moor Farm

quarry

91

Throwleigh Common

map 40

Blackaton Brook

1

leat

Shilstone Tor

90

2

Kennon Hill

3

4

Forder Brook

map 38

0   100   200   300   400
METRES

65

66

MAP 40
RIVER TAW AND COSDON HILL

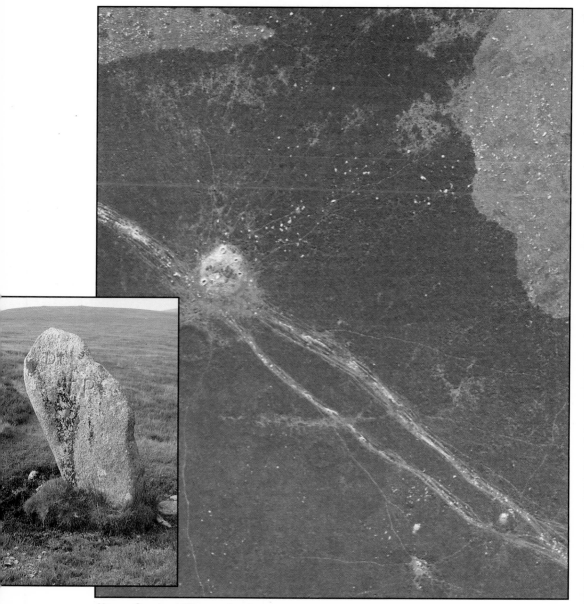

Above: Cosdon Hill summit cairns
Inset: White Moor stone

MAP 40

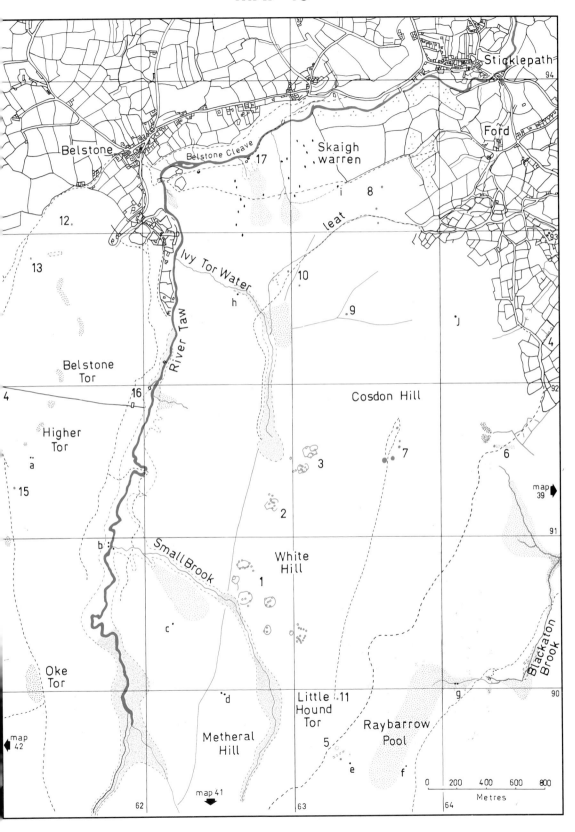

Sticklepath

94

Ford

Belstone

Belstone Cleave   17   Skaigh
                              warren

12   Ivy Tor Water   i   8

13   leat

                                        93

Belstone   10
Tor   h
                              9   J

4   92
16
                    River Taw   Cosdon Hill

Higher   6
Tor
a   3   7

15   map
                                               39
                        2
                                               91
b
            Small Brook   White
                           Hill
                    1

Oke   c
Tor

map   d   Little 11
42   Hound
            Metheral   Tor   Raybarrow
            Hill   5   Pool   9   90

map 41   e   f
                                    0 200 400 600 800
    62   63   64   Metres

Blackaton Brook

MAP 41
THE UPPER TAW
AND WALLA BROOK

Cosdon Hill stone rows

MAP 41

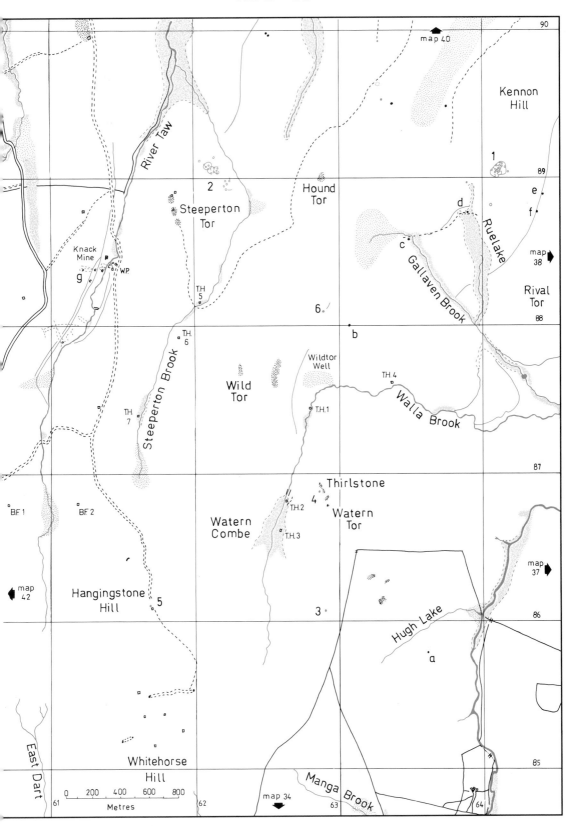

Kennon
Hill

River Taw

map 40

1

89

Hound
Tor

e

d

f

Steeperton
Tor

2

map
38

c

Knack
Mine

Gallaven Brook

Ruelake

Rival
Tor

g

W.P.

88

T.H
5

6

b

T.H.
6

Steeperton Brook

Wildtor
Well

T.H. 4

Wild
Tor

Walla Brook

T.H.
7

T.H.1

87

Thirlstone

BF 1

BF 2

Watern
Combe

T.H.2

4

Watern
Tor

T.H.3

map
37

map
42

Hangingstone
Hill

5

3

Hugh Lake

86

a

Whitehorse
Hill

0   200   400   600   800

Metres

East Dart

map 34

Manga Brook

85

61

62

63

64

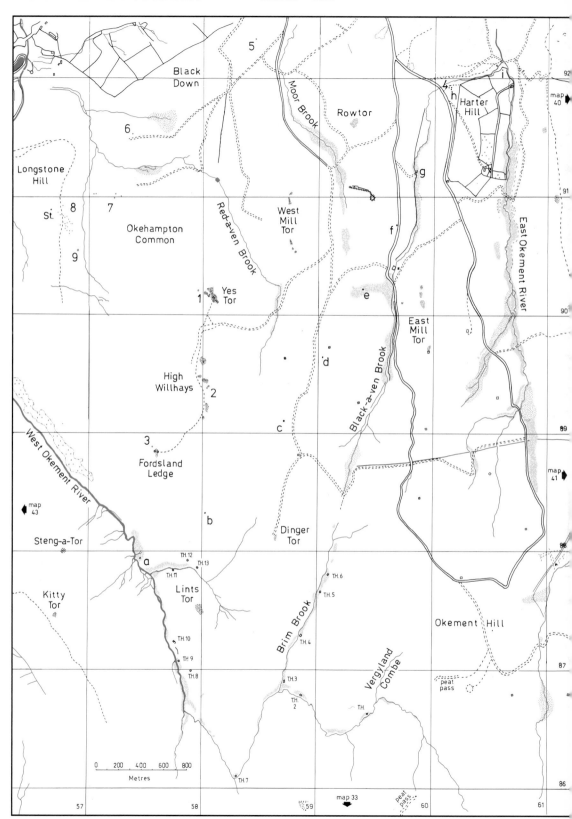

Black
Down

5

Moor Brook

Rowtor

map
40

Harter
Hill

h

92

i

6

g

91

Longstone
Hill

West
Mill
Tor

Red-a-ven Brook

East Okement River

St.

8

7

Okehampton
Common

f

9

1

Yes
Tor

e

East
Mill
Tor

90

d

Black-a-ven Brook

High
Willhays

2

3

c

89

West Okement River

Fordsland
Ledge

map
41

map
43

b

Steng-a-Tor

Dinger
Tor

88

a

TH.12

TH.13

TH.11

Lints
Tor

TH.6

TH.5

Kitty
Tor

Okement Hill

TH.10

Brim Brook

TH.4

TH.9

87

TH.8

Vergyland Combe

TH.3

peat
pass

TH.
2

TH.

0   200 400 600 800
Metres

TH.7

map 33

peat
pass

86

MAP 43　　　THE LYD VALLEY

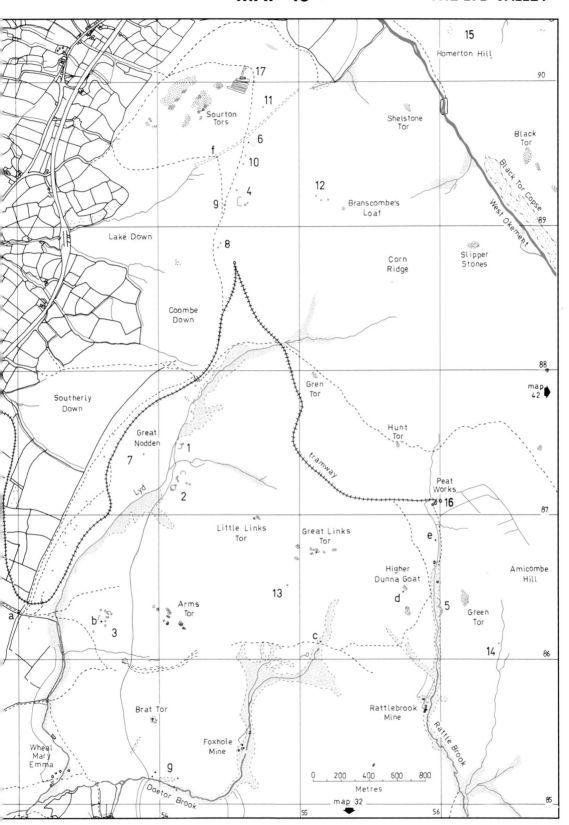

15

Homerton Hill

90

Sourton
Tors

17

11

6

f

10

Shelstone
Tor

Black
Tor

Black Tor Copse

West Okement

89

12

4

9

Branscombe's
Loaf

Slipper
Stones

Lake Down

8

Corn
Ridge

Coombe
Down

88

Gren
Tor

map
42

Southerly
Down

Hunt
Tor

tramway

Great
Nodden

7

1

Lyd

2

Peat
Works

16

87

Little Links
Tor

Great Links
Tor

e

Higher
Dunna Goat

Amicombe
Hill

d

Arms
Tor

13

a

b

3

c

5

Green
Tor

14

86

Brat Tor

Rattlebrook
Mine

Rattle Brook

Wheal
Mary
Emma

g

Foxhole
Mine

0　200　400　600　800

Metres

map 32

54

Doctor Brook

55

56

85

Sourton Tor ice works

MAP 34

TH 1-13 Tin Streaming along the Upper East Dart and West Dart Head

Neither of the main branches of the Dart was a prolific source of tin. The only large streamworks along the East Dart involves both banks of the river at Broad Marsh, so much so that the exit through Sandy Hole Pass had to be walled and deepened. The lower reaches of Lade Hill Brook have been streamed for a short distance above the junction where a bottle-shaped beehive hut has been built amidst the tinners' mounds, well preserved with a narrow entrance leading into a corbelled circular chamber (c. 3.0 x 2.0 m). The normal type of tinners' hut, **TH1** (c. 7.0 x 2.5 m), rectangular in plan, is to be found at the upper end of streamworks along the north bank of the main river near Sandy Hole Pass. This comparatively long narrow building is also in very good condition, its walls, banked-up outside, still over a metre high and with a doorpost at the entrance in the south-east corner. Nearby the Vitifer mine leats are taken off, both clearly visible as far as Winney's Down Brook, after which the upper one virtually disappears for much of its circuitous course to the mire at the head of Lade Hill Brook.

A tinners' hut, **TH2** (c. 6.5 x 3.0 m), now almost engulfed by the bog, lies opposite Broad Marsh Stream, and another, **TH3** (c. 5.3 x 2.8 m), about 150 m from the junction. Further up is a curious little shelter, **TH4** (c. 1.8 x 2.8 m), three of its sides the usual drystone walling, much of it tumbled within, built against a large boulder serving as the other long side. Pebble mounds accompany Broad Marsh Stream as far as an old watercourse joining from the west, which after an interval has been streamed to above its source. Here the walls of **TH5** (c. 4.5 x 2.5 m) have been deliberately dismantled and the stones strewn in all directions. One of the Phillpotts peat passes commences at the upper end of this gulley, little more than a track with a memorial stone at each end crossing the watershed into the valley of the West Dart.

Above Broad Marsh a substantial leat leaving the north bank next to a conspicuous rock outcrop is soon lost in the soft ground but its purpose is far from clear. The last two major tributaries draining the east side of Cut Hill join the East Dart a short distance apart on the opposite bank. Tinners' huts on the edge of isolated patches of pebble mounds accompany both streams, **TH6** (c. 4.5 x 2.5 m), with a curved outer wall perhaps for a garden, and **TH7** (c. 3.2 x 2.0 m) rather better preserved at the head of a streamwork with walls up to a metre high and visible entrance. Further upstream the prospectors had little success but nevertheless needed shelter whilst gaining what profit there was: **TH8** (c. 5.5 x 2.0 m) on the right bank 200 m above Kit Rocks and **TH9** (c. 5.0 x 2.3 m) and **TH10** (4.9 x 2.2 m) a kilometre and more higher up.

Summer Brook, one of several streams which join the West Dart near Flat Tor, is the site of a pair of tinners' huts 5 m apart, **TH11** (c. 4.5 x 2.2 m) and **TH12** (c. 5.3 x 2.7 m) which seem to have been connected by a wall. Their foundations remain but not the collapsed walls, so presumably the stones have been carted away for use elsewhere, even in this remote situation. Just above the junction at least one corner of **TH13** (c. 4.8 x 2.0 m) still stands over a metre high with an entrance, unusually, facing away from the river. This building is at the lower end of a 200 m streamworks involving both banks of the West Dart.

TH14-16 North Teign streamworks

Tin streaming along the North Teign begins 700 m from its source at a tinners' hut within some pebble mounds on the north bank. The walls of the building, **TH14** (c. 3.1 x 2.4 m), stand a metre high with an entrance protected by a porch. Streamworks begin in earnest as the river alters course to the north-east, widening past where the Varracombe Brook leat

MAP 34

winds through the workings eventually to add its contribution to the Vitifer mine leat, to the deep excavations around the junction with Marsh Hill Brook. The tinners' hut, **TH15** (c. 4.2 x 2.0 m), half a kilometre up the latter also has a protecting wall outside the entrance.

The lower courses of the next two left bank tributaries have both been streamed, Varracombe Brook **TH16** (c. 3.2 x 2.5 m) and, much more extensively, Manga Brook. The latter flows entirely within the Teignhead Farm newtakes, one of the most isolated farms on Dartmoor, built about 1780 and occupied until it was requisitioned by the War Office in 1943[11]. The buildings are now ruinous like its neighbour Manga Farm downstream. Below the farm buildings are the remains of a blowing house (c. 13.0 x 3.4 m) beside the North Teign, but only the wall facing the river stands to any height. The building is identified by the mould stones, one of them a large slab with two moulds, just within the doorway, next to a huge block taking up much of the interior, probably part of the furnace. The remaining half of a second mould lies at its base and another smaller one has been placed on top of the riverside wall opposite. There are no convincing signs of the wheel pit but the leat to it is visible in places, partly overlain by the same wall.

Below Manga Farm ruins the river descends rapidly, free of tinning activity as far as Hugh Lake where deeper ore deposits were encountered. Pebble mounds recommence and for six hundred metres the 2 m high banks were cut back from the river creating a gully eighty metres and more wide. At the lower end of the excavations a leat taken off the right bank soon divides into two, the upper channel, from its depth, being a later construction. Both end abruptly on the hillside though they may originally have been intended to connect with the leat at about the same level on the far side of Stonetor Brook. After an interval shallow streamworks reappear, continuing up both branches of the Brook and alongside the main river as curved parallel ridges as far as its junction with the Walla Brook.

Statts House and Mute's Inn

Several small buildings, probably peat cutters' huts of no great age, are to be found on Marsh Hill and its south-east extension on Winney's Down. Best known is Statts House (c. 4.5 x 2.0 m) right on the summit where it can be seen from a considerable distance. The walls, 1.5 m high, were probably built with stones taken from the cairn with which it shares the hilltop and have obviously been refurbished from time to time. One end is curiously rounded and the lintel has fallen in front of the fireplace at the other, sited next to the doorway in the south-east corner. A short distance north-west is the memorial stone at the upper end of a Phillpotts peat pass, 300 m long but soon becoming indefinite as it descends the hillside towards Broad Marsh. A second building (c. 4.3 x 1.8 m) with one end rounded, similar to Statts House, lies 350 m to the north, and an even smaller one, 2.3 m square, near the source of Winney's Down Brook.

Another group of buildings, at least seven, is to be found on Whitehorse Hill as far south as Quintin's Man, an area much favoured by the peat cutters. These are squarish in plan and smaller than the typical tinners' hut, up to 3 m across, and are sited near the hilltop rather than beside streamworks. The ruin nearest the summit with a fireplace at one end and a superb view eastwards is known as Mute's Inn (c. 3.0 x 2.0 m) and, according to Burnard[23] was erected in the early nineteenth century. Two peat passes visible from each other open onto the firm ground on the summit where peat cutting has lowered the ground considerably. Both are provided with pairs of memorial stones, a short western section, and a deep 250 m cutting down the eastern slope enlarged for use as a track to the observation post on the hilltop. The Sandpath, a raised causeway some two hundred metres long built across the bog by an earlier generation of moormen, is visible from the lower end of the latter.

MAP 35

MAP 35 Fernworthy Forest and White Ridge

1 Metherall settlement (fig. 35.1)

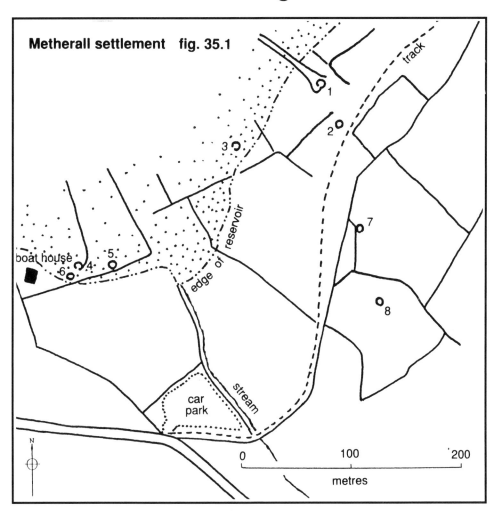

Metherall settlement   fig. 35.1

The site of Metherall Farm was occupied at least as far back as the Bronze Age, perhaps a continuity broken only by comparatively short intervals down to the present. Some of the field walls have been rebuilt on the earliest foundations either as bank and ditch or later drystone walling. The lower fields alongside the South Teign are now submerged by the reservoir but the prehistoric settlement covered a large area extending uphill from the river bank to the lines of orthostats, one of them including the Heath Stone, beyond the present enclosures south of the road. Eight large huts all with diameters over 7.5 m survive within the fields, some probably re-used as farm buildings at various periods and two of them certainly by the tinners as workshops or stores in the sixteenth century. Four huts are now

MAP 35

submerged close to the edge of the reservoir though these periodically reappear when the water level falls in summer. Despite some nineteenth century damage to their walls by stone workers most of them are in excellent condition and give a good idea how spacious such dwellings could be. They were much admired by the early Dartmoor writers and the settlement was one of the first on the Moor to receive a detailed description.

Huts 1 to 5 (fig. 35.1) were excavated in 1934-6 by R.H. Worth prior to the flooding of the reservoir. Hut 1 (8.6 m) was the only dwelling approached from the riverbank via a passageway, mainly 5 m across but widening near the hut joining it on the south beside the entrance. The interior has been excavated down to the original floor level, about 1.5 m below the top of its massive wall. The jambs still stand on either side of the paved entrance with two steps down into the interior. The floor had been greatly disturbed and only three flint flakes and a few pot-boilers were found, but despite some charcoal there was no trace of a hearth.

Some of the wall stones of hut 2 (7.7 m) are particularly massive, one measuring 3.7 m long and standing about 2 m high. A flint spear head and a hammer or whetstone were found, together with some Bronze Age pottery shards and a scatter of charcoal. From the original floor level of hut 3 (9.0 m), also of massive stones and with an entrance to the south-east, came a hammer stone, flint, pot-boilers and charcoal. Above this was a layer containing both tin ore and slag mixed with charcoal, some pieces of sixteenth-century pottery and a very worn Henry VII penny. Worth considered the hut to have been re-used as a tin store and workshop in the early sixteenth century, as was hut 4 (7.5 m). Here also a layer of tin slag mixed with charcoal and sixteenth-century pottery was found above the original floor level from which a typical Bronze Age assemblage was collected: pot-boilers, a number of flints, pottery shards from at least two vessels, charcoal and what appeared to be a whetstone.

Worth concluded that the exceptionally large circle 5 (10.1 m) was the remains of a cairn with all the small stones removed, though in appearance it is not dissimilar to the huts. Features he considered unusual were that the wall-stones on the inside were set more evenly than normal and were shorter than those forming the outer face, and that there was an inner ring of small slabs. The wall on the south edge where the entrance to a hut would be expected was too badly damaged to determine the matter. The only probable contemporary finds were some flint chips and four quartz crystals but none of the usual household waste such as pottery or charcoal. Beneath the rubble floor another exceptional feature was a large flat slab covering a shallow depression in the subsoil containing charcoal, which Worth interpreted as an interment pit.

Hut 6 (7.4 m) is also submerged but, like 7 (8.4 m) and 8 (8.6 m) within the fields uphill, has not been excavated.

2 Lowton Brook East settlement

The neighbouring settlement upstream from Metherall occupies the slopes above Lowton Brook, the first track off the perimeter road within the Forest cutting through the site. Two huts lie beside the track, the first now cleared of trees, but only about a third of its circumference still stands. Beside it is a large circle (10.0 m) of similar construction to circle 5 at Metherall, with its shorter inner wall face almost complete and the tops of a few small earthfast slabs showing above the turf within. Worth supposed that this may also have been a cairn with all the loose stones removed but the abutting enclosure wall on the east side is more likely to be associated with a hut. Most of the perimeter of another enclosure survives within the trees downhill outlined by orange-topped posts, and a little further along two more huts of large stones, but much damaged, are visible above the track.

MAP 35

3 Lowton Hill East

A few low banks can be seen on the hillside a short distance outside the plantation. All large stones have been removed but the outline of at least one enclosure is recognizable and the site is probably the last remnant of an ancient settlement.

4 Lowton Brook West

Major prehistoric settlements occupied the slopes on the northern spur of Assycombe Hill, between the Lowton and Assycombe Brooks. Much has been irrecoverably lost, first to the enclosures surrounding Assycombe and Lowton Farms which were already abandoned and ruinous by the middle of the nineteenth century, long before the afforestation of the hillside which has been much more damaging.

Eleven huts can be found, with some difficulty, in small clearings approachable from the nearest track. The largest hut (9.1 m), furthest to the north, has been incorporated in a later field wall and so survives almost intact, though one stone lying at the centre has a neat series of five slots cut along its length in preparation for use as a gatepost. The others are of medium to large size (5.0-8.0 m) with entrances, where visible, opening to the south-east. Short lengths of walling attached to several huts are soon lost within the trees but are obviously part of their surrounding field walls.

5 Assycombe Brook settlement

Over the ridge to the south-west the Assycombe settlement is equally fragmentary. Most of the eight huts (3.5-8.5 m) have only recently been recovered from the plantation, together with some slight remnants of their field walls. Some had been incorporated within Assycombe Farm newtakes, one pair taking up so much of the interior of one of the smaller fields that they must have been re-used as farm buildings.

The largest hut (8.5 m), less than 3 m from the lower end of the stone row, was the only one not to have been overplanted. It was excavated by Baring-Gould and Burnard in 1894 in an attempt to discover the relationship between the rows and the huts but they were disappointed to find that it had already been thoroughly dug into as a source of stone. Nothing useful was found but they left it in better condition than it had been by rebuilding part of the wall.

6, 7 Fernworthy West and Hemstone Rocks settlements and cairns

The lower Forest track from Fernworthy to the moorgate opposite Grey Wethers stone circle passes about midway between two compact settlements on the hillside. Trees have recently been felled around the north settlement uphill from the track, **6**, revealing the outlines of six huts, but so far nothing of their surrounding fields. Only the largest hut (7.0 m) furthest uphill had not been overplanted. The rest are evenly spaced below it but have been considerably damaged, their diameters, where measurable, ranging from 4 to 5 m across.

The Hemstone Rocks settlement lies below the track some 200 m to the south-west, **7**. Eight huts 3 to 6.5 m in diameter can be found in small clearings within the plantation, all of them having been overplanted which has caused considerable damage. Several short lengths of field walls are visible, disappearing into the trees where they cannot be followed. This was probably the site which the Dartmoor Exploration Committee began to excavate

MAP 35

on a July day in 1900. They had cleared out one hut, finding only charcoal, and were starting on others when a thunderstorm 'drove the explorers off the ground'.

The same report, the seventh, records that the Committee excavated four cairns in the vicinity, not relocated, together with one of a group of three huts which may have been part of the same settlement. A flint knife was found within a cist, all that remained of one of the cairns. The other three covered a central pit containing charcoal but one of them also contained burnt bone and two pieces of flint. The excavated hut produced a flint scraper and a cooking stone.

8 White Ridge North settlement (fig. 35.2)

This settlement of two separate enclosures with an outer wall on the south-east side is in very poor condition. The banks are nowhere more than 0.2 m high and the east side of A has entirely disappeared. A pair of huts, now low circular banks 3.5 to 4.0 m across, occupies each of the enclosures. On the edge of the settlement uphill the two channels of the Birch Tor and Vitifer mine leat wind their way around the hillside.

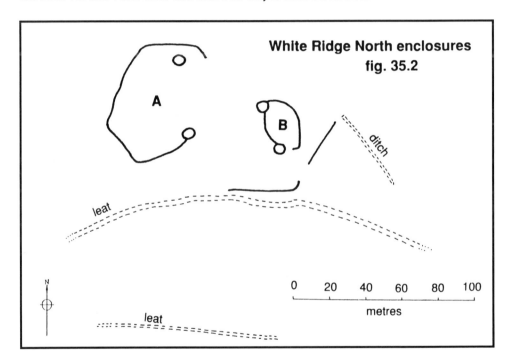

White Ridge North enclosures
fig. 35.2

9 Lade Hill Brookhead settlement and cairn

About fifteen huts grouped closely together can be found immediately south of the damp ground around the source of Lade Hill Brook. All the huts are small, 3 to 4 m across, most of them with little more than the tops of their walls showing above the turf. The only trace of associated fields in conjunction with the huts is a short run of slabs between the uphill pair.

In 1898 the Dartmoor Exploration Committee excavated a previously untouched cairn somewhere in the vicinity of the settlement '700 yards south of Grey Wethers'. It was of insignificant height even then (5.0 x 0.2 m) and has not been relocated. A pit below the cairn contained nothing but a small amount of wood charcoal, the burial having entirely disappeared.

MAP 35

10-12 White Ridge South-west settlements and cairn (fig. 35.3, 4, 5)

Three independent settlements developed around the higher slopes on the south-west side of White Ridge, separated one from another by lines of orthostats set into low banks. Their complicated interior field pattern suggests that there was a period of considerable expansion before they were finally abandoned.

Settlement **10** (fig. 35.3), on a south-east facing slope next to a dried-up spring, contains five huts in a fair state of preservation. The floor of hut 1 (8.3 m) was found to be paved when it was excavated by R. Burnard in 1893 but he concluded it had been a storehouse as no artefacts were recovered and there was no trace of a fireplace or cooking pit. The jamb stones are collapsed towards each other at the entrance on the south-east side, which was about 1.2 m wide. Huts 2 (4.5 m) and 3 (3.7 m), excavated by the Dartmoor Exploration Committee two years later, were more productive. Both contained some coarse pottery and a number of cooking stones, and the former a few flint flakes. Three more flint scrapers were picked up beside the Stannon Brook nearby. A curved interior wall can be seen within hut 4 (8.8 m) which also appears to have been dug into, but little more than the tops of the wall of hut 5 (4.0 m) can be seen above the turf.

Immediately below this settlement the downhill wall of a much more recent enclosure includes one side of a longhouse (10.5 x 2.9 m) which, unusually, is aligned along the slope. The circuit wall is butted on to the end walls of the building and obviously post-dates it, the entrance having been blocked up. A second building (15.5 x 3.8 m) of post-medieval

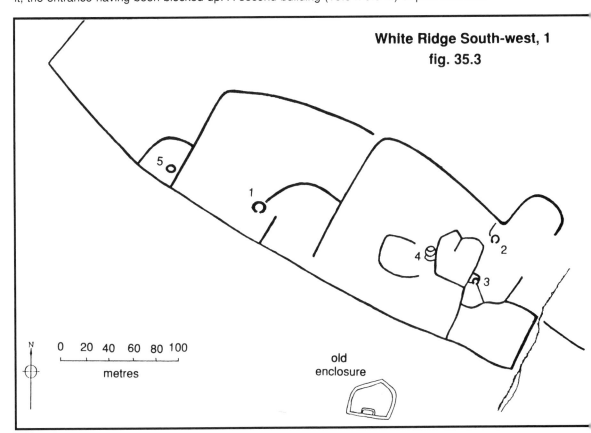

White Ridge South-west, 1

fig. 35.3

5

1

4

2

3

N

0   20   40   60   80   100

metres

old
enclosure

MAP 35

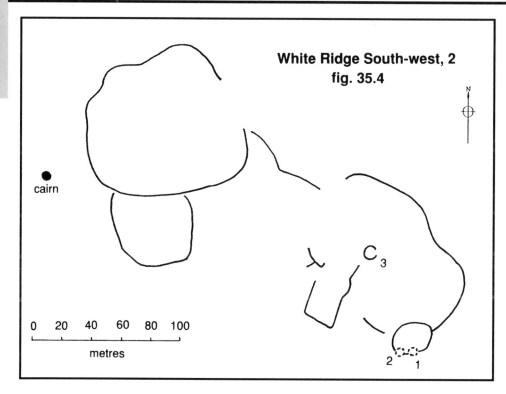

White Ridge South-west, 2
fig. 35.4

N

cairn

0   20   40   60   80   100

metres

C 3

2   1

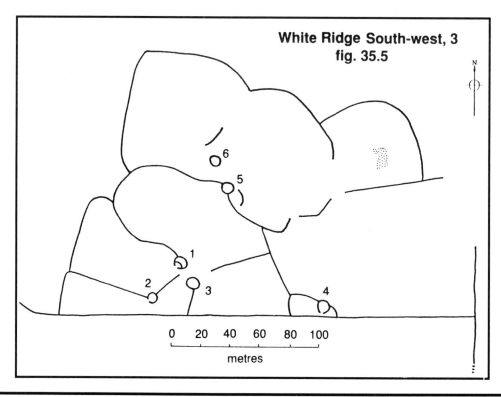

White Ridge South-west, 3
fig. 35.5

N

6

5

1

2   3

4

0   20   40   60   80   100

metres

MAP 35

date is located at the head of a tiny combe 150 m to the south-west, its walls still standing to over 1.5 m high. The two entrances face each other in the centre of the long sides and a pair of slabs within the building are probably the remains of a fireplace. The ruins of yet another building (6.8 x 3.6 m) can be seen on the opposite side of the field wall to the south-east of the latter.

The walls and huts of settlement **11** (fig. 35.4) are much more difficult to identify on the ground as all the banks are very low, mostly less than 0.2 m high, with only occasional orthostats standing above the turf. It appears to have been deliberately dismantled as long sections of bank are completely missing and more huts might be expected from the large area enclosed. Some loose stones lying roughly in circles on the eastern edge are probably the scant remains of a pair of huts, while most of the base course of a third (7.0 m) lies 60 m away in the centre of the enclosure. A turf-covered cairn (6.5 x 0.4 m) lies on the hillside 25 m outside the western enclosure, trenched across the centre revealing a stony interior.

Settlement **12** (fig. 35.5) with six huts is much better preserved than settlement **11** and is separated from it by a reave which continues downhill to the edge of the soft ground around Lade Hill Brook. Four of the huts were excavated by the Dartmoor Exploration Committee in 1896, though apart from hut 1 few details were given in the rather skimpy report of their investigations. Hut 1 (6.5 m) produced several cooking stones, flint flakes and some fragments of coarse pottery, as well as two small but unidentified worked stones. A curved wall can be seen crossing the interior and a jamb stone stands at the entrance. A small amount of charcoal and a flint were recovered, probably from hut 2 (4.5 m), whose main feature is the pair of massive jamb stones collapsed together at the entrance. Of the other four huts, with diameters ranging from 4.5 to 6.9 m, two were excavated but nothing was found in one and only a cooking stone in the other.

Several short lengths of reave can be found on the hillside north of the settlements as far as the South Teign, and a few others, apparently submerged by the peat, are visible on aerial photographs.

13 Broad Down North-east settlement and cairn

A prehistoric settlement once occupied the spur of high ground which forces the East Dart northwards around the eastern corner of Broad Down before resuming its southerly progress. Two huts alone remain (both c. 5.5 m), reduced to rings of small stones around flat interiors, together with a short section of enclosing bank. The larger uprights have all been removed, probably to build the nearby newtake wall. Nearer the summit a cairn (6.5 x 0.5 m) with central pit has been spared demolition, its exposed stones of larger size than usual.

14 Templer's Newtake (fig. 35.6)

A rather unusual site was chosen for this enclosure, on a steepening bank above the river with much of the interior taken up by a large natural depression. Downhill are a number of tinners' trial pits and the dry ditch of Powder Mills leat winding around the hillside below. The uphill enclosure wall is clearly visible from the edge of the newtake as far as a stony area which then forms part of the boundary. The lower wall on a steeper gradient is little more than a step in the hillside and ends at a small rock pile. The northern boundary seems to have been completely removed, perhaps to provide material for the newtake walls. Only one hut (c. 4.0 m) has been found within the enclosure, on the lip of the depression.

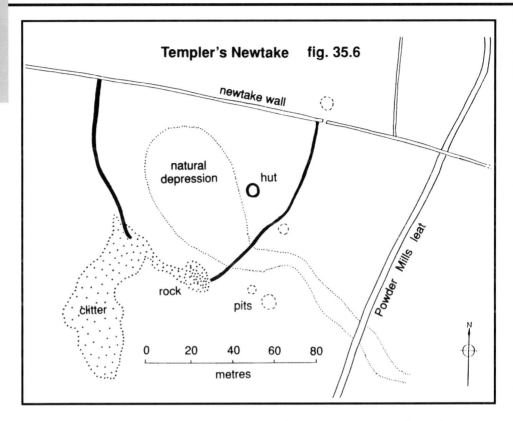

MAP 35

Templer's Newtake   fig. 35.6

newtake wall

natural depression   hut

Powder Mills leat

rock

clitter

pits

N

| 0 | 20 | 40 | 60 | 80 |

metres

15 Fernworthy stone circle, rows and cairns (figs. 35.7, 8)

What remains of this group of monuments, a stone circle, three stone rows and five cairns, which once must have rivalled Merrivale and Shovel Down as a ceremonial centre, lies in the miserable little clearing grudgingly allotted them by the Forestry Commission. Though all the stones are comparatively small, this interesting complex deserves better than the poor setting it occupies at present alongside the old track to Teignhead Farm. The stone circle and cairns 2-5 (fig. 35.7 and 35.7A, page 233) were excavated by the Dartmoor Exploration Committee in 1897 who produced an excellent plan of the site the following year. This shows that much damage had already been caused prior to afforestation by the Fernworthy Farm newtakes whose outer enclosure wall can be seen below the trees on the other side of the track.

The monuments are grouped around the stone circle, sited on level ground but overlooked from the gentle slopes to east and west. It was probably the earliest structure here, built perhaps nearly 4000 years ago, and apart from the two stones missing on the south side, has remained unmolested down the centuries with all the surviving stones still in place. Twenty-seven small stones stand in a circle 20 m in diameter (centres) slightly flattened around the north-west quadrant, the tallest on the south and diminishing in height around to the opposite side. Excavation of the interior revealed that the original ground surface was everywhere covered by a layer of wood charcoal, evidence that the circle had once been the scene of numerous fires. Perhaps, as the excavators supposed, of funerary feasts or the pyres of the departed.

Stone row 1 (fig. 35.8) starts 140 m north of the stone circle, orientated towards its western edge. The 1898 plan shows a mound with a stone alongside as its northern

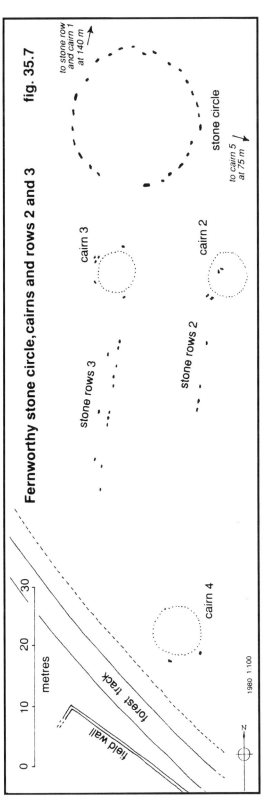

Fernworthy stone circle, cairns and rows 2 and 3   **fig. 35.7**

to stone row and cairn 1 at 140 m

stone circle

to cairn 5 at 75 m

cairn 3

cairn 2

stone rows 3

stone rows 2

cairn 4

field wall

forest track

metres

0   10   20   30

1980 1:100

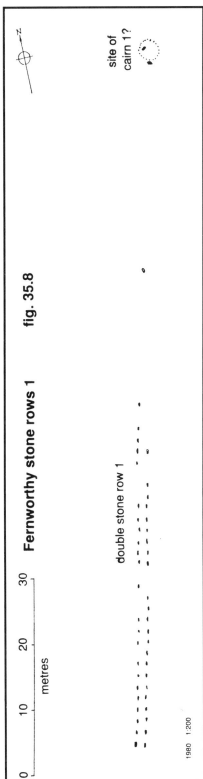

Fernworthy stone rows 1   **fig. 35.8**

N

site of cairn 1?

double stone row 1

metres

0   10   20   30

1980 1:200

163

MAP 35

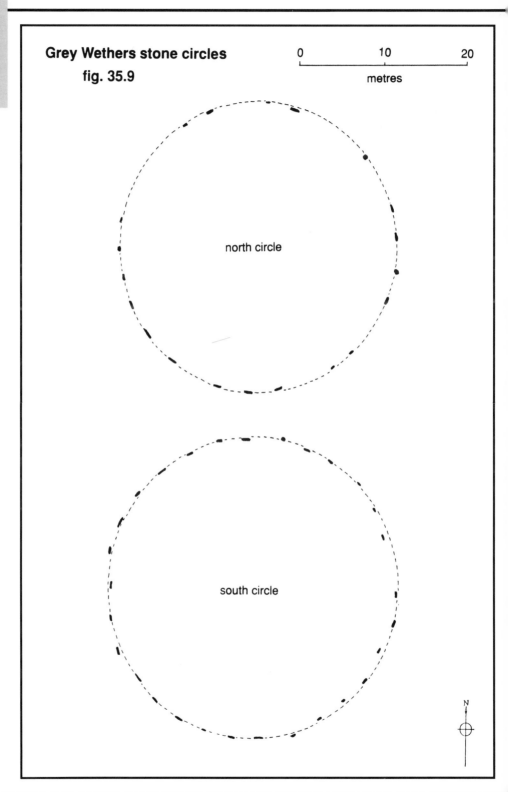

Grey Wethers stone circles
fig. 35.9

0   10   20

metres

north circle

south circle

N

MAP 35

terminus, probably a cairn, 1, with a retaining circle. This stone is still visible together with another at an angle, perhaps one side of a cist, but the cairn is totally obscured by brushwood. The northern half of the row was at one time overplanted and all but a single flat slab has disappeared, perhaps buried under the turf. The southern half remains much as it was with regularly spaced stones and few gaps, ending abruptly at disturbed ground. Page, writing in 1889,[38] noticed some prehistoric enclosures east of the row but no trace of these can be seen here within the trees.

Cairn and stone row 2 (fig. 35.7) have also recently been cleared of trees. An end and side slab of a cist are exposed within the cairn from which the excavators recovered 'masses of burnt bone', though previous diggings had left no accompanying artefacts. The tops of four stones are all that are visible of a double row orientated towards the edge of cairn 4. Cairns 3 and 4 covered pits dug in the subsoil, but here also treasure-seekers had been at work and only a tiny flint chip was found in the latter. A double row with thirteen stones still in place is aligned from cairn 3, roughly parallel with the others, and cairn 4 may well have been similarly equipped before the newtake wall was constructed.

Cairn 5, separated from the others on the summit 75 m east of the edge of the stone circle, produced more interesting results as it was found to be intact. The stones were replaced after the excavation and only a shallow central depression now records the disturbance. Trenches were cut at right-angles across the cairn revealing a pit at the centre 1.2 x 2.2 m across and 1.0 m below the original ground level. This contained a small piece of bronze with a wooden handle, perhaps part of a knife or spear head, a V-perforated conical button made out of Kimmeridge shale, and a flint knife, but no trace of the human remains which no doubt accompanied them. Amidst charcoal on the floor of the pit was the crushed remains of a beaker, originally protected by a few slabs around it, and a few shards of a second pot. There is no record of a stone row but three stones of a surrounding circle of slabs stand 2 m outside its base and others probably lie prone beneath the turf.

16-18 The Grey Wethers stone circles, enclosures and cairns (fig. 35.9)

The builders chose a spectacular site when they erected the stones of the twin Grey Wethers circles on the ridge below Sittaford Tor, **16**, an unusual position on the parting between three rivers, the North and South Teign and Lade Hill Brook. Despite numerous excavations of stone circles the purpose of many of them is still unclear and the necessity for two built so close together only compounds the mystery. Before 1909, when the circles were restored by Burnard[51], only nine stones stood erect in the north circle and seven in the south, the rest lying where they had fallen or buried beneath the turf. Packing stones at their base identify the re-erected slabs. If the reconstruction was reasonably accurate the circles may have been intended to be identical with the centres due north and south of each other (in fact they are less than 2° off). Each had thirty stones, one more than at Fernworthy, and differ in diameter by only 0.7 m from a mean of 32.9 m (centres), a variation easily accounted for in the restoration. The shallow pits in the peat within the circles are the result of trial excavations undertaken by the Dartmoor Exploration Committee in 1898 who found, as at Fernworthy, a layer of charcoal covering the original ground surface.

South of the circles but out of sight is another enigmatic monument, an oval enclosure 40 x 48 m across surrounded by a stony bank 0.6 m high and spread to 4.0 m, **17**. A single large slab lies within. The enclosure was sited across an old watercourse which once drained into Lade Hill Brook but presumably it was already dry when the bank was constructed. The bank was breached and its bed re-cut when the Varracombe leat was dug in the early nineteenth century, carrying water from the North Teign to supplement the

MAP 35

supply of the Birch Tor and Vitifer mine leat traversing the base of the hill. The bank has been damaged where stone has been carted away leaving large gaps in the wall. It has been suggested that two of these gaps are original and the structure was a henge, with opposing entrances, though without the inner ditch associated with these monuments.

Such small circular or oval enclosures of prehistoric date without associated huts are not very uncommon on Dartmoor, and may well have had a ceremonial function. A smaller one lies within sight a little over 200 m to the south-west **18**. It is almost exactly half the diameter of the last, 22 x 24 m across but is in better condition. A single entrance with a jamb stone still in place faces west, towards the river. In 1902 the Dartmoor Exploration Committee dug a few trial pits within this enclosure and examined the entrance but 'nothing was found' except a long narrow stone which still lies near the centre. The surrounding hillside is remarkably free of large surface stones, at least at present, and it is tempting to suppose that this monolith may have purposely been dragged here to be set upright.

Also unusual is the cairn lying about 55 m south-east of the larger enclosure. The surface is uneven as though it has been dug into, and its present sub-rectangular shape 8 x 14 m across may be a distortion of the original. Numerous small stones show through the turf within the body of the mound, many of them set upright though not in any obvious pattern, and several larger slabs are aligned along its lower edge.

A more conventional cairn (c. 5.0 x 4.0 m) lies nearly 250 m north-east of Grey Wethers. The Dartmoor Exploration Committee found that it had been undisturbed before they excavated it in 1898, but the usual central pit, 0.8 m deep, contained nothing but charcoal.

19 Assycombe Hill stone rows (fig. 35.10)

This double stone row, overgrown but otherwise in excellent condition, is similar to its neighbour on Hurston Ridge a kilometre to the east. The pair of rows descend the hillside from a cairn with cist to end at a single blocking stone across the south row. A shallow depression here, as though some peat has been carted away, may explain the absence of a companion stone across the north row. At the higher end an outer retaining circle encloses the cairn and an inner ring of slabs surrounds the cist, only one side slab of which remains alongside the empty pit.

Probably only eleven stones are missing out of an original 144, neatly paired, though the distance both between and along the rows is remarkably uneven. All are small except for those nearest the cairn, the tallest of which is at right-angles to the rows. This stands across the foot of the cairn with packing stones at its base where it was re-erected when the rows were restored in the 1890s. A curious feature is that the rows are aligned well to the south of the cairn centre, the north row towards the cist and the south row nearer the edge of the cairn as though a later addition. Alternatively a third row may have been planned but never built on the other side of the central row. Crossing the rows about halfway along is a prehistoric bank, now reduced to a step in the hillside, and probably contemporary with the nearby huts. The shorter intervals between the adjacent pairs of stones suggest that these may have been moved slightly backwards out of the way by the hut dwellers wishing to cause minimum disturbance to the monument.

20 White Ridge stone rows (fig. 35.11)

The battered cairn and double stone row which descends the south side of White Ridge is one of the least spectacular on the moor, having served as a useful source of stone. Of the forty-one stones that remain in place few show much above ground level, presumably not worth the trouble of digging out. Another eighteen have fallen and most of these have a covering of turf. As they descend the steepening gradient the rows gradually widen from 0.9

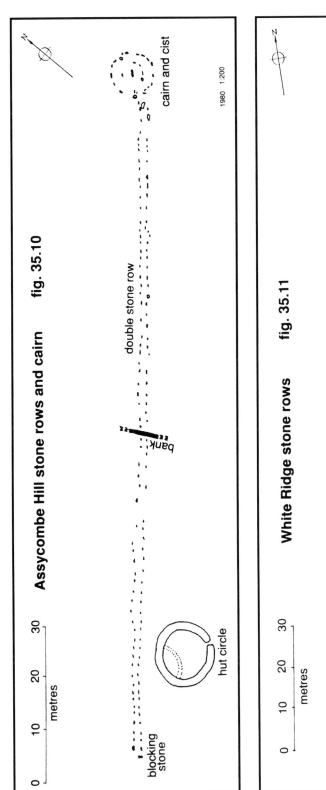

Assycombe Hill stone rows and cairn   fig. 35.10

N

cairn and cist

1980 1:200

double stone row

bank

hut circle

blocking
stone

0   10   20   30

metres

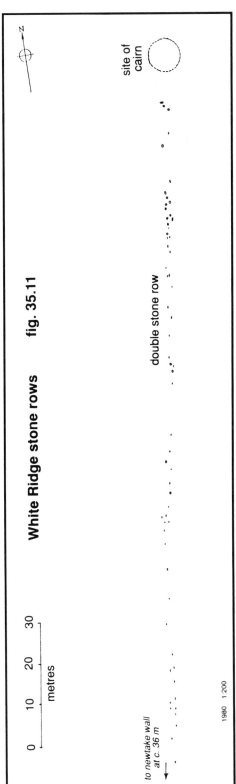

White Ridge stone rows   fig. 35.11

N

site of
cairn

double stone row

0   10   20   30

metres

to newtake wall
at c. 36 m

1980 1:200

167

MAP 35

to 1.5 m apart and their orientation deviates a few degrees to the west, once the upper end is lost to view, before resuming the original alignment lower down the slope. The present length is 167 m from the centre of the cairn, but the original length is unknown as the stones thin out southwards near Stannon Newtake wall without any obvious termination. The stones have been almost entirely removed from the cairn at the uphill end a few metres beyond the first fallen slabs of the rows. All that remains is a slight mound about 8 m across with a flat surface except for a rim of rubble around the western edge, and it is just possible that the interment remains undisturbed at the centre.

21 Cairns in Stannon Newtake (figs. 35.12,13)

Two cairns are to be found within the newtake north-east of Stannon Farm, the stones of the retaining circle of the uphill one standing out clearly on the hillside (fig. 35.12). Two of these have been lost opposite the double-banked ditch which passes close alongside, but six remain set fairly accurately in a circle with diameter 3.9 m (centres). All four sides of an empty cist survive in place at the centre, though the cover has disappeared. The single slab 6 m south-west of the circle may be an outlying part of the structure.

On the flatter ground 130 m downhill to the west is a less conspicuous cairn (6.0 x 0.7 m) which was excavated by Burnard in 1896 (fig. 35.13). Two trenches were driven across the centre from the north-west and north-eastern edges, the latter revealing an off-centre pit dug in the subsoil below the cairn. This was 0.4 m deep and was filled with charcoal and ash intermixed with a few pieces of burnt bone and a single flake of sharpened flint.

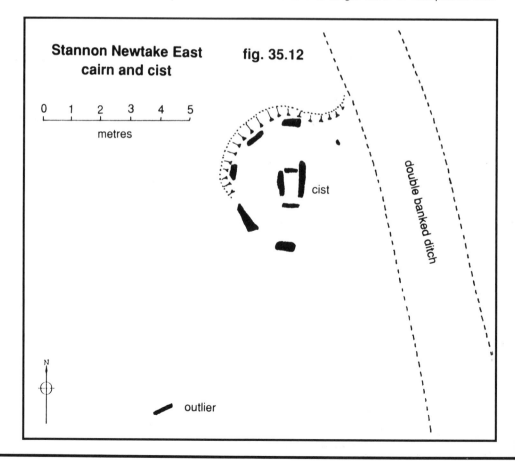

Stannon Newtake East cairn and cist

fig. 35.12

0 1 2 3 4 5
metres

cist

double banked ditch

N

outlier

MAP 35

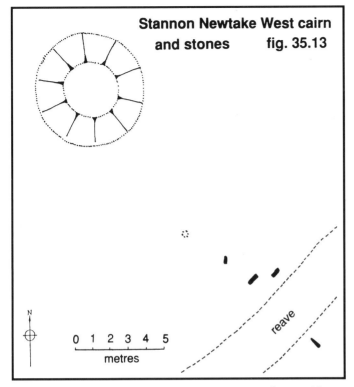

Stannon Newtake West cairn and stones   fig. 35.13

N

reave

0 1 2 3 4 5

metres

Apparently associated with the cairn are two stones (0.9 and 0.6 m high) set facing it 10 m to the south-east with a smaller one at an angle nearer the cairn and the top of another just showing above the turf on the other side of a prehistoric reave. This slightly alters course opposite the cairn. The excavation plan shows a fifth buried stone in line with the others. The two largest may be the blocking stones at the end of a double stone row, the rest having been cleared from the site, though the orientation along the hillside rather than downslope from the cairn would be unusual. At least one of these has probably been re-erected as packing stones are visible at its base.

The remains of either a third cairn or possibly a hut circle in the vicinity, reported many years ago by the Rev. H. Breton, have not been relocated.

22 Thornworthy cairn and cists

The cairn and well-preserved cist on the southern slope of Thornworthy Down, just 10 m from the edge of the reservoir, has a better recorded history than most. Although a conspicuous 1.5 m high when first noticed, and then excavated by S. Slade of Torquay in 1878, it was found that it had not previously been dug into. The mound covered one cist at the centre and a second slightly smaller one on the south-east side. They were set at an angle of about 30° to each other but the longer sides of both were orientated, as, usual, within the N.W./S.E. quadrants.

The excavator cleared out the central cist first, finding only a flint knife, and at a later date a flint scraper. The other was left exposed but unopened in anticipation of a visit by William Pengelly, famous for the excavations he was carrying out at Kent's Cavern. In the meantime the cist was ransacked and all that was recovered from the contents, which had been thrown to one side, were two more pieces of flint and some fragments of pottery.

The central cist was left in place with the cover propped open. The other was transported to Torquay Museum and reassembled in the hall where it can still be viewed.

a The D Stone

This tall, shaped pillar stands on the summit of Assycombe Hill 25 m outside Fernworthy plantation. Lightly cut on the west face is the letter *D* which usually indicates a Duchy bound, but this stone is well within the present boundary of the Forest and must have some other significance.

MAP 36

MAP 36 East Shovel Down and Thornworthy Tor

1 Kes Tor settlement (figs. 36.1,2)

Though of no great size its position on the eastern extremity of the high moorland makes Kes Tor a prominent landmark from a considerable distance. A large prehistoric settlement covers all but its south-western slopes, originally excluding the rock itself though this was later partly incorporated within the enclosed area. These Bronze Age farmers were not however the first to find this part of the valley attractive, for thousands of flint implements of neolithic and even mesolithic date have been collected from within the Batworthy enclosures opposite. The site is well known as Batworthy Lane cuts through the ancient boundaries, visible on either side of the road and extraordinarily well preserved considering the proximity of present farmlands. Many of the modern field walls still follow the course of the original ones down the eastern slopes. Some of them, composed of large upright slabs like those due east from Kes Tor rock, were well enough constructed in prehistoric times to have remained in use almost unaltered. Usually there is a slight gap on the moorland side of the junction where stones have been removed.

How far the settlement extended downhill to the east is uncertain but it probably descended at least as far as the 320 m contour, some 400 m below the highest point of the moorland boundary. The alignment is maintained this far, the walls gradually altering course eastwards, and some ten large-diameter huts can still be found within the area presently enclosed. Northwards the boundary banks are lost on the steep slopes down to the North Teign which seems to have formed the limit of open-ended fields in this direction.

A continuous axial north-east/south-west reave curves around the hillside midway between Kes Tor rock and the Round Pound, mirroring the course of the river below as far as Batworthy Brook. It may well have continued further for a reave reappears on the opposite side of Batworthy enclosures, eventually ending on one at right angles east of Stonetor Brook. The original western boundary of the settlement seems to have been a north-west/south-east reave based on this axial reave which passes just to the east of Kes Tor rock. The junction of the connecting bank from the three rather irregularly-shaped fields to the west is slightly offset and these must have been a later addition. Southwards the lower strips within the present fields may have merged with those around Middle Tor but a well-marked boundary reave provides a definite termination to the moorland part of the settlement. The latter ends at a pile of stones on the floor of the valley to the west, fifty metres beyond the cross bank of the last strip.

The majority of the huts and smaller fields lie on the nothern slopes of the tor, the only area with a considerable amount of surface stone and small rock outcrops. Four huts (1-3,5) here were excavated by Lady Fox in 1951 and 1952 with a surprising result. One of them was the large hut within the Round Pound, 1 (fig. 36.2), a small enclosure up to 34 m across but solidly enough built to cause the road to be diverted around its perimeter. The hut (11.4 m), the largest in the settlement, had been occupied by iron workers, two hollows in the subsoil being identified as a furnace which still contained some slag, and a forging pit. Neither are now visible but were on the right of the doorway. Otherwise its structure was typical of the larger round houses with cobbled entrance, stone sill and steps down into the interior which was partly paved. A fire once smouldered against the opposite wall and a central hollow draining under the lower wall gathered drips from the roof. A Bronze Age flint arrowhead was found just outside the entrance and amongst the debris on the floor were some pottery shards, twenty-one pieces of flint one of which may have been used as a sickle, and a whetstone.

Kes Tor settlement   fig. 36.1

North Teign River

Batworthy Brook

Batworthy

Kes Tor

0   100   200   300
metres

171

MAP 36

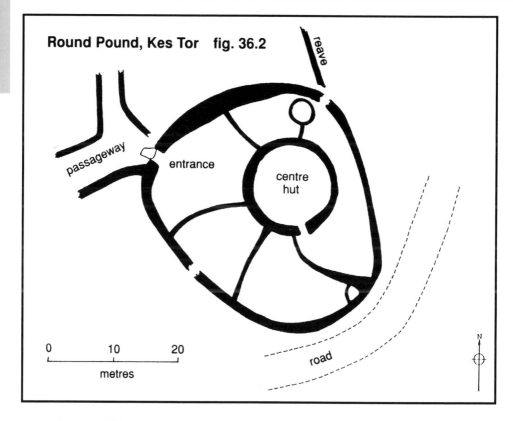

Round Pound, Kes Tor   fig. 36.2

reave

passageway

entrance

centre
hut

road

0   10   20

metres

N

An anvil, ten pebbles – some showing signs of wear – and two hammer stones may well have formed part of the ironworkers' kit. Many centuries after they abandoned the building, perhaps in the twelfth century, a shepherd built a crude shelter against the inner wall in which the excavators found a fireplace and fragments of a cooking pot. They suggested he may have converted the pound into a sheepfold and been responsible for building the five radial walls across the intervening space. These were constructed from stones fallen from the hut wall some time after it had been abandoned.

The Pound is shared by a much smaller hut (3.0 m), or possibly an un-roofed pen, on the north side. This was also excavated but nothing was found to indicate its function or date, though probably it was contemporary with the central hut. The curved foundations of an even smaller structure can be seen in the angle between the south radial wall and the outer circuit.

Round Pound itself differs only in scale and size of stones from similar structures on the moor. Its massive wall spread to 4 m across and nearly 2 m high externally on the north side encircles the hut asymmetrically, the straighter eastern side overlying a reave approaching from the north-west. The gaps in the east and west walls are later damage, the original entrance being through the north wall from a passageway across the fields. The entrance was excavated revealing a step down to the outside, still visible, but there was no sign of postholes for a gate so it must have been closed by a hurdle or something similar. The entrance passage is flanked on either side by three courses of large horizontal slabs and was apparently covered by a lintel, the massive stone that has slipped forward and now blocks egress. It would have been only about 1.2 m high.

Outside the Pound a passageway leads in both directions to the edge of the fields, cutting across at least two reaves and so presumably constructed some time after the fields

MAP 36

were laid out. The shorter western section has some particularly large blocks in its wall and opens opposite Batworthy Brook. Eastwards two narrower lanes branch off uphill approximately in the direction of the pair of huts 2 and 3 on the opposite side of the road. Both are in poor condition, 2 (8.2 m) having little more than the inner face in place and the partly-buried hut 3 (6.5 m) with the entrance, next to a jamb stone, blocked by a fallen slab. The passageway widens considerably to 16 m half-way along before abruptly narrowing again, stopping short of a pair of huts, 4 (7.7, 8.0 m) in the neighbouring strip. These are both reduced to their foundations with only a few stones remaining around circular platforms levelled into the hillside.

Hut 5 (8.3 m) also excavated by Lady Fox was found to be unexceptional. At the entrance a step down on to a cobbled area to the interior faced a fireplace near the opposite wall. The site had first been levelled into the hillside and the inner wall slabs levered into position along a continuous shallow trench rather than into individual sockets. A turf roof was supported on a ring of seven wooden posts around a central upright. Some broken pottery was found near the hearth and in one of the post holes. Two whetstones were also recovered, together with flints, part of the base of a quern stone for grinding grain, and, a common find within many huts usually explained as playthings or gaming pieces, a large number of quartz crystals.

A curved wall cuts off an opposite corner of the same field around two circular banks, 6. The smaller (4.6 m) is of the usual construction but the other ring of slabs (c. 9.0 m) seems too slight to have supported a roof and it may well have been a simple animal pen. On the opposite side of the cross wall many of the stones have slipped sideways off the wall of hut 7 (5.9 m) and a large slab now blocks the entrance into the paddock. Hut 8 (9.0 m) was built of massive stones but part of its east wall is missing. It was trenched at the same time as hut 5 but nothing of interest was found and there is now no sign of it having been disturbed.

North-eastwards on the other side of a cross bank about half a dozen slabs are arranged around a circular levelled area, all that remains of hut 9 (c. 6.2 m). Its strip was bounded by passageways on either side but only its upper end survives above the present field margin. Lower down the poor remains of three large huts, 10 (8.2, 8.7, 9.4 m), from which many wall stones have been removed can be seen on the other side of the fence. Better preserved is hut 11 (9.1 m) at the junction of the next two fields to the south where half the circumference has been incorporated into the present enclosure walls. In contrast to these and the pair of ruined huts, 12 (7.2, 4.5 m), near the rock outcrop uphill, hut 13 (8.4 m) is in a splendid state of preservation. The exceptionally thick wall, up to 3.5 m across, has a complete inner facing of massive granite slabs, opening into a paddock on the south-east side. Equally impressive is hut 14 (8.9 m) next to two smaller ruined companions (6.3, ?m). Together with hut 15 (5.8 m) these last five buildings lie beside a long narrow passageway opening into one of the strips uphill. The lower end of the passageway is lost near the field margin but its original course seems to be retained in the present track off the moor which descends to Teigncombe.

Apart from the two small buildings 16 (5.2 m) and 17 (4.5 m) in the corner of strips uphill the rest of the huts east of Kes Tor are below the present field margin. Two huts, 18 (8.0, 5.5 m), lie within the first field next to the passageway with remnants of paddock walls. On the steeper hillside farther south a large hut, 19 (8.5 m), has survived against the odds, its massive blocks perhaps too large for easy removal, supporting a field wall around its rim. Two fields further in the same direction are the barely recognisable remains of another building (**map 36**), probably of large size but only a few blocks of the outer wall are visible around the lower edge of its mud-filled interior. The hut (c. 9.0 m) marked on Ordnance Survey maps due east of Kes Tor has an almost complete inner face of megalithic proportions, a gap on the south-east side no doubt the site of the entrance. Another (c. 9.5 m) a short distance downhill has been almost totally robbed of wall stones.

MAP 36

Beyond the western boundary reave the huts and fields seem to be later additions to the settlement with comparatively few upright slabs and all apparently robbed. Passageways from the direction of Batworthy Brook run to the north of the square field surrounding the pair of huts at 20 (3.8, 4.6 m) and the two (c. 6.6, ?m) in the neighbouring field, 21. Three more huts, 22 (4.4, 4.6, 7.6 m), the largest with an interior dividing wall, are associated with the larger fields to the south.

2, 3 Settlements south of Kes Tor

A single strip projects westwards from the Kes Tor boundary reave, sub-divided by cross banks and occupied by three huts along the uphill side, **2** (fig. 36.3). All have entrances facing south-east, hut 1 (5.8 m) opening into its own small enclosure and hut 2 (4.6 m) with a curved interior wall. Hut 3 (6.4 m) is the largest of the group and a fourth hut (5.9 m) on the opposite side of the reave has been severely damaged by a trench through its walls.

South eastwards from this group a pair of widely separated reaves continue the alignment to the south-west, one of them passing through the rocks of Middle Tor before visibly ascending the opposite slope on to Thornworthy North settlement. The two reaves are joined below the crest by a cross bank blocking one end of a passageway. The latter, 4.5 m across at this point, widens to 7.0 m before being lost within the present fields to the east where no doubt huts associated with the enclosure once existed.

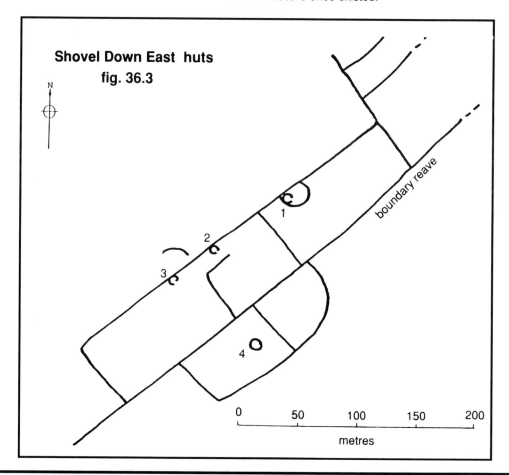

Shovel Down East huts

fig. 36.3

N

boundary reave

1

2

3

4

0   50   100   150   200

metres

MAP 36

South of Middle Tor little remains of the prehistoric settlement, **3**. Ditched banks cross the spur to beyond Frenchbeer Rock showing that the moorland here was enclosed and then abandoned in more recent times. The present fields encroach far up the eastern slope and the little valley to the west has been streamed for shallow deposits of tin. Only those stones too large to move or of no use elsewhere have been left in place along the ancient field boundaries or around the two remaining huts on the summit. Much of the inner face of the north hut (6.2 m) survives but less than half the other (7.7 m) a few metres away, though here a huge pillar which was once part of its outer wall still stands in place. The sites of other huts nearby are visible on aerial photographs.

4 Shovel Down Central settlements and cairns (fig. 36.4)

Westwards from the head of Batworthy Brook the ground rises gently up onto the central plateau. The saddle between is crossed by a long north-west/south-east reave which runs from the North Teign through the centre of the stone row group towards a tributary of the South Teign, separating the Kes Tor and border settlements from those on the higher ground to the west. A cross reave originates on this one near the stone circle, orientated towards the south-west and forming the base line of a number of fields reaching almost to the summit of the Down. These seem to form three independent groups (A, B, C) joined together by a sinuous upper bank.

The eastern group, A, of four huts (4.6-7.7 m) occupy four or five small fields bounded by low banks with occasional slabs in line. The largest and best preserved hut lies closest to the summit, apparently built before the field walls were constructed as these curve in to

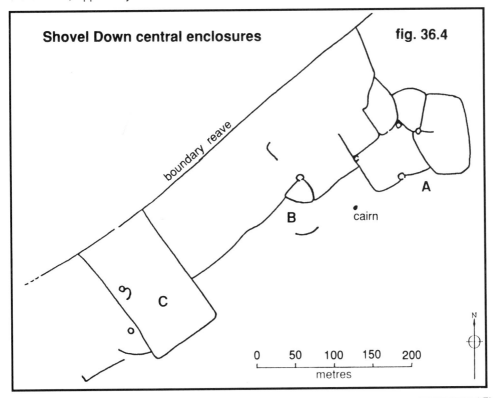

Shovel Down central enclosures   fig. 36.4

boundary reave

B   cairn   A

C

0   50   100   150   200
metres

N

MAP 36

meet it. The entrance into this field is still preserved, a pair of slabs set sideways across the downhill wall. Forty metres outside the south-west corner a small solitary cairn (5.0 x 0.3 m) has been dug into, the displaced stones subsequently returned to the central pit where they lie in a loose pile. Another cairn (6.5 x 0.3m), apparently undug, lies on the open hillside 250 m north of the enclosures downhill from several very low mounds, all possible burial cairns.

Some fifty metres to the west a winding bank connects this group of fields with a far more substantial triangular enclosure, B, where a single hut (5.0 m) with a jamb stone still in position opens into one of the lower corners. Unconnected a short distance away are several lengths of walling which obviously once formed the boundaries of other fields. The hillside here is noticeably clear of surface stone and the appearance of these banks suggests they were most likely dismantled in antiquity, perhaps to provide material for the triangular enclosure.

A further bank leaves this enclosure to the south-west, eventually butting onto the large rectangular field, C, based on the lower cross reave. Here are the foundations of two large huts (7.8, 7.0 m), one of them with the remains of a paddock wall, together with some outer banks which suggest this site may once have extended even further in this direction.

5, 6 Thornworthy Tor North and South settlements (figs 36.5,6)

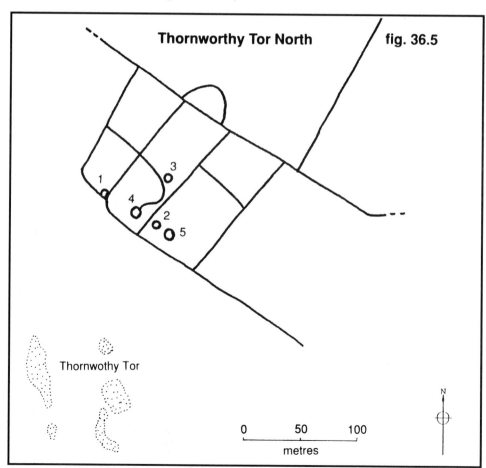

Thornworthy Tor North — fig. 36.5

Thornwothy Tor

0   50   100
metres

N

MAP 36

Most of the surface stone has been cleared from the vast newtake surrounding Thornworthy Tor, reducing the two prehistoric settlements on the north and south slopes to barely visible banks. The outline of the north settlement, **5** (fig. 36.5), of five huts within a trio of rectangular fields is still intact. Two small (c. 3.5 m) and two medium (c. 6.5 m) huts are reduced to low circular banks, though hut 5 (9.5 m) retains several wall slabs too massive to have been required for use elsewhere. Reaves lead outwards from the fields towards the Central Settlement **4** and the Middle Tor field-system, interrupted by the mires around the sources of Longstone and Thornworthy Brooks which have probably increased in size subsequent to the tin workings downstream.

The walls of the settlement south of the tor, **6** (fig. 36.6), are even less obvious, with some of the banks discontinuous on either side of a central reave. Apart from hut 1 (6.0 m), which has been dug into, the other six (4.5-7.5 m) are little more than circular patches levelled into the hillside. Originating on Longstone Brook are two leats which cut across the site, the upper one carrying water to Thornworthy Farm. The lower leat, much older and almost overgrown, empties into the higher end of a tinners' gully beside Crown Hall stream.

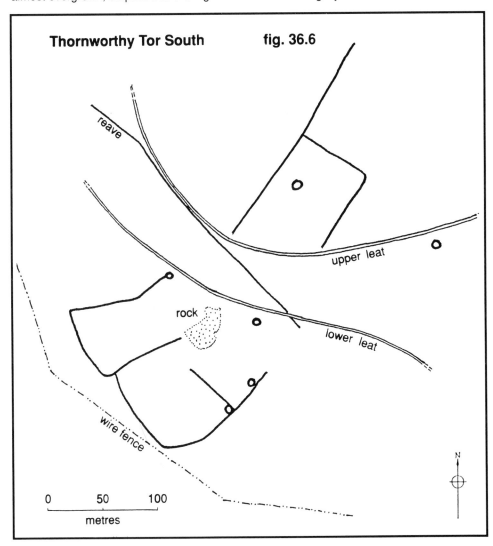

Thornworthy Tor South   **fig. 36.6**

reave

upper leat

rock

lower leat

wire fence

0 50 100

metres

N

MAP 36

6 Shovel Down stone circle, rows and cairns (fig. 36.7-14)

This most complex of all the surviving Dartmoor ceremonial centres, consisting of a stone circle, a single stone row and five double stone rows, was laid out across the central ridge of Shovel Down (fig. 36.7). Situated so close to the edge of the moor it is not surprising that many stones have been robbed from the rows, particularly towards their ends opposite Batworthy and Thornworthy newtakes, though some of the missing ones are no doubt simply buried beneath the turf. A hollow rutted track from Batworthy corner cuts through the centre of the site, and everywhere patches of roughened surface are evidence of centuries of peat cutting. Although much survives today the first damage to the monument occurred in the Bronze Age not long after the stones had been so carefully set up, when one of the main parallel reaves was constructed from the bank of the North Teign south-eastwards to Longstone mire. It was driven straight across the site without deviating, though no doubt with some regret, as minimal damage was caused to the rows except perhaps where a cairn at the head of row 3 was incorporated in the bank. This was a typically strict application of the reave builders' passion for parallel lines and right-angles as even a slight re-alignment downhill would at least have avoided the centre of the group.

Presumably cairns and rows were added as required but there seems to have been no overall geometrical arrangement of the group apart from their roughly north-south alignment. The badly damaged stone circle (fig. 36.8) confined in the corner of the later Bronze Age enclosure was probably the first monument to be built. Only three slabs remain standing, flat-topped like the Grey Wethers, but the tops of two more fit neatly on the perimeter of a circle 17.7 m in diameter, and others lie nearby. The slope is comparatively steep for a stone circle, 7°, and much of the flat interior has been stripped for peat.

Of the stone rows grouped closely together east of the circle, row 1 (fig. 36.9) differs in many respects from the rest. The only single row, it far exceeds the others in length, measuring 540 m between its present ends. It extends from Batworthy corner southwards over the ridge, where it wanders off its original alignment like the nearby reave, almost as far as the Longstone. No cairn is to be seen in line and its original length is unknown, though any stones beyond the Longstone are likely to have been robbed at the same time as those from row 6. Undoubtedly many stones remain hidden under the surface in the long gaps in the row. The ninety-nine visible ones are exceptionally small with the tops of many of them at ground level and others exposed only where the turf has been removed. The largest stone is a flat slab 1.05 m long, perhaps significantly near the highest point of the ridge.

Rows 2 to 6 are double and may all have been of the Hurston Ridge type. That is, with stones neatly paired across the rows gradually increasing in height towards a cairn at the upper end. The lower terminal when complete was typically a 'blocking stone' set at right-angles across each row though none survive on Shovel Down, or a large standing stone like the Longstone.

A long gap follows the two isolated stones at the lower end of Rows 2 (fig. 36.10) but numbers increase substantially towards the cairn where twelve pairs stand in place. Forty stones remain altogether and from the intervals between those still erect at least 192 have been removed to serve some other purpose. The final stones of the row next to the cairn are two large pillars, 3.6 and 2.2 m long, both flat and the former with the letters *GP* cut on the surface denoting its function as the boundary between Gidleigh and Chagford parishes. The cairn (fig. 36.11) at the uphill end is known as the Fourfold circle from the four concentric rings of stones which surround the central pit. A slight rise within the outer ring is all that remains of the mound, most of the smaller stones from the body of the cairn having been carted away. The rings are elliptical rather than truly circular with the longer axis in the

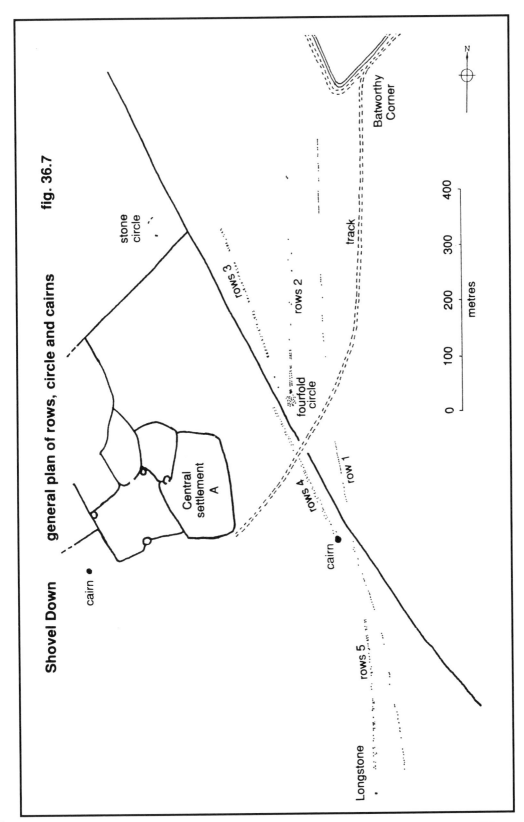

Shovel Down   general plan of rows, circle and cairns   fig. 36.7

stone circle

rows 3

rows 2

fourfold circle

track

Batworthy Corner

N

0   100   200   300   400

metres

cairn

Central settlement A

rows 4

row 1

cairn

rows 5

Longstone

MAP 36

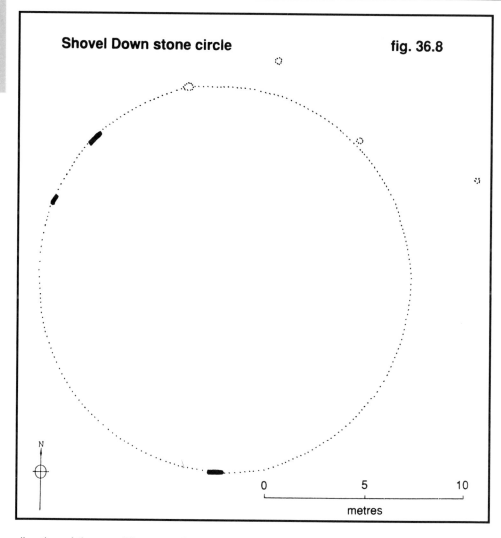

Shovel Down stone circle　　　　　　　　　　**fig. 36.8**

N

0　　　　　　　5　　　　　　　10

metres

direction of the row. The outer ring has a diameter of about 9 m and contains ten stones, the others six, eight and five stones respectively, though all have several gaps.

No terminal defines the end of the double row 3 (fig. 36.12). The lower end may not have continued much further for the stones are increasing in size here and set closer together, and the reave crosses the upper end of the rows roughly where a cairn might be expected. There is now no sign of the cairn in line next to the Fourfold circle marked on Worth's plan (1931) but possibly one was included in the line of the reave which is much spread and ill-defined at this point. Stone rows were not laid out with quite the geometrical precision of the reaves and this alignment shows a marked curvature to the west downhill. The ends are not intervisible and as usual the rows wander off line as the upper end becomes hidden by the slope of the ground.

The best preserved of the group is double row 4 (fig. 36.13). Sixty-one stones are in place, nine have fallen and thirty-two are missing between the present ends, the only major damage having been caused by the sunken track two-thirds of the way down. The rows lead uphill to a cairn (7.0 x 0.3 m) with a central pit which once contained a cist, now no longer visible. Below the track the majority of the pairs are intact, one of the penultimate

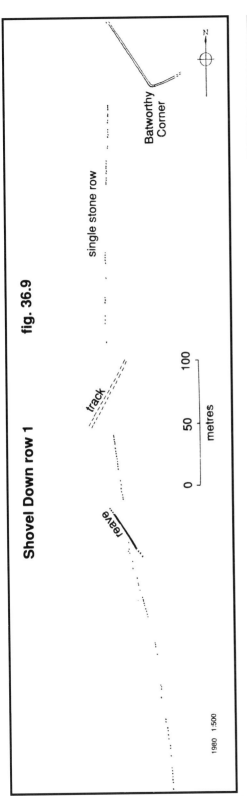

Shovel Down row 1   **fig. 36.9**

Batworthy Corner

single stone row

track

reave

0   50   100
metres

1980 1:500

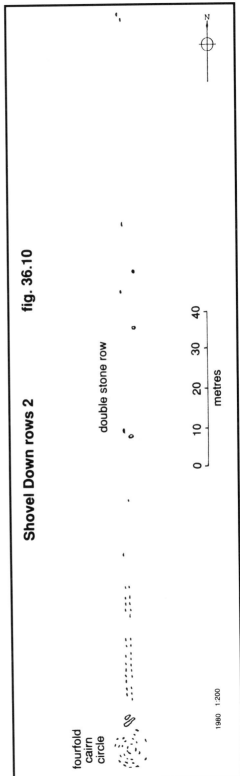

Shovel Down rows 2   **fig. 36.10**

double stone row

fourfold
cairn
circle

0   10   20   30   40
metres

1980 1:200

181

MAP 36

ones being the tallest in the rows. Blocking stones at right-angles might be expected here if the rows were complete but there is no indication that they ever continued beyond the last pair, 118 m from the centre of the cairn.

Double row 5 (fig. 36.14) descends the opposite slope from near the crest of the ridge to the Longstone 148 m away. At the uphill end the first two pairs of stones are noticeably taller than the rest, a feature normally associated with an impending cairn, but not the slightest trace of one remains. Most of the stones barely show above the turf and the spaces left by missing or buried ones progressively increase downhill, with a final gap of about 20 m before the Longstone. Like row 3 the orientation differs between the ends, altering course about midway as the upper end is lost to view.

The gigantic Longstone, 3.1 m high, stands at the lower end with its face set across the rows like a blocking stone. It now does duty as the point where the parishes of both Gidleigh and Chagford meet the Forest and the letters *GP*, *DC* and *C* have been cut on appropriate faces. It has been supposed that the Longstone is identical with the boundary mark on the border of the Forest called Heighestone (Highstone) in 1240 and Henston or variations of it in later Perambulations. The neighbouring boundary points are very uncertain and this doubtful attribution causes the Forest border to make an awkward detour eastwards. In 1609 the Highstone was described as 'lying near Fernworthy hedges' a good distance to the south-west, having apparently fallen at some time after 1240. There is no record of the Longstone being re-erected and a flat, but as yet undiscovered, menhir near the Fernworthy stone circle and rows, like those associated with the ceremonial complexes on Shovel Down, Merrivale and Drizzlecombe, would both improve the description and return the Forest boundary to its normally direct route around the centre of the moor.

Practically nothing remains of double row 6, most of the stones having been removed to build the nearby newtake wall some time prior to 1848, though their pits could still be seen in the turf ten years later. The rows ran southwards from the Longstone, possibly as a continuation of 5 as there is no trace of a cairn at this end, though one might have been entirely removed along with the rows. They ended about 170 m

Fourfold circle   fig. 36.11

0 1 2 3 4 5
metres

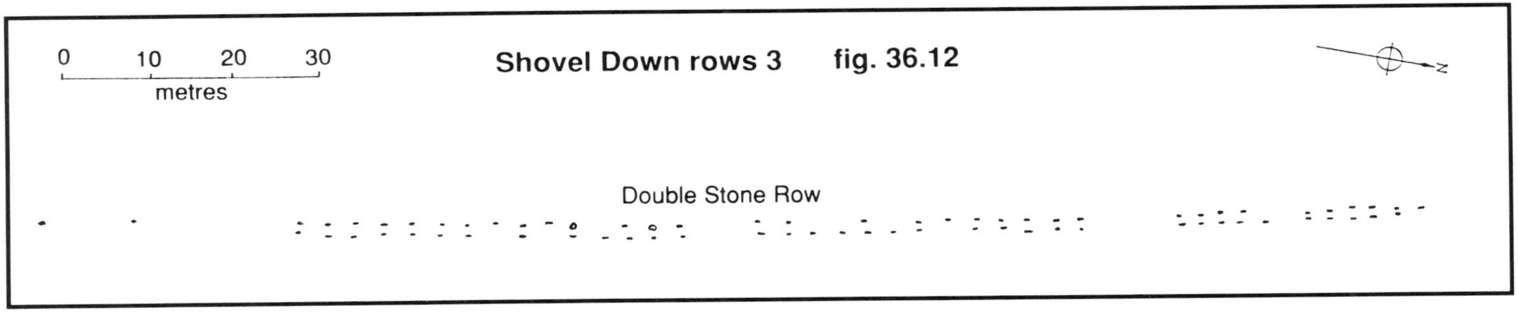

Shovel Down rows 3   fig. 36.12

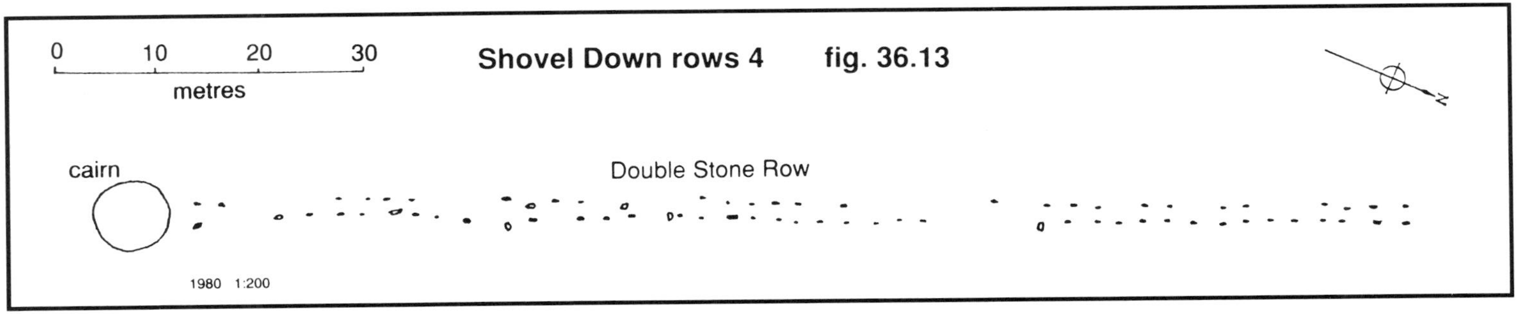

Double Stone Row

N

0 10 20 30
metres

Shovel Down rows 4   fig. 36.13

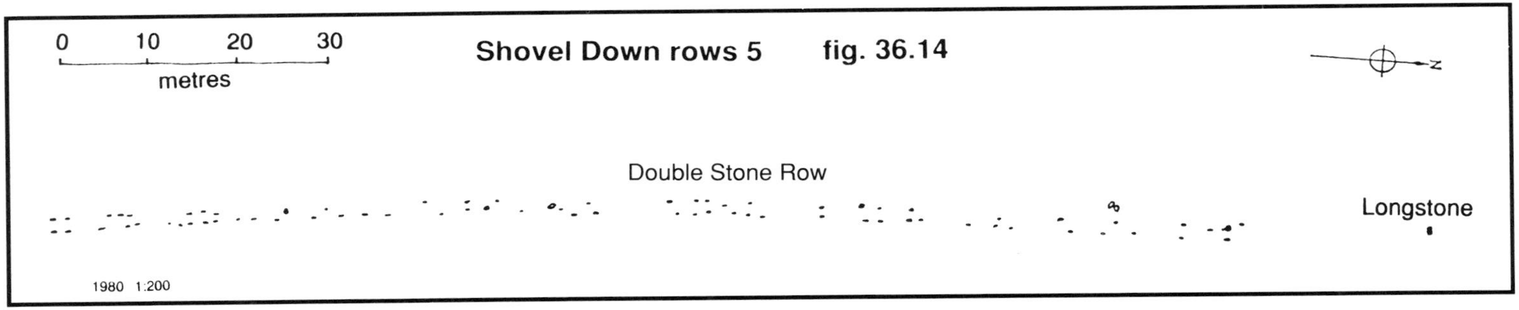

Double Stone Row

N

0 10 20 30
metres

cairn

1980 1:200

Shovel Down rows 5   fig. 36.14

Double Stone Row

Longstone

N

0 10 20 30
metres

1980 1:200

Double Stone Row 1

MAP 37

away at the Three Boys stone, 1.4 m long, the last of a trio which once stood here, now leaning precariously earthwards. This stone faces across the line of the rows and may well have been a blocking stone. Some trivial remnants survive between it and the Longstone which were perhaps buried at the time the other stones were removed. The tops of three stones are visible about 50 m south of the Longstone and another 20 m short of the Three Boys but perhaps more still lie hidden beneath the turf. Nothing is now to be seen of the continuation of these rows south of the Three Boys orientated towards Fernworthy, recorded by Ormerod in 1858.

A hundred metres downhill from the Three Boys is a single slab set in the earth with a pit alongside which Worth interpreted as one side of a cist, but there is no other indication of a burial mound here. More definite remains of a cairn lie 20 m west of the Three Boys, an irregular mound thoroughly dug into with the upcast making a second mound on the north side.

a Cow Bridge and the Teign Tolmen

North of the Fourfold circle the boundary between the parishes of Gidleigh and Chagford continues to the large flat slab, **a**, known as Cow Bridge at least as early as 1843 when the name was recorded on the Tithes map[11]. Propped up beside Batworthy wall, between the leat and stream, the stone has the letter *G* cut into the surface.

The Teign tolmen, (**map 37.b**) is a curiously worn granite slab with a hole through it about 1 m across, overhanging the river just below the clapper bridge. Tolmens, or holed stones, were a favourite with some of the early antiquaries because of their supposed Druidical association, said to have survived in such country customs as 'drawing children through a round hole made in flat rocks to cure the rickets' (W. Borlase 1769). This example, the best of the holed stones on the moor, attracted the attention of nineteenth century Dartmoor explorers because of the proximity of Scorhill stone circle, only a short distance uphill. Upstream, single-span clappers bridge the Teign and Walla Brook, the former replacing one washed away by a flood in 1826.

MAP 37 West Shovel Down and Stonetor Hill

1 Stonetor Brook East settlement (fig. 37.1)

Gentle north-eastern slopes provide the setting for a very well preserved settlement with a splendid view over the North Teign basin. Slight damage has been caused by a short and apparently pointless wall, now ruinous, which overlies one of the earlier banks on the western edge of the settlement, and by an almost overgrown leat which cuts across the south-east corner. Reaves to the south and east confine most of the huts and smaller fields against the eastern branch of Stonetor Brook, expansion downstream being inhibited by waterlogged ground on the flatter valley floor. About fourteen huts are crammed together within rectangular fields, many of which have been subdivided by stone fences into tiny portions around the huts. Another seven huts lie outside the reave boundaries.

The largest hut in the settlement, 1 (8.0 m), with both jambs in place 0.8 m apart, is approached by a funnel-shaped passageway from the direction of the river but blocked as usual by a cross-wall at its lower end. A single line of stones follows the contour of the hut around the west side as far as the entrance leaving a space about a metre wide outside the

MAP 37

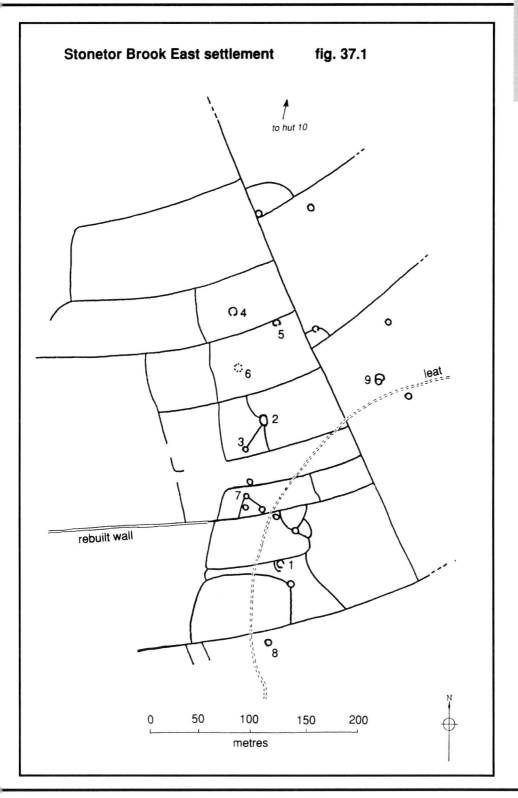

Stonetor Brook East settlement   fig. 37.1

to hut 10

leat

rebuilt wall

0   50   100   150   200

metres

N

MAP 37

hut wall. Hut 2 (9.3 x 5.1 m) is rectangular with rounded corners, a most unusual shape for a hut, and contains a large slab set on end near the centre of one of the long walls. It shares the field with a smaller hut, 3 (5.5 m). Jambs still stand at the entrances of huts 4 and 5 (both c. 6.0 m), those of the former being exceptionally large, and a few stones on the arc of a circle south-west of the latter may be the remains of another dismantled hut. Three smaller huts (3-4 m) surround hut 7 (c. 5.5 m), all of them despoiled, like the nearby banks, by the builder of the ruined wall which descends for no obvious reason down the slope.

Completely detached from the settlement and close to a ditched embankment 250 m to the north-east is what seems to be an isolated hut of medium size, 10 (5.0 m) but of no particular distinction, merely a circular bank with a number of stones showing around the edge. No fields are associated but a few metres away stand two large slabs facing each other 3 m apart, obviously artifically set but with no discernible purpose.

2, a, b Stonetor Hill North settlements (fig. 37.2), cairns, and boundary stone

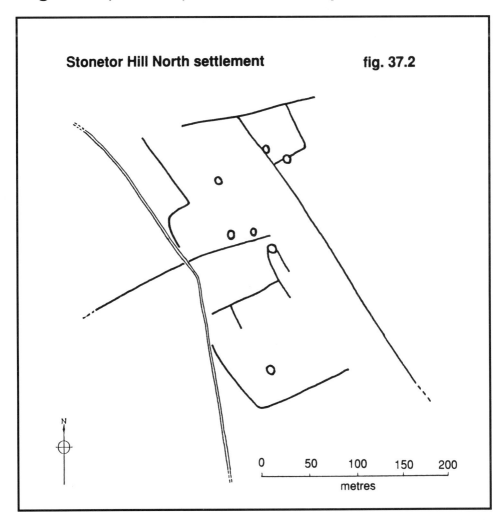

Stonetor Hill North settlement   fig. 37.2

0   50   100   150   200

metres

MAP 37

This settlement has suffered grievous harm from the building of the newtake wall across Stonetor Hill overlying part of its perimeter. All the slabs of useful size have been removed from the prehistoric field walls which are either reduced to very low banks or in places have completely disappeared. The seven medium to large huts (c. 6.0-9.0 m) are in similarly poor condition, little more than circular platforms levelled into the hillside surrounded by slight banks with very few wall stones left in place. The eastern border of the settlement seems to be a reave running south-eastwards, from above Stonetor spring over the watershed to the source of Crown Hall stream, though the latter section remains hidden within the most recent extension of Fernworthy Forest.

A separate farmstead consisting of a single hut (c. 6.0 m), paddock and rectangular field lies amidst the clitter on the northern tip of the hill, apparently unconnected with the larger settlement and perhaps the potential nucleus of a new one.

Two rough slabs stand in line on the level ground below the settlement, the watershed between Crown Hall stream and the eastern branch of Stonetor Brook. The east stone, **a**, is inscribed with the letters *GP* and marks the boundary between Gidleigh parish to the north and the Forest. The boundary continues eastwards to the Longstone where Chagford parish joins the other two. The two stones do not appear to form part of any prehistoric structure and were a nineteenth-century addition to the Forest boundary, though why two stones were erected is a mystery. The Teign Tolmen, **b**, is included in **map 36**. Another curiosity is the substantial bank which starts south of the stones and curves around the hillside along the contour to the east of them as a ditch before cutting through Stonetor Brook East settlement. Presumably a leat, it now starts well away from any source of water, but was probably intended to tap the western branch of the brook on the other side of the hill and for some reason was never completed.

On the edge of the leat on the hillside opposite the settlement a jumble of stones is probably the remains of a cairn with a cist. A second cairn (7.0 x 0.6 m) lies 50 m above it, better preserved but with the usual treasure seekers' trench across the centre.

3 Stonetor Brookhead settlement (fig 37.3)

An exceptionally large number of huts are grouped around the head of the western branch of Stonetor Brook which flows through the settlement. Waterlogged ground swamps those nearest the stream but the majority of the thirty-eight huts lie on the clitter-strewn slopes above the west bank, their walls shrouded in heather but otherwise damaged only by the passage of centuries rather than the hand of man. Two-thirds of the huts are small with a diameter of less than 4.0 m across.

An axial reave bisects the settlement, entering the forest to the south-east in the direction of the South Teign and continuing in the opposite direction over Long Ridge before being lost near the newtake wall. Huts were constructed close to the Stonetor side of the reave, the isolated one to the south being the largest in the settlement, 1 (c. 7.5 m). Parallel-sided fields similar to those elsewhere on Shovel Down were laid out on this side. West of the reave some of the large group of huts in the centre of the settlement are joined together by short walls forming irregular paddocks. All these huts are small except for 2 (c. 7.0 m), and 3 (5.2 m) which has a rectangular yard on one side. The string of paired huts mounting the hillside to the south are slightly larger, mostly about 5.0 m across, but apart from the outer wall around hut 4 these are without any enclosure at all.

The axial reave can be traced part way across the modern field to the north, passing close to a small building (4.0 x 3.0 m) just outside it, and the foundations of two animal pens, or possibly buildings, within. The lower field next to the brook is now a swamp but, higher up, its ridged surface has been partly cleared of stone suggesting it has been

MAP 37

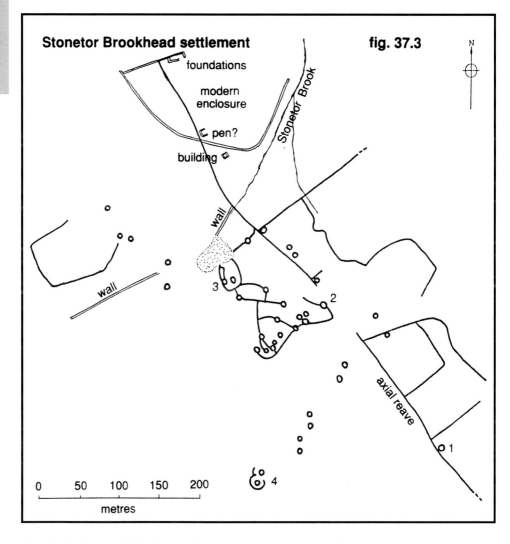

Stonetor Brookhead settlement   **fig. 37.3**

N

foundations

modern
enclosure

pen?

building

Stonetor Brook

wall

wall

3

2

axial reave

1

4

0   50   100   150   200

metres

ploughed. South of this field, and probably contemporary with it, a ruined cornditch wall connects the Stonetor Brook with the North Teign, separating off the north end of Long Ridge. The reave emerges on the far side of the field, continuing as the uphill boundary of at least three strips which descend obliquely towards the brook.

4 Stonetor Brook West settlement (fig. 37.4)

One of the banks originating near the north end of the Brookhead axial reave descends the hillside to the stream where it forms the southern boundary of this settlement of eight huts. Walls of four small fields infiltrate the boulders strewn over the hillside on the steep slope above the junction of the two branches of Stonetor Brook. The site, like Stonetor Brookhead, was presumably chosen for the easy availability of surface stone, a commodity noticeably absent over much of the Down. The slabs had merely to be shifted sideways to form the perimeter of walls but no great effort was expended in clearing the fields. The huts, of medium size (4.0-5.7 m) and mostly in good condition, are levelled into the hillside.

MAP 37

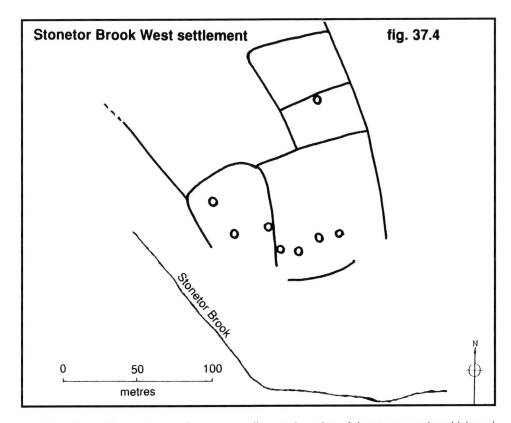

Stonetor Brook West settlement

fig. 37.4

Stonetor Brook

0   50   100

metres

N

Below the settlement a peculiar structure lies on the edge of the streamworks which end a short distance upriver. Three heavy slabs, one of them displaced, form the top of a rectangular stone box about 2 m long and open at both ends. In this remote spot its most likely function would seem to have been a tinners' cache.

5 Shovel Down North-west corner settlement and cairns (fig. 37.5)

The perimeter walls of this settlement are reduced to low banks, discontinuous in places and not easy to follow on the ground. The five huts are all of medium size (5.5-7.0 m) and are similarly overgrown, only the double-slabbed wall of hut 1 standing clear of the turf. This latter is approached via a passageway which seems to continue towards the three huts near the centre of the compound. Downhill a leat off the North Teign winds around the base of the hill to end at a turf-covered mound of rubble. From the western side of the settlement a reave curves away towards the river, though it now terminates at the edge of streamworks some 50 m short of it, thus enclosing the tip of the ridge for the exclusive use of the settlement.

Southwards six small burial mounds, in line, occupy the ridge, no doubt built by the inhabitants of the nearby settlements. The nearest contains a central cist but like the others has been dug into and its cover slab displaced sideways onto the mound. Four more are grouped togther 100 m further uphill and another lies 45 m from the newtake wall.

MAP 38

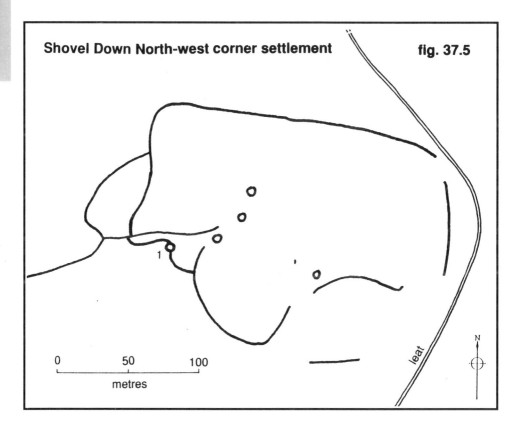

Shovel Down North-west corner settlement   fig. 37.5

0   50   100

metres

MAP 38 Buttern Hill and Scorhill

1-7 Prehistoric settlement on Buttern Hill and Scorhill

On the other side of the North Teign beyond Kes Tor (**map 36**) the reave settlements continue along the eastern borderland on to Buttern Hill. As at the former site numerous flint artefacts of mesolithic and neolithic date show that earlier peoples had previously frequented this area.

Although somewhat lower than Kes Tor and Buttern Hill, for some reason Scorhill seems to have been almost ignored by the Bronze Age farmers, any settlement there might have been on the eastern slopes, for which there is no evidence, having been lost within the present fields. Below the western summit, only a solitary hut, **1** (c. 5.0 m), has been found from which Scorhill circle can just be seen, and a reave is orientated across its lower slopes. The latter would have met the North Teign opposite Shovel Down central reave (**map 36**) but this end has been destroyed by tinners' workings and the higher end is lost close to the stone circle. It may originally have curved nothwards to join a well-preserved 200 m section along the western side of the ridge between Scorhill and Buttern

MAP 38

Hill, and even continued as the western boundary reave of the Buttern Hill settlement. The abrupt termination of a number of field walls here, **2**, and the dearth of boundary banks across the ridge, seemingly an attractive site, is puzzling. If ever present, perhaps hedges were grown as an alternative to walling because of a lack of suitable surface stone, though there is a plentiful supply on the eastern side of Buttern Hill. Alternatively later stone collection from this part of the moorland may have been particularly thorough. Certainly the corrugated ground surface shows that peat cutters have been at work, and shattered monoliths like those in the two stone circles show the gate-post maker's handiwork too.

Six small huts are associated with the open-sided fields on the southern end of Buttern Hill, **2** (3.0-4.5 m), all built of small slabs and much overgrown. Another pair uphill, **3** (c. 3.5 m), identified as cairns on the Ordnance Survey map, are also probably huts where the inner facing has collapsed allowing the wall packing to spread over the interior. Three long reaves, originating on or near the settlements' western boundary reave, cross the summit and descend the eastern slope to the centre of the settlement. Unfortunately a well-cleared squarish newtake, **4**, has been built over the first of these, destroying any structure that may have existed within. The reave reappears on the north side next to a large hut (8.3 m), mostly complete and levelled into the hillside. Another (9.2 m) outside its south-west corner has a straight interior cross wall but has lost all the stones around its lower half. Even less fortunate is the hut and short length of walling on the hillside 80 m south of the newtake, with barely a quarter of the circumference remaining, its two door slabs curiously detached from the rest.

Southwards a number of low banks run towards the field margin, three of them continued downhill by the present walls though how far these overlie the ancient banks is uncertain. Only a single hut (c. 10.0 m), the largest in the settlement, survives within the upper fields, but a rectangular paddock surrounding another lies just north of the corner cut through by the Bradford leat. The latter hut (c. 7.0 m) would be in fair condition but for the two wall slabs tipped over to make a clapper across the leat. To the north the ground slopes more steeply down to the flat valley floor, a boggy area never enclosed in ancient or modern times. Well above the waterlogged ground is a large hut, **5** (9.2 m) in the corner of a field built on to a reave but now detached from the rest of the settlement. The smaller stones have toppled from the hut and lie around its base but the wall is still substantial, 1.7 m wide, and the entrance clearly visible on the south-east side.

The heart of the settlement seems to have lain on the north-east side of Buttern Hill in the area now occupied by the strangely shaped newtake, **6**. Its peculiar plan was dictated by the underlying reave patterns which radiate out in various directions as they re-emerge on the moorland side. Some of the walls within the newtake have been added to here and there but are otherwise little altered since they were erected in prehistoric times. Shorter detached lengths show where others have been partially demolished. Four large huts survive, a fifth marked on the Ordnance Survey map within the south field having been recently cleared and the stones piled around the perimeter. The lowest hut (8.8 m) has been dug into, the upcast heaped on one side of a deep central pit. Uphill the centre hut (8.5 m) is at the lower end of a passageway which rather oddly meets it asymmetrically and not apparently opposite the entrance. The two upper huts (7.4, 9.0 m), built of large stones, were both severely damaged when the wall alongside was re-constructed. Attached to the reave outside the south corner of the newtake is a curved bank surrounding a small-stoned hut (5.5 m), and another (5.6 m) with about a third of its circumference missing can be found against the reave in the neighbouring strip.

A reave emerges alongside the Bradford leat midway along the north side of the newtake, gradually climbing the hillside towards Forder Brook. About 250 m along, a bank descends the hillside to a roughly rectangular enclosure sited where the gradient eases, now much overgrown and barely recognizable, **7**. Two flattened stone areas along the

MAP 38

uphill side are probably all that is left of a pair of huts and the raised ring of stones on the north side, marked as a cairn circle on the Ordnance Survey map, is more likely to be the site of another.

8 Scorhill stone circle, rows and cairns (fig. 38.1)

The siting of this circle near the bottom of the hill only 250 m from the North Teign, with the view from it limited to the west and south-west, is unusual. The other stone circles have a grander outlook being sited in a more prominent position higher on the hillside or on the saddle of a ridge, yet from the size of its stones it must have been the most impressive of those that have survived. Unfortunately it stands too close to the edge of the moor to have escaped considerable damage, the interior having been churned up by tracks passing through the circle on the descent to Walla Brook bridge. At least three of the flat stones, like many in the vicinity, show evidence of having been deliberately split, and another on the west side, 1, has a neat row of jumper holes down the centre preparatory to being converted into gateposts. A breach in Gidleigh leat 50 m to the west has been repaired by four or five long slabs which may well have come from the circle. Another prehistoric casualty is the nearby reave, cut by tracks and banks in several places along its course from the river before finally fading out 20 m east of the circle.

One advantage of its accessibility though is that the circle has been frequently described over the past century and a half. These records show that there has been no major deterioration during this period and that most of the missing stones had gone by the early nineteenth century at the latest. One of the largest stones, 2, finally toppled over about a hundred years ago but twenty-three of the remaining thirty-four still stand in place on a true circle 27 m across. The original number of stones is difficult to estimate as the intervals between them are irregular, those around the southern half being much more closely spaced, but a likely number would be about sixty. There is no obvious grading in the heights of the stones still in place, the largest being an impressive menhir 2.2 m tall on the north-west side, 3. This must have been at least rivalled by the flat pillar, 4, displaced south of the circle by the track, now nearly 2 m long, but with a series of jumper holes across its base showing that it has been considerably shortened.

Scorhill is one of the group of seven stone circles aligned in a curve around the north-east border of the moor, lying midway between the neighbouring circles of Buttern Hill and Shovel Down 1.25 kilometres to north and south. The intervals between the others, Little Hound Tor, Fernworthy and the Grey Wethers (two circles), is a fairly constant 2 kilometres, suggesting each was constructed as part of a comprehensive design and hence contemporary in planning and execution.

Within sight about 120 m to the south-east of the circle is a mound with central pit (c. 7.5 x 0.8 m), probably the much damaged remains of a burial cairn. The west side in particular has been rutted by the wheels of vehicles climbing the slope up from the bridge across the leat. Four stones around its lower edge stand clear of the mound and the tops of others are visible through the turf. More interesting is a similar mound (c. 7.0 x 0.5 m) on the other side of the leat, also visible from the circle. The pit has exposed a slab near the centre, probably one side of a cist, and the three or four stones around the perimeter are the last of a retaining circle. Starting at the lower edge two parallel lines of slabs almost hidden under the turf, the remains of a double stone row, are orientated directly downhill towards the river. The first six slabs of the west row and four in the eastern are in place, but the ground has been disturbed by peat cutting and stone pits further down and the rest have been lost. This association of stone circle and stone rows elevates the site into an important ceremonial centre like those at Merrivale, Fernworthy and Shovel Down.

MAP 38

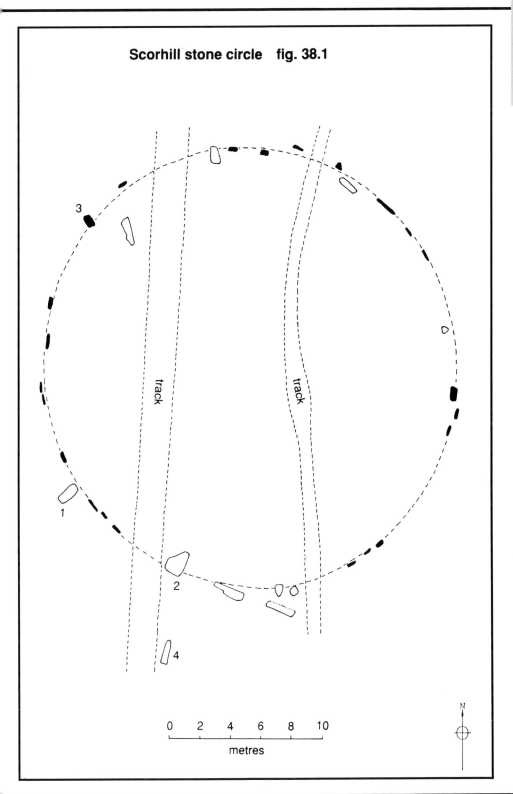

Scorhill stone circle   fig. 38.1

3

track

track

1

2

4

0   2   4   6   8   10

metres

N

MAP 38

9 Buttern Hill stone circle (fig. 38.2)

Though only slightly less in diameter than its neighbour on Scorhill the smaller stones used in constructing this circle make it much less impressive. The site is overlooked from the slopes to east and west but would have been prominent on the skyline from a considerable distance if approached up the valley from the south. The largest stone lies on the south-west side, 2.05 m long, but like several of the others has been worked on by the stone cutter. Of the twenty-three stones that were obviously part of the monument, including those buried beneath the turf, five alone remain standing, the tallest being only 0.6 m in height. The other eighteen lie as they fell and no attempt has been made at restoration. The erect slabs stand accurately on a circle 24.8 m in diameter and the intervals between the three adjacent stones on the north-east side indicate the original number to have been about forty.

Turf has been stripped from the surface within the circle but there are no deep pits and the interior is flat and apparently undamaged. There is now no sign of the small cairn 6 m inside the southern perimeter recorded by R.N. Worth in 1894. He also described a second smaller stone circle about 20 m in diameter 'a short distance on the slope to the westward', with four or five stones erect around a fallen menhir. A number of stones on the hillside do show above the turf but none appear to be artificially arranged.

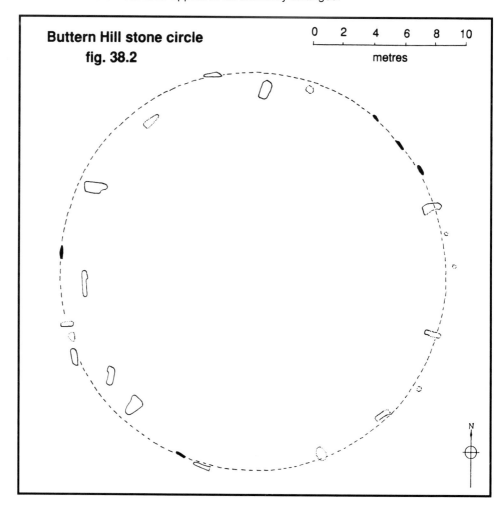

Buttern Hill stone circle

fig. 38.2

0   2   4   6   8   10

metres

N

MAP 38

10 Scorhill cairns

Two cairns lie about 15 m apart on the north side of Scorhill, out of sight of the stone circle. Both have been dug into but the proximity of fields only about 50 m away and the ancient droveways leading on to Gidleigh Common nearby have no doubt contributed to the damage. One of the latter leads to Creaber pound to which stray cattle and horses were taken during the Forest drifts, serving the same purpose for the northern quarter of the moor as Dunnabridge pound (**28.1**) for the rest.

The cairns are of similar size but now much spread with pitted surfaces and are only 0.4 m high at most. A third of a well-spaced retaining circle survives around the south cairn, and a few slabs of an inner concentric ring about 2 m smaller in diameter. The other cairn has lost any stone surround it may have had.

11 Gidleigh chambered cairns (fig. 38.3)

In 1975 two chambered cairns were recognized on the east slope of Buttern Hill lying about 450 m apart. Both had been dug into at some time in the past, exposing part of their interior structure. The south cairn **11** is the best preserved with a clearly defined passage of two pairs of stones, about 2 m long by a metre wide, and opening towards the south-west (210°). The other end is restricted by a pair of cross slabs at the entrance to the chamber (fig. 38.3). Beyond these lies a large and partly turf-covered flat slab and the tops of several others which show just above the surface of the ground in the body of the mound, probably the chamber walls. The upcast from the interior has been thrown out downhill, distorting the shape of the mound so that the tomb is now well off-centre.

The structure of the north cairn, immediately downhill in the line of a prehistoric field wall, is by no means so clear. There are a number of slabs obviously artificially set on a mound, which may form part of a chamber, but the remains have been disturbed and are very ill-defined.

a Gidleigh parish boundary stone

This tall pillar on the boundary between Gidleigh and Throwleigh is mentioned in **map 41.**

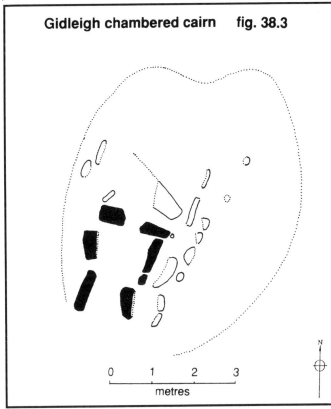

Gidleigh chambered cairn   fig. 38.3

0   1   2   3

metres

N

MAP 39

MAP 39 Throwleigh Common

1 Throwleigh Common settlement (fig. 39.1)

Beneath the bracken on the east side of Throwleigh Common lies one of the best preserved settlements on the moor. Like others along the eastern borderland from Holne Moor northwards, parallel reaves divide the settlement into long narrow strips partitioned by cross banks into rectangular fields. The pattern is not as neatly laid out as at sites like Horridge Common, apparently because the ancient surveyor of the three northern reaves did not check his alignments down the changing profile of the hillside here, although he corrected them on the lower slopes above Moor Farm.

The smaller enclosures around the huts lie at the centre of the settlement well down the eastern slopes. Outside these are the large strips and fields which are strictly confined within boundary reaves on the south-west and north-west sides. The latter reave continues beyond the settement onto Kennon Hill where it takes a zig-zag course southwards around two more groups of huts **2, 3** before terminating on Gallaven Brook, a total length of four kilometres. The south-west boundary reave originates on this one and can be followed as far as a tributary of Forder Brook which is approximately on the same alignment. The brook may have been regarded as a notional boundary but the settlement appears to have been still expanding in this direction when it was abandoned.

The downhill extent of the settlement is uncertain as the reaves become progressively more difficult to follow nearer the road. Open-ended strips and detached banks imply that it continued further but soil movement has overwhelmed some of these on the steeper slopes and numerous tracks and ditches cut across the lower field walls. One reave can be traced to the edge of the Moor Farm enclosures where the alignment is taken up by a number of the present field walls on both sides of the road, suggesting that the prehistoric reaves once continued as far as Blackaton Brook. The pattern is not repeated within the present fields further south but the pair of large huts, 16 and 17, are also likely to have been included within the strips. Further damage to this part of the site has been caused by the quarry and dump opposite Moor Farm, the Bradford leat which was cut across the site in the early part of the sixteenth century[57], and to a lesser extent by a medieval longhouse, 19 (c. 15.0 x 3.7 m), which incorporated the lower end of a reave as part of its wall.

The site has survived because the moorland above the road was never enclosed by later fields as has happened to the neighbouring settlement north of Blackaton Brook. Even the lower fields here reach 360 m which, if continued across Throwleigh Common, would have obliterated most of that part of the settlement containing the huts. The entire site would have disappeared under the higher fields at 400 m.

An axial reave through the centre of the settlement, parallel with the north-west boundary reave, separates the fields on either side. Its uphill section is doubled to form a passageway, 5 to 6 m wide and still clearly visible, ending at the settlement boundary but not obviously blocked here as is usually the case. It bounds large fields on one side and, no doubt, others were intended to be enclosed in the large open area to the south, but these were never built. At the centre of the settlement the passageway abruptly curves away downhill to the north-east but a modern track has demolished the banks at this point. Four large huts, 1 (9.3 m), 2 (7.4 m), 3 (8.0 m) and 4 (8.9 m), the first two with small gardens attached, line this section of the passageway giving the impression of a village street. Another hut, 5 (8.5 m), its walls mostly turf-covered, was built within the same group of fields.

Many huts south of the axial reave are equally large. Hut 6 (7.5 m) and the group of three within the next strip, 7 (6.1, 6.3 and 8.5 m), the largest of which retains its jamb

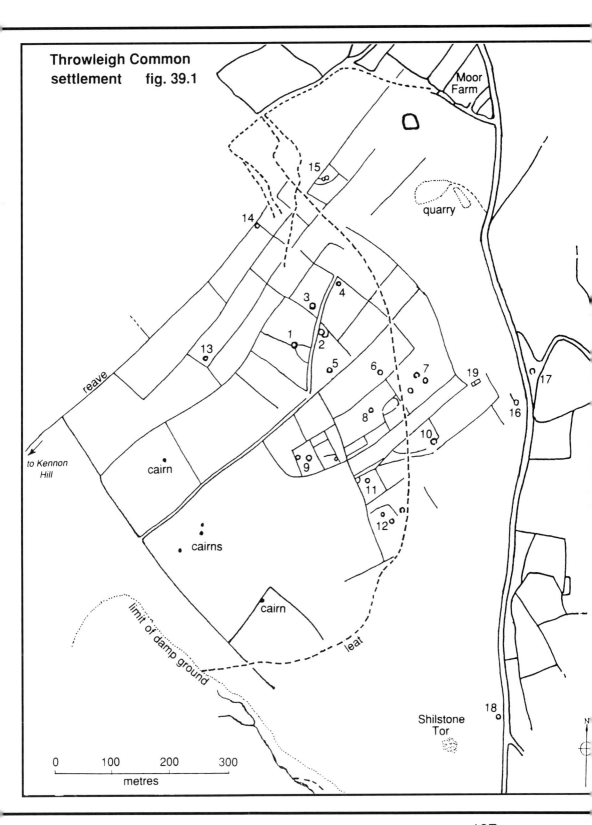

**Throwleigh Common
settlement   fig. 39.1**

Moor
Farm

quarry

15

14

reave

3
4

1
2
13

5
6   7
19

8   10
16
17

cairn

9
11

12

cairns

cairn

limit of damp ground

leat

to Kennon
Hill

Shilstone
Tor

18

0   100   200   300

metres

N

MAP 39

stones, are all solidly built. An arc of stones at 8, perhaps a quarter of the circumference, is all that remains of another large hut at least 9 m across. Immediately downhill from the latter is a curious pear-shaped enclosure, too large to have been roofed and with a pair of entrances on opposite sides clearly defined by cross slabs. Its walls are massive enough to have deflected the course of the Bradford leat around it. Within the same strip uphill are two smaller and less well defined huts, 9 (4.5 and 4.2 m), and possibly the remains of a third, much damaged.

The prize example in this settlement though must be hut 10 (10.5 m) which, unlike the others, is clear of vegetation and shows Bronze Age building technique at its best. The builders may not have intended it to last upwards of three millenia but the courses of massive blocks remain in place much as they were laid, despite the attentions of a recent stone-cutter. The largest block in the wall, 2 m long and ideal for a pair of gateposts, has been split and part of it carted away. The corridor-like entrance through the walls, 2.3 m thick here, must have made the interior rather gloomy.

Below the hut a rectangular field has been cleared of surface stone which has been collected into a pair of clearance cairns at the centre. Uphill a well-defined passageway curves away to the edge of the strip, below a small square field. A free standing hut, 11 (c. 4.5 m), lies near the centre of this and an arc of stones across one corner may be a second building or possibly an unroofed pen or store. Three more huts occupy the next strip to the south amid a patch of surface stone, 12. The largest, (7.0 m), separated from the other two (5.7, 6.3 m) by a cross wall, is well preserved with door jambs in place.

Huts 13 (4.5 x 2.9 m) and 14 (6.5 m) lie in the corner of strips on the north side of the settlement. The former is now a low circular bank only, bereft of wall slabs. At 15 a D-shaped enclosure surrounds a hut (6.4 m) with a small annexe (c. 2.0 m) built onto one side. The largest huts of all lie close to the road, their massive stones useless for other purposes and too much trouble to demolish. A short length of wall attached to hut 16 (9.6 m) shows that it probably was once included within the strips, as may have been hut 17 (11.5 m), though 18 (11.0 m) seems always to have been isolated from the rest. These last two huts were as big as any on the moor.

On the other side of the hill, out of sight of the settlement but still within its boundaries, is a cairn cemetery which may well have been the burial ground for the hut dwellers. Five cairns 3.5 to 7.5 m across but no more than 0.3 m high can be found, together with a number of smaller mounds not shown on the plan. None appear to have been deliberately dug into though one has been damaged by a cart track.

2-4 Kennon Hill North-east settlements

The north-west boundary reave on Throwleigh Common continues beyond the settlement, **1**, onto the northern spur of Kennon Hill. Here it alters course to the south along the eastern flank of the hill, picking a curiously winding course between the prehistoric huts and enclosures and apparently defining their access to the water supplies in the Forder and Blackaton valleys. The reave initially makes a wide sweep eastwards around what is now a slight walled and incomplete enclosure open on one side, with no associated dwellings. It then detours sharply uphill to the west of a group of five huts with irregularly shaped enclosures built on a particularly stony patch of the hillside, **2**. General overgrowth of turf and bracken, in the summer especially, make these structures difficult to distinguish amidst the many small clitter streams which descend the slope. The huts are remarkably uniform in size, 3.0 to 3.5 m in diameter, spaced within the enclosures.

Southwards the reave divides, still a substantial bank, one branch returning in the direction of Throwleigh Common but disappearing at the edge of the soft ground. The other

MAP 39

branch alters course sharply in the direction of the Kennon Hill settlement (**map 41**), at the same time acting as the uphill boundary of a second group of ten huts, **3**. These are noticeably larger, 3.8 to 7.5 m across and are otherwise unenclosed. The structure furthest downhill next to the track has a single prominent slab on one side and a raised interior, which suggests it may be a cairn rather than a dwelling.

On the opposite side of the reave are two sides of a rectangular enclosure, **4**, which was probably built onto it. A circular enclosure 14.5 m in diameter has been built across one corner and the grass-covered foundations of a hut (5.0 m) lie on the perimeter.

5, 6 Cosdon Hill East settlement and Shilley Pool cairn

Prehistoric settlement north of Blackaton Brook may well have been as extensive as that on Throwleigh Common but here the present fields extend up to the 360 m contour, 60 m higher than those around the Common. All but the large uphill fields have been obliterated and even these have been robbed to provide material for the later walls. The present regular field pattern, somewhat smaller than elsewhere and with a similar orientation to the reaves uphill, suggest that the ancient settlement extended down to the stream on the valley floor below. These however have been energetically cleared and a pair of large huts, **5** (both c. 9.0 m), levelled into the hillside are all that survive within a bracken-covered field. The gradient is particularly steep here, 22°, and only the massive size of their boulder walls has saved them from disappearing below the surface.

Uphill and just outside the present field margins a circular enclosure 23 m in diameter surrounded by a bank 0.2 m high has been fitted into the ancient field pattern, but without any associated huts. A ruined cairn is now the sole occupant of the next block to the south, **6**. A large central hollow down to ground level has revealed two flat slabs, possibly the remains of a cist. The boundary reave between this and the neighbouring field beside Blackaton Brook continues uphill beyond them, ending on the flatter ground near Cheriton Combe. Nearby, towards the junction of the two streams, an oval structure (c. 6.0 x 4.5 m) of comparatively recent date appears to have been deliberately slighted, probably because of the danger to livestock. This strip includes the only other hut (4.2 m) to survive on this part of the moor, on the edge of its own irregularly shaped enclosure. A reave crosses the strip at right-angles and continues south of Blackaton Brook to connect it with the Throwleigh Common settlement. Its course is interrupted by the slight remains of two earlier enclosures, one of them partly rebuilt, which were accepted as part of the boundary.

The Bronze Age farmers were by no means the first to settle in the valley which was extensively occupied from mesolithic times onwards. Numerous flints have been found within the fields on the opposite slope, particularly around Middle Week Farm where nearly 5000 pieces have been picked up.

MAP 40

MAP 40 River Taw and Cosdon Hill

1-3 Prehistoric settlements in the Lower Taw valley (figs 40.1, 2, 3, 4)

Nine settlements, five of them single enclosures, three multiple and one at least partly enclosed, occupy the western slope of Cosdon Hill and its White Hill extension. All lie within little more than a kilometre between Small Brook and the head of Ivy Tor Water and are sited east of a reave which runs from the head of the latter southwards to Steeperton Brook. The reave seems contemporary with the Small Brook enclosures, approaching to within 15 m and apparently separating them from the flat valley floor around the Taw.

The five lower Small Brook enclosures **1** (fig. 40.1) are all single, containing from one to nine huts. The circuit walls, now up to 0.5 m high, were never very substantial, the width between their outer faces varying between 1 to 1.2 m across. All the huts of enclosure 1 lie on the periphery, its peculiarly angular plan apparently designed merely to connect them together. The huts are small (3-4.5 m), the gap between the pair on the north side possibly being an original entrance. Two more lie uphill outside the enclosure.

The single hut (3.5 m) of enclosure 2 lies on the edge of a paddock, about 12.5 m across, which is included in the outer enclosure wall. A pair of tall pillars, one flat the other leaning, in the paddock wall opposite the hut look as though they once formed a monumental entrance. The curved bank which leaves the opposite side of the enclosure was perhaps originally connected with the reave which approaches to within 15 m and can be seen mounting the hillside to north and south.

The lower edge of enclosure 3 has been partly destroyed by tinners' workings around Small Brook. A large hut (7.8 m) with interior divisions is centrally placed and a second lies immediately downhill with a tall jamb stone at the entrance. Two more are in the circuit wall and a fifth just outside. The reason for constructing enclosure 4 on the steeper slope higher up the hillside is not obvious as there seems to be adequate room alongside the Small Brook. Its south wall is more substantial than around the other enclosures but other sections have almost disappeared. The huts are small, up to 3.5 m across where measurable. Enclosure 5, comparatively well preserved, contains three huts all about 3.5 m across.

Uphill from these enclosures and out of sight is a different type of settlement of about twenty huts (fig. 40.2). Two huts within the clitter have small enclosures attached, part of the boundary being formed by surface rocks, but the main group is crowded closely together on the flatter ground above. These were at least partly enclosed for a bank curves around the lower border of the settlement and short sections appear above the turf elsewhere. The largest hut 1 (8.0 m) with a pair of jambs at the entrance lies at the upper edge of the settlement, the rest varying in size from 3 to 7 m across. A few metres to the north of hut 1 is a mound 5 m across with a central depression which is probably a cairn rather than a hut circle, but there is no sign of the ruined cist reported to be nearby.[10] The site is very overgrown and further banks and huts are likely to lie below the surface.

350 m north of the Small Brook group is a very overgrown multiple enclosure, **2** (fig. 40.3), with nine huts. The circuit wall has disappeared in places and the huts (3.0-7.5 m) are no more than low circular banks, though the largest is divided internally.

A further 200 m to the north-east two more multiple enclosures occupy the slightly sloping ground above Ivy Tor Water, **3** (fig. 40.4). Although too remote to have been robbed for stone the walls are difficult to follow amidst the heather and bracken and most of the huts are in poor condition. Thirteen huts (3.0-7.0 m) can be found associated with the

MAP 40

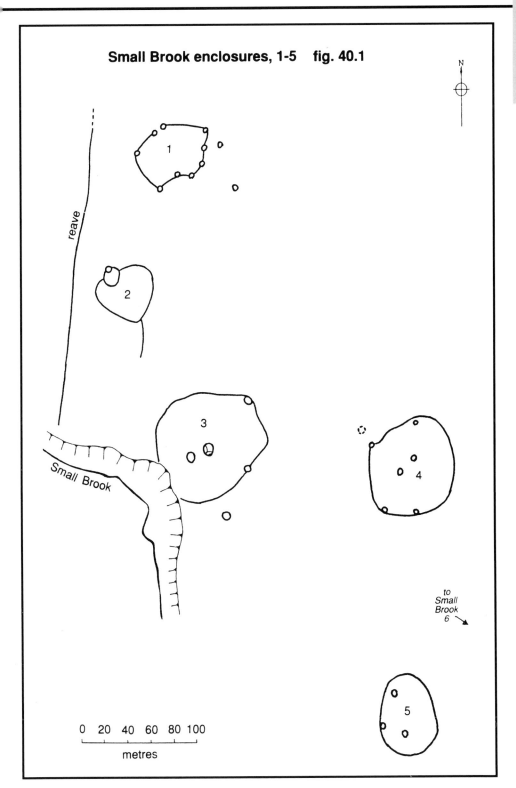

Small Brook enclosures, 1-5   fig. 40.1

reave

Small Brook

1

2

3

4

5

to
Small
Brook
6

N

0 20 40 60 80 100
metres

MAP 40

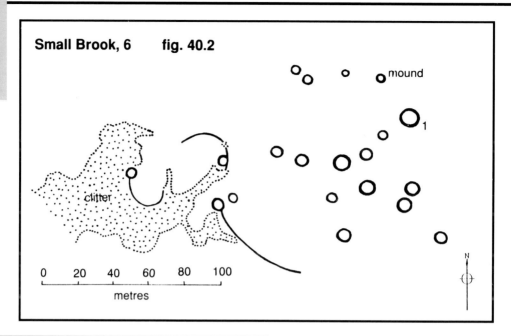

Small Brook, 6   fig. 40.2

clitter

mound

1

0 20 40 60 80 100

metres

N

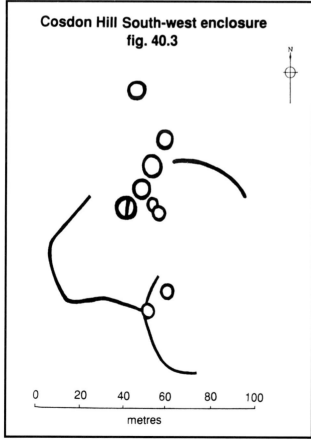

Cosdon Hill South-west enclosure
fig. 40.3

N

0 20 40 60 80 100

metres

southern enclosure, the larger ones built into the circuit wall and the smaller ones inside connected by banks. The largest of all, 1 (7.0 m) with a massive wall 0.5 m high lies significantly apart from the rest on the flat ground downhill. The walls of the north enclosure are rather easier to follow but, strangely, all five huts are comparatively small (2.5-5.0 m). A break in the boundary at its lowest point may be the original watergate.

4 Cosdon Hill north-east settlement

Even less of the prehistoric settlement survives on the north-east flank of the hill than it does further south (**map 39**), for here the highest of the present fields reach the 400 m contour. One field alone has not been completely cleared and preserves the last remnant of what was probably an extensive field system. Two lengths of walling together with the lesser parts of three large huts about 9.5 m in diameter are all that remain.

MAP 40

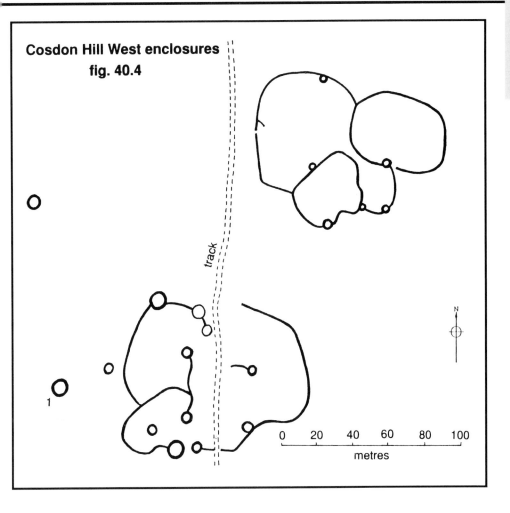

Cosdon Hill West enclosures
fig. 40.4

track

N

0   20   40   60   80   100

metres

1

5 Little Hound Tor stone circle and cairn (fig. 40.5)

The stone circle south of Cosdon Hill stands on the saddle between the two Hound Tors. Only when approached up the steeper slopes from the west is it out of sight until quite close, and from the circle itself there is an extensive view in all directions except the north. The monument now appears in good condition but only thirteen stones were standing before it was 'taken in hand' by the Dartmoor Exploration Committee in 1896 when they re-erected the other five. There are spaces for two more but no socket hole was found in the north-west gap and the Committee concluded that there never had been a stone here, which would be an exceptional feature and is perhaps open to doubt. They did not excavate within the circle and, apart from some shallow depressions, the interior appears to be undamaged. Most stones are thin slabs fitting fairly accurately on a circle 20.2 m across through their centres. The stones range in size from 0.3 to 1.15 m high, though several have had the tops broken off, with no particular pattern to their position in the circle. As at other circle sites a cairn lies close by, a heather-covered mound 8.5 m across with a slight dip in the surface where it has been dug into.

MAP 40

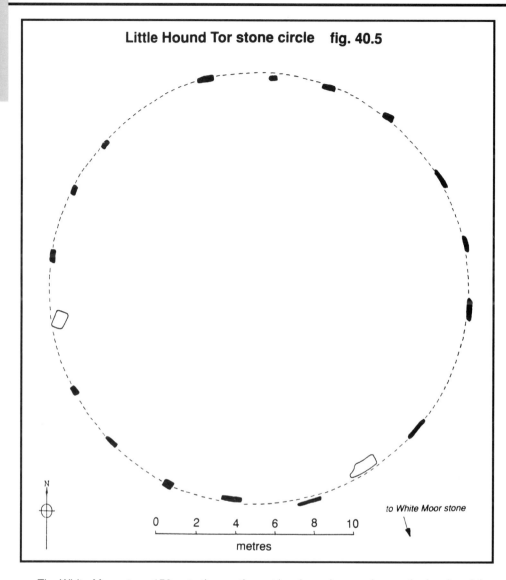

Little Hound Tor stone circle   fig. 40.5

N

to White Moor stone

0   2   4   6   8   10

metres

The White Moor stone 150 m to the south-east is a boundary marker on the border of the Forest but at 1.6 m high it seems too large to have been stolen from the circle. A rather awkward detour is made to include it in the boundary suggesting it was already in position before being adopted as a marker. The stone may originally have been an outlier contemporary with the circle, perhaps re-erected as it is no longer orientated towards it or the cairn.

6 Cosdon Hill stone row (fig. 40.6, 7)

When first erected at the head of Cheriton Combe this triple alignment of stones descending from a cairn must have made an impressive spectacle. The site on the east side of Cosdon Hill is a good one, on a natural shelf of the hillside before the gradient steepens again up to the summit. The upper end of the rows is in fine condition despite the evidence of stone

MAP 40

working in the vicinity, and the local wall builders have well resisted the temptation of a convenient source for their material. Some damage has been caused to the middle section where the South Zeal peat track crosses the alignment but even here two stones remain stranded in position between the ruts. Below the track the stones rapidly thin out and decrease in height, many showing just above ground level. Very likely most of the missing stones remain in position but completely covered by turf, and it may be hoped that this end is also substantially intact, preserved for future exploration and display.

The length from the centre of the cairn to the last visible stone is 146 m, but if the large triangular slab lying across the rows further downhill is taken to be a blocking stone at the original termination the length increases to 176.5 m. Heights gradually increase uphill towards the cairn. The tallest are those nearest the cairn and a pair 0.8 m high, 24 m from its edge stand almost opposite a large slab set outside the rows to the north, the significance of which is unclear. Packing stones at the base of the former suggest that these have been re-erected, possibly incorrectly, at right angles to the rows. Along the western half the stones of the north row are noticeably taller than the other two, 0.4 m on average as opposed to 0.34 and 0.33 m high. The distance between the three rows remains fairly constant along the length of the alignment at 1.4 m, but the distance between the stones along the rows decreases with their height eastwards, from 1.6 m to 1.3 m. Despite being intervisible throughout its length there is a noticeable curve to the north of about 3° as the alignment progresses eastwards.

Cairn at head of Cosdon Hill stone rows   fig. 40.7

cist 1

cist 2

0 1 2 3 4 5
metres

Cosdon Hill stone rows   fig. 40.6

cairn

triple stone row

slab

tracks

metres

0 10 20 30

1980 1:200

large flat slab

MAP 40

Uphill the rows end symmetrically at a ruined cairn (fig. 40.7), the middle row orientated towards its centre. The cairn is unusual in that it contains a pair of cists sharing a common end slab. Two slabs only remain of one of these but the components of the other are all present, including the cover slab. Five stones of an outer retaining circle surround the mound but little is to be seen of the inner ring reported by the Dartmoor Exploration Committee in 1896. The Committee excavated what was left of the cists which had been exposed on the surface but found they had already been dug into and apparently no finds were made. They also re-erected an unknown number of fallen slabs in the rows including those at right-angles in the middle and south rows next to the cairn. The end stone of the north row was already in this position when the site was first described by Worth four years earlier.

Nothing was found in a second cairn excavated by the Committee 'on the side of Cosdon', an unhelpfully loose description considering the size of the hill, and this cairn has yet to be re-located.

Ramsley Hill and Oke Tor stone rows

R.N. Worth confidently asserted that stone rows once existed on Ramsley Hill, near South Zeal, on the evidence of George French who worked at the Ramsley copper mine. The mine workings had substantially destroyed whatever structure existed here by about 1870 except for a few stones apparently still visible in 1896. Even these have not been relocated but a pitted and bracken covered cairn (10 x 0.7 m) survives on the northern tip of the hill about 60 m above the chimney.

The same writer described an alignment of stones on the west side of Oke Tor which he suggested was the remains of a single row. The stones remain just as he described, north-west of the tor about 100 m below the crest, consisting principally of two slabs on edge about 40 m apart and a pair of 'menhirs' lying flat a short distance downhill. There is no evidence that the latter ever stood erect and as stones similar to the former are fairly common on this hillside the site seems more likely to be a natural arrangement.

7-11 Cairns on Cosdon Hill (fig. 40.8)

Having attained the summit of Cosdon Hill the walker is rewarded not only with a magnificent view over much of North Devon but by an interesting variety of burial monuments laid out along the ridge, **7** (fig. 40.8). An enormous amount of labour must have been spent on collecting the stones for the largest cairn, 1. It was probably the first structure to be built as it occupies the very highest point and now supports a trig. station. The original dimensions are impossible to estimate as the stones have been thrown out in all directions, partly to accommodate a number of shelters around the edge, but it is now up to 3 m high and spread to 27 m across. A circular setting at the eastern foot of the cairn may be the foundations of a hut circle or a more modern erection like that associated with one of the large cairns on Corndon Tor.

Not so obvious is the large ring cairn 25 m to the east, 2. A nearly circular bank 1.6 m wide of the usual double-slabbed construction, surrounds an area 21 x 22.5 m across. The interior appears to be at ground level, with a number of shallow pits but no sign of any interior structure. A similar but smaller ring cairn, 3, lies 90 m to the north. The bank 1.2 m wide has an outer kerb of close-set slabs surrounding an interior 16 x 15.5 m across. Nothing now can be made of the few slabs partly covered by turf that lie near the centre but in Rowe's time (1848) he describes them as arranged in a square, eight feet across, surrounding a 'coffin'. A more typical cairn, 4, 55 m to the north has been dug into at

MAP 40

the centre to reveal a carefully structured interior. Two slabs on the edge of the pit are probably the sides of a cist. The pile of stones a few metres away not yet covered by turf is probably of recent origin, though it is included in Grinsell's list as a cairn. The fifth cairn, 5, is still well preserved with a flat top surrounded by an outer kerb of stones, most of them in place. A concentric inner ring of slabs is exposed in places and near the centre a shallow pit no doubt provided the material for the modern stone heap.

At the north end of the hill an inconspicuous turf-covered cairn, **8**, with shallow central depression lies on the hillside just above the enclosed land. On a slight knoll 150 m further uphill are the probable remains of a second cairn, now reduced to a scattered pile of stones around a single set slab. Above the track a further 100 m in the same direction are two slabs facing each other 1.7 m apart with a pair of longer stones lying between. They are obviously artifically set and may be the last vestige of what was a well-known stone setting called the Eight Rocks which existed on the hillside until sometime in the nineteenth century. This was probably the retaining circle of a cairn like the Nine Stones on Belstone Common and the stones were said to dance to the sound of South Tawton church bells.[10] The surrounding area has long been swept clear of all available surface stone to provide material for the nearby enclosure walls.

Almost halfway to the summit a damaged cairn, **9** c. 7.0 m across, lies in the angle between two reaves, the upcast from the central pit forming a second mound on the downhill side. One reave winds around

Cosdon Hill summit cairns   fig. 40.8

the side of the hill from its origin in the damp ground around Ivy Tor Water, to be lost in the stony ground on the north-east flank of Cosdon. The branch reave descends towards the source of a tributary of the Taw though it fades out some distance short of it. Cairn **10** c. 7.5 m across with a slight central depression, lies about 70 m east of a much longer reave, sited on a slight knoll on the hillside to make it more conspicuous. This boundary line includes the straight upper course of Ivy Tor Water and can be easily followed for nearly 4 kilometres to Sheepstor Brook. Cairn **10** overlooks a small cairnfield with at least seven members one or two hundred metres downhill to the west. All are inconspicuously small, 3 to 4.5 m in diameter rising to 0.3 m at the most, and appear to be undamaged. A partly polished flint axe of late neolithic form was found further down the slope in the late nineteenth century.

A possible cairn **11** lies on the summit of Little Hound Tor, which is really only a slight rise of the southward extension of Cosdon Hill. The low mound crowned by a modern stone

MAP 40

heap is, at best, only partly the work of man as a large natural block is exposed on one side. The stones piled on its surface were obviously obtained from the trench to the centre. The summit of the 'tor' is entirely free of rocks despite the story that an artificial one was once built here to extend the boundary of the Forest and hence the grazing of the farmer who rented it.[19]

12-15 Belstone Common cairns

The cairn, **12**, on the highest point of Watchet Hill above Belstone has suffered badly from the curiosity of casual diggers. The pits at the centre have reached ground level and probably little of the original structure remains where it was placed. The upcast has been thrown outside in ragged heaps around the edge, increasing the diameter to about 14 m from probably one nearer half that size.

A tinners' gully separates the hilltop cairn from the well-known Nine Stones cairn circle, **13** (fig. 40.9) on the slopes close above the Belstone track. It stands on the edge of an area of clitter which may have helped preserve the prominent retaining circle from destruction. The latter consists of sixteen stones rather than nine, though one has been uprooted outside the circle, another lies buried and two more on the south side are leaning almost flat with just their tops showing. The curious arrangement of close-set slabs on the north-west side and the rest being irregularly spaced around the circumference seems to have been the original design. The full complement of stones are probably present as there is only a single socket hole adjacent to the fallen slab and it seems unlikely that alternate stones would have been robbed. Apart from the fallen slab 1.75 m long which must have stood higher, the erect stones are of comparable size, 0.5 to 0.8 m tall, the two small slabs at

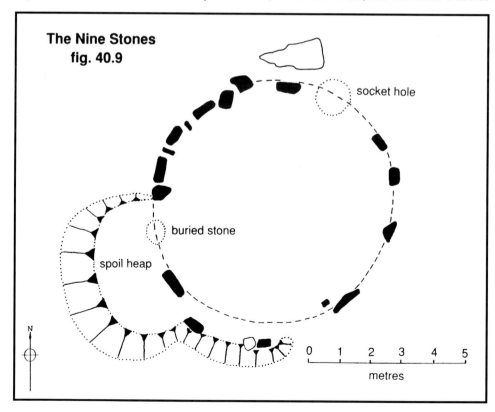

The Nine Stones
fig. 40.9

socket hole

buried stone

spoil heap

N

0 1 2 3 4 5
metres

MAP 40

right-angles to the ring merely helping to fill the gaps between the taller stones. Naturally the interior has been dug into and judging by the size of the spoil heap outside the western edge the centre of the mound would have reached as high as the stones. Slabs of unknown size show just above the uneven interior which could possibly be the sides of a cist.

Nearly a kilometre to the south-west on the almost flat ground near Cullever Steps is a smaller cairn circle, **14**. About a third of the retaining circle is missing, the rest set as a kerb only 4.5 m in diameter surrounding a substantial mound. A large block has been exposed in a deep pit at the centre and a flat slab 1.7 x 1.2 m across, propped against the outside of the mound, may well be a displaced cist cover. Nearby a flint knife of Early Bronze Age date was found lying on the surface after having been exposed by heavy rain.

Irishman's Wall can be seen descending Belstone Tor to the east, its foundations continuing across the valley floor to Cullever Steps and East Okement Farm, the latter built about 1878. It was erected in the early nineteenth century[10] as the northern boundary of one of the largest enclosures attempted on the moor, 600 Ha. in extent. The wall continues southward over the tinners' mounds alongside the Black-a-ven for three kilometres before accompanying the military track back to Steeperton Gorge on the Taw. Much of the enclosed area is within the Forest but also includes small parts of Belstone and Okehampton Commons. According to Crossing the commoners, not surprisingly objecting to this loss of their rights, pulled down their sections of walling before the circuit was completed.

On the summit of the ridge south of Higher Tor and just beyond the Belstone Common boundary stones is a well preserved cairn 8.5 m across, **15**. The tops of a retaining circle show within the edge of the mound which appears to be undamaged except for the deep pit at the centre. Within it two slabs remain of the cist, the backing stones of one of them clearly visible within the body of the mound. In 1889 the contents of the cist were investigated by Dr Prowse with the aid of his walking stick, but someone had been there before him and the only finds he made were some fragments of 'bony tissue' which he concluded were the last remains of an interment.

16, 17 Tin and copper mining in the Taw valley, and Skaigh Warren

The valley of the Taw has seen far more activity than its present air of peaceful solitude suggests, for both tin and, more recently, copper have been extracted from the river bed and its banks. The tinners steadily worked their way up the main stream and along its tributaries, the deposits confined to a narrow band lower down and expanding upstream towards the source. The first deposits were obtained from a few hundred metres just outside the Belstone enclosures where the river has been diverted from its original channel. Sited amongst the waste heaps on the west bank are the foundations of a building, **16**, probably Thomas Tuckfield's combined knacking mill and blowing house, in action at least from 1521 to 1535, for which he paid a rent of 3d.[11] The lower walls still stand, recessed at one end and with a flight of steps in the opposite corner ascending to the top of the bank above. The supply leat from the river is not clear but the short return north of the building is still well preserved. Upstream waste mounds commence once again beyond the junction with Small Brook, expanding enormously at the bifurcation of the river at the base of Steeperton Tor where the tinners are also known to have been active in the middle of the sixteenth century.[58]

A narrow band accompanies the upper Small Brook, with deeper gullies below the prehistoric settlements and again at the boundary of Commons and Forest. Ivy Tor Water also yielded its quota of ore, particularly from the wide excavation around its spring up to

MAP 40

3 m below ground level. A small area of streaming around the head of Blackaton Brook, insignificant in extent, has interfered with the drainage of the shallow valley south-east of Cosdon, turning the naturally soft ground into what is reputed by some to be the worst bog on the moor, Raybarrow Pool. Its middle reach above Cheriton Combe has been excavated to a depth of 4 m.

Three centuries after the tin streamers had worked out their claim and departed the valley re-awakened to the sound of the picks wielded by a new generation of miners, this time working the copper lodes further down the valley. Copper mining became an important industry in the nineteenth century and numerous mines were opened around the fringes of the moor. The western edge was the most productive but the area around Belstone and Sticklepath here on the north side of the moor was also of considerable importance. Slight remains of the Ivy Tor and Taw River mines can be found on opposite sides of the river in Belstone Cleave. The right bank track passes two adits of the former, one of them still accessible, and the foundations of buildings below the site of the shaft, **17**. Uphill are the nineteen buries of Skaigh Warren, apparently of nineteenth century date and owned by the Duchy. More foundations and leats can be found downstream on the opposite bank where an enormous 70 foot water-wheel was installed for draining the shaft. The mines were abandoned in 1892 when the workings were flooded.[46]

Ford Farm mine was active for a few years after 1897, producing both copper and arsenic, its most obvious relic being the leat taken off Ivy Tor Water which accompanies the track around the north side of Cosdon. Remains of other copper mines can be seen alongside the A30, on Greenhill west of Sticklepath, and the massive dumps of Ramsley mine, still for the most part bare of vegetation, which loom over the road as it curves around the base of the hill before entering the village (neither shown on map). A stack on the hillside serves as a landmark for miles around but the engine shaft with its parapet has been concreted over and what little remains of the buildings is shrouded in thick undergrowth. Ramsley mine was worked from about 1850 to 1880 and re-opened 1900-1911, steam power being used in the latter period. The mine was of some importance, employing up to ninety-seven men in its best year[8] and producing in excess of 10 000 tons of copper ore.

a-j Boundary stones

The parishes of Belstone, South Tawton and Throwleigh were each energetic in setting up stones along their borders with neighbouring commons and more particularly with the Forest. None are likely to be of very early date, though the churchwardens' accounts quoted by St Leger-Gordon[59] show that at least some of the South Tawton boundary stones were erected in 1752. Their present boundaries encroach upon the Forest, for all the early Perambulations start and finish on Cosdon Beacon which is now well within South Tawton Common. The stones are cut with the parish initials, *T* standing for both Throwleigh and South Tawton, which also uses *ST*, and *DC* for the Duchy of Cornwall.

At **a** two stones of different sizes (*BBP* and *BB*) stand a few metres apart, presumably erected on separate occasions; **b**, three stones (*BB, ST* and *ST*), South Tawton having a stone on each side of the Taw; **c**, (*T*) stands on the edge of a small stony mound which is included in Grinsell's list of cairns, as is a similar pile 90 m to the north west; **d**, two tall pillars (both *T*) about 20 m apart with a third much smaller slab in line to the west; **e**, the White Moor stone (*T/T/DCTP*) marks the junction of the Forest with Throwleigh and South Tawton. The latter pair share stone **f** (*TST*) but have separate stones at **g** (*ST* and *TP*) which stand on tinners' mounds about 10 m apart. Stone **h** (*BB*), 20 m from Ivy Tor Water, stands on South Tawton Common. Stones **i** and **j** (*SZ1/DC1* and *SZ2/DC2*), also on the Common, reflect the Duchy's claim to Cosdon Hill.

MAP 41

MAP 41 The Upper Taw and Walla Brook

1 Kennon Hill settlement and cairn

A multiple enclosure settlement lies south of the summit of Kennon Hill, on an even slope facing down the Ruelake valley. The reave from Gallaven Brook onto Throwleigh Common winds across the hillside to the east, and on the valley floor Whitemoor Marsh, around the head of Forder Brook, separates it from the prehistoric enclosures on Buttern Hill. The settlement is very overgrown but the boundary walls are continuous and do not appear to have been robbed. At least fourteen huts can be counted, each 3-4 m across, connected together by a network of banks which form paddocks between them.

Another isolated hut (5.5 m) lies 200 m downhill to the south and slight traces of other unconnected enclosures can be seen nearer the summit and in the hollow between Kennon Hill and Rival Tor. Rather closer is a heather-covered cairn (6.0 x 0.7 m) a few metres from the head of Ruelake pit. A pair of slabs is visible within the body of the mound and a slight central hollow shows that it has been dug into, though not apparently very thoroughly.

2 Steeperton Tor settlement

Despite the height above sea-level, 460 m , the north-eastern flank of Steeperton Tor supported a considerable prehistoric settlement, unusually distant from their nearest neighbours almost 2 kilometres away on Cosdon Hill. The site is very overgrown but at least in this position, far from the nearest newtake or track, was safe from those in search of stone. Some eighteen huts can still be found ranging in size from 3.0 to 5.5 m in diameter, many with just the tops of their walls showing above the turf, and no doubt others are completely buried. The majority are clustered around four small enclosures, badly defined in places, with two free-standing huts to the north. A short distance south-east, fragments of walling associated with another group of five huts show that these also were at one time provided with fields.

3-6 Cairns on the high moorland

The massive cairn on the southern tip of Watern Tor ridge, 50 m below the highest point, has remained free of vegetation so that its stones stand out as a prominent landmark against the background of green turf, **3**. These are of a useful size for newtake walls but the builders of the nearby enclosure, approaching to within a hundred metres, commendably resisted this easily available source. The cairn is 24 m across and 3.5 m above ground level on its downhill side where stones thrown out from the central pits have increased its original height considerably. No doubt many of the displaced stones have rolled back into the cavities but the excavations do not seem to have reached anywhere near ground level and so the lower levels may be undisturbed.

Out of sight of this cairn on the northern tip of the hill is the spectacular rock ridge of Watern Tor leading to the Thirlstone. Just uphill from the latter at the foot of the rocks is a small heather-covered cairn (4.5 x 0.4 m) with a flat slab lying on its surface, **4**.

The cairn (c. 18 x 1.8 m) visible on the summit of Hangingstone Hill across the valley to the west, **5**, has been severely damaged by the Observation Post built into its southern edge, which appears to have had part of the cairn material used in its construction. There is

MAP 41

only a shallow central pit but the base of a flagpole sunk into the mound at this point suggests that the interior has been considerably disturbed as well. Downhill, almost due north, the Ordnance Survey map shows the position of another cairn less than a hundred metres from the track but this has not been located.

In 1902 the Dartmoor Exploration Committee recorded a 'ruined cairn ... with a very fine Kistvaen' that they had excavated 'about a mile beyond Watern Tor'. Though cairn **6** (6.5 x 0.5 m) is considerably less than this distance and now appears undamaged it is almost certainly the one referred to. It lies on the saddle of the ridge north-east of Wild Tor with a short bank from the north-north-east curving in towards it as described, about 50 m long but fading away in the opposite direction. The excavators must have reburied the cist and carefully reformed the mound into its present smooth outline. The cist would have been exceptionally large, for the single side and end slabs which remained were 2.2 and 1.3 m long respectively, exceeded only by Merrivale in size. Two flat stones nearby were both assumed to be cover slabs. The excavation showed that a pit about 0.5 m deep had been dug into the floor of the cist which contained only a small amount of wood charcoal.

a-f Gidleigh parish boundary stones

From the pair of slabs at the foot of Stonetor Hill (**map 37**) the Gidleigh/Lydford parish boundary crosses the North Teign to Manga Rock, **a** (*GP*), the largest of a group of natural boulders on the hillside overlooking Hugh Lake. The boundary continues to Hawthorn Clitter, one of several patches of surface stone visible on the opposite slope, and then on to Thirlstone (*GP*), the 'holed' rock on Watern Tor. From here the O.S. maps show the next boundary point to be Wildtor Well where both Lydford and Throwleigh parishes meet Gidleigh, excluding a perfectly good boundary stone **b** (*GP/DCTP*) on the summit of Hey Down half a kilometre to the north-east. The Gidleigh/Throwleigh boundary continues to two more slabs **c** and **d** (both *GP*), beside the track near the heads of Gallaven Brook and Rue Lake, and then another, **e** (also *GP*) out of sight on the south-east slope of Kennon Hill. The latter is a triangular slab propped up on a reave and was probably originally placed here in prehistoric times. A large slab, **f** (*G*) lying on the reave about 120 m downhill may have been an earlier boundary mark. Neither of these is shown on the Ordnance Survey map. The last stone in the series is a more modern pillar with a latin cross cut into one face, (**map 38 a**) (*G/†*) overlooking Whitemoor Marsh, from which the boundary continues down to and along Forder Brook.

TH1-4 Tinning along the Walla Brook and its tributaries

Upriver from the streamworks, at its junction with the North Teign, the Walla Brook meanders along the flat valley floor, its waterlogged northern bank receiving the run-off from Buttern Hill and is thus approached only with difficulty. On firmer ground piles of discarded pebbles accompany the river up to its confluence with Gallaven Brook, its heavily streamed tributary. For the next three kilometres the Walla Brook was unproductive, its main interest to the tinners being as a water supply to supplement the flow along Gallaven Brook. The first leat, obliged to travel a considerable distance around the tip of Hey Down, is now very indistinct and even entirely lost in places. Some 200 m higher up a better-preserved leat, still bridged by clappers, is taken off at the edge of a small patch of tinners' waste to empty into the upper end of a gully on the south side of Gallaven Brook. Yet another leat can be

MAP 41

traced along the hillside above Wildtor Well, orientated towards the dip between Wild Tor and Hey Down. This is probably the old Gidleigh Mill leat, which must have skirted Gallaven Mire to the north before descending the flanks of Kennon and Buttern hills, though it cannot be traced so far. It is now a shallow ditch mainly recognizable by the displaced blocks which accompany its course. This last leat left the Walla Brook a short distance above a small streamworks with remains of a tinners' hut (**TH1**) alongside.

The only significant deposits of ore along the Walla Brook were at Watern Combe where it flows sluggishly for several hundred metres through long lines of pebble mounds. Here the stream bed has been lowered by up to 4 m before exiting through a narrow defile which has been walled and deepened to increase flow and avoid flooding the workings. Two primitive buildings can be found amidst the waste mounds within the gully, the first **TH2** (2.8 x 2.0 m) halfway down the side of the excavation with an entrance facing upstream towards a semi-paved track up which the tin must have been carried. The gables of the second hut **TH3** (3.2 x 1.5 m) have been rebuilt on older foundations, though its siting near the valley floor suggests it post-dates at least the earliest workings. Little more than the foundations remain of a fourth building of uncertain function, **TH4** (c. 9.0 x 4.0 m), much larger than the usual tinners' hut, which was built into the hillside on the north bank of the Walla Brook some distance below Wildtor Well.

Though the Gallaven Brook can be stepped over at almost any point, this little valley was continuously productive from its source below Gallaven Mire to the junction with the Walla Brook. The stream bed was lowered by up to 3 m along its middle course and it is along this section that the Bradford leat ascends the side of the gully from its take-off point upstream. This is one of the longest leats constructed by the tinners, said to be 20 kilometres overall though rather less than half of this is on the moor. Except for some short stretches where it passes through fields still in use its moorland course is traceable as far as Shilley Pool on Blackaton Brook (**map 39**). It was constructed in the sixteenth century to supply mine workings now covered by Bradford Pool, at Shilstone north of Chagford, but an interesting court case in 1699[57] deprived the tinners of its use and only that section up to Scorhill continued to carry water.

A prodigious amount of work was also carried out along the only tributary of Gallaven Brook, Rue Lake. It has been streamed to well above the point where it emerges on to the surface and a leat taken off the former just below the mire was fed into these upper workings. A well-used track from the ford overlies about half its course but the eastern section running into the top of the gully is clearly visible. The excavations are over 100 m wide in places, narrowing abruptly at the higher end and ending finally at a pit 4 m deep.

g, TH5-7, BF1, 2 Knack Mine and tin streaming along the Taw and Steeperton Brook.

Only small patches of tinners' mounds occur alongside either the River Taw or Steeperton Brook upstream from the massive excavations around their junction at the apex of Steeperton Tor. These medieval streamworks by no means exhausted the potential of the upper Taw valley and at a later date, probably in the fifteenth or sixteenth centuries, the gullies and ditches were excavated above the west bank, the most southerly provided with a hillside reservoir. Underground working probably started in the late eighteenth century when the mine seems to have been known as Wheal Virgin, the letters *WV* being inscribed on a large slab, **g**, in the upper end of one of the gullies. It was subsequently known as Knack or Steeperton mine and what is known of its later history has been described by Tom Greeves.[58]

MAP 42

Desultory interest in the mine continued on and off throughout the nineteenth century until 1876 when new proprietors secured and extended the old levels. The following year a large amount of money was expended on equipment and machinery such as stamps, and most of the remains on the east bank below the ford belong to this period. These have been somewhat damaged by the military track but above the platform beside the river can be seen the filled-in wheel-pit with its tail-race emptying back to the stream and the site of one of the three round buddles. These were served by two well preserved leats, the upper running towards the wheel-pit and the lower taken off 250 m upstream at the eastern end of a dam across the Taw. The two-roomed building levelled into the opposite hillside no doubt housed the miners during the working week, doubling as a mine office and forge[58], and immediately upstream are the adits and shaft. Despite this expenditure only small amounts of tin were raised and the workings were finally closed and the company put into liquidation only two years later, in 1879.

Tinning along Steeperton Brook was confined to a number of small streamworks beside the river, three of them accompanied by tinners' huts. **TH5** (3.2 x 2.2 m), just below the ford, is one of the best preserved examples with all four walls standing to 1.5 m high, a cupboard recess at the far end and the lintel lying in the doorway. The ground around **TH6** (4.8 x 2.7 m), set well back from the bank, has become waterlogged since it was built and the doorway and interior features are obscured by heather and rushes. Only a few courses are visible of **TH7** (5.0 x 3.0 m) at the higher end of a more substantial streamwork which has lowered the bed by up to 2 m.

The small buildings, **BF1** (2.6 x 1.3 m) and **BF2** (2.3 x 1.8 m) on the summit of the ridge between the two rivers and within sight on the east slope of Okement Hill are well away from streamworks and are more likely to have been the home of peat cutters or shepherds. The first is bottle-shaped with a narrow passage leading to a corbelled chamber; most of the roofing slabs have collapsed and the lintel from over the doorway lies at the entrance. Ground level reaches the top of the back wall of **BF2** and here also the lintel has fallen across the doorway. The deep turf ties to the north are obviously of comparatively recent date.

MAP 42 Okehampton Common, East and West Okements

1-9 Cairns on Okehampton Common

With their preference for the most prominent sites around the edge of the central moorland the builders of the larger cairns not surprisingly chose Yes Tor with its splendid view over much of North Devon and Cornwall. A cairn, **1**, 29 m across, north-west of the summit rocks is now a mass of small stones piled up around a huge pit at the centre. A trench across the north side seems to have reached down to bedrock. Almost as much labour must have been spent on this unrecorded excavation as on its original construction. Also considerably damaged is a second large cairn between two rock piles nearer the summit, now a formless mound of stones many of which have slipped downhill and are much pitted exposing some of the natural blocks underneath. Flint implements including knives and arrowheads of the Bronze Age and earlier have been found on the Tor, and indeed over much of Okehampton Common.

MAP 42

A ridge connects Yes Tor with the rock piles on High Willhays, at 621 m the highest ground in southern England. A roughly circular bank, with a break through the wall, built against the base of one of the smallest of these outcrops, **2**, may be the gutted remnant of a cairn or possibly an enclosure of prehistoric date. Layered slabs visible beneath the heather surround a flat peat-covered interior. The next outcrop to the south also has an artificial feature, a short double line of slabs on end around a mass of small stones, but despite its remoteness has also been too badly damaged to identify. From here the summit track continues on to Forsland Ledge, a rock outcrop well down the hillside to the south beside which is a substantial cairn, **3** (10.0 x 0.4 m). Its outer rim appears to be intact but the centre has been dug into where some of the larger stones have been raised on end, giving the superficial appearance of a cist.

Of similar size (10.0 x 0.6 m) but on the far side of Okehampton Common is a cairn, **4**, about 15 m from the boundary stones on the northern tip of Harter Tor. Not surprisingly in this position, 100 m from East Okement farm newtakes, a large cavity has been dug at the centre down to ground level. Between it and the pitted cairn on Black Down overlooking Moor Brook, **5** (7.5 x 0.8 m), is the only prehistoric reave so far noticed on this part of the moor, a short stony bank 90 m long supporting a few upright slabs. Below the cairn a track continues on to the western promontory of the same hill which separates Red-a-ven Brook from one of its tributaries. Thirty metres from the track just north of the summit the pit at the centre of cairn **6** (6.5 x 0.6 m) has exposed two small earthfast slabs, the end stones of a cist about a metre in length. The cover and side stones have disappeared. The Red-a-ven descends a deep cleft between it and the foot of Yes Tor, a sheltered coombe with several apparently suitable bankside settlement sites though no stone-built dwellings were ever erected here. Two or three small cairns, **7** (5-6 m), occupy the crest to the south, all of them damaged and one with a slab about 9 m from its base which may have been artificially set. Downhill to the west two long mounds of small stones, 9 m and 12 m by 4 m wide, are of uncertain date and function.

From here the rounded outlines of cairns in the Bronze Age cemetery on Longstone Hill stand out on the skyline to the west, **8**. At least two dozen mounds from 2 to 7 m in diameter and up to 0.6 m high lie within 300 m along the east side of the ridge, some of the smaller ones oval rather than round and dfficult to distinguish from natural hillocks. All have been dug into causing considerable distortion to the shape of many of them. Distant about 200 m to the south and not closely associated with this group is a much more substantial cairn, **9** (13 x 0.9 m).

The hillside is exceptionally clear of large surface blocks but on the summit of the ridge above the cairns is a flat pillar (**St.**) about 2.5 m long which it has been suggested may be the longstone which once stood upright to give the hill its name. If so, it must have fallen many years ago as turf is beginning to cover it and there is no sign of a socket hole. One puzzle concerning all these cairns and those on Homerton Hill nearby (**map 43**) is the whereabouts of the settlements of the people who built them. The nearest known sites are small ones over three kilometres away on the west side of Corn Ridge and in the Lyd valley, an area itself well provided with burial mounds. Valleys such as those of Red-a-ven and Black-a-ven Brooks appear to provide plenty of suitable areas but no settlements have so far been located anywhere between the rather doubtful site beside **TH10** on the West Okement and the River Taw. Possibly their dwellings were purely of timber construction or more likely were well down the lower slopes and have been cleared from within the present fields and enclosures.

Crossing recorded two more cairns in the area, though within the Forest boundary, neither of which have been relocated; a small one south of East Mill Tor near the ruined wall and 'the remains of a large tumulus' on the summit of Okement Hill.

MAP 42

TH1-13 Tin Streaming along the West and East Okements

The West Okement rises on the edge of Cranmere Pool, now merely a dry hollow in the peat, having been drained, probably in the early nineteenth century, as a danger to sheep.[38] Like the Tavy most of the ore was recovered from small pockets in the stream bed or in narrow bands accompanying it, the only really large deposits being encountered along its tributary, Lints Tor Brook. Tin streaming could hardly have been the usual lonely occupation along this river and there seems to have developed something of a 'tin rush'. No less than thirteen buildings associated with the waste mounds can be found and no doubt others once existed that have since decayed beyond recognition.

Pebble mounds begin to appear as the river rounds the northern tip of Black Ridge, involving both sides just beyond the first right bank tributary descending Vergyland Combe. One corner of a tinners' hut here has collapsed **TH1** (c. 5.0 x 2.8 m) but the rest is banked up outside and still stands over a metre high. The narrow entrance faces downstream and is given some protection by a slab set vertically outside it. Further down, only an end wall of **TH2** (c. 4.0 x 2.0 m) is visible having been almost overwhelmed by the mounds that were later heaped up around it.

TH3 (c. 5.0 x 2.2 m), almost hidden under vegetation, lies a short distance up the next right bank tributary, Brim Brook, which has been streamed almost to its source. Amidst the debris further up was a larger building **TH4** (c. 9.0 x 4.0 m), twice the usual size. A recess in the far wall was probably for a fireplace but the walls have been reduced to their foundations, apparently deliberately, and the stones scattered over the interior. It has been suggested[54] that this building was associated with the nineteenth-century tin mine Wheal Providence 'at the bottom of Dinger Hill' in which case Dustings shaft should be nearby but has yet to be relocated. Both **TH5** (c. 5.0 x 2.2 m) and **TH6** (c. 5.0 x 2.0 m) have inner chambers divided off by cross walls.

Downstream the river is forced southwards by the pointed spur below Dinger Tor, an unproductive stretch barely worked over by the tinners. A few small mounds at the apex where the river turns back to the north-west is the site of a primitive little shelter with a rounded lower end, **TH7** (c. 3.0 x 2.0 m), built into the base of the hill. Three more huts lie about midway between here and Lints Tor Brook. **TH8** (c. 3.4 x 2.4 m) set well back from the river, has been severely damaged and the north wall of **TH9** (c. 4.4 x 3.0 m) has almost disappeared, though this building was constructed of larger blocks than normal. **TH10** (c. 5.0 x 2.8 m) is still a substantial building with walls up to 1.5 m high and an outer enclosure attached to the south side that perhaps surrounded a garden plot. Immediately upstream the curved stony bank parallel with the river and the pair of circular foundations uphill, each about 3 m across, may equally well be of prehistoric or more recent date.

For the first 300 m both banks of Lints Tor Brook have been thoroughly turned over by the tinners. Hidden amongst the rubble mounds and intersecting channels are the foundations of a crudely built shelter, **TH11** (c. 2.5 x 1.4 m), no more than some loosely piled blocks on one side of a large boulder and open at one end. A similar structure, **TH12** (c. 2.3 x 1.3 m), lies on the opposite side of the brook, but neither of these really warrants the title of 'building' and are quite unlike the normal type of tinners' hut. More interesting but in no better condition is the two-roomed building on the edge of the clitter upstream, **TH13** (both c. 3.0 x 3.0 m).

Shallow streamworks continue downriver as far as Black Tor Copse, beyond which few deposits of tin were encountered (**map 43**). A small area of disturbance on the left bank opposite the centre of the copse must have been a disappointment, for the construction of the well-preserved leat emptying into its upper end, taken through some very stony ground, must have required more labour than the workings. Better luck was to be had at Croker's

MAP 43

Pits around the small tributary draining the north end of Corn Ridge. It was served by a leat taken off Vellake Brook, itself with a deep excavation at its source.

All three moorland tributaries of the West and East Okements have been streamed, particularly Moor Brook below the ford where the shallow parallel ridges are up to 100 m wide, and Black-a-ven Brook. The military road crosses the latter at New Bridge about midway along its course, at the point where the workings expand enormously around a wedge of untouched ground. Here some wide excavations leave the valley floor up the western hillside for 300 m to Curtery Clitters. Between these two rivers is a modern relic of the Army's use of the moor, the target rails and bunkers on Rowtor Ridge. In Crossing's day the guns sited on Halstock Down swept this ridge and he recommended a viewpoint under West Mill Tor 'from where the artillery practice could be safely watched'.

These streams however were relatively inconsiderable sources of tin compared with the East Okement, which together with the Taw and Lyd were the most productive on the north moor. Streamworks only begin below the first tributaries, the bed of the right bank feeder having been lowered by several metres within an enormous gully which extends up the hill beside the road. Downstream from the upper ford the river meanders across the wide valley floor through the mounds and diversion channels known as Rithy Pits. The heaps of discarded pebbles increase in size, developing into a spectacular moonscape where the track fords the river at the corner of East Okement farm. The farm wall now closely follows the course of the river over the top of the workings until the gully, ever deepening, ends abruptly at an enormous pit fully 7 m below the right hand bank.

a-i Okehampton Parish boundary stones

A line of lettered boundary stones from Sandy Ford on the West Okement north-eastwards to Cullever Steps on the East Okement defines the boundary between Okehampton Parish and the Forest. More than half of these are paired, with a small slab at the foot of a tall pillar which was presumably a more easily visible replacement. Each is inscribed with *OPB* on at least one face, the exception being stone **f** which has the letters on different faces.

MAP 43 The Lyd Valley

1-3 Prehistoric settlement in the Lyd valley

No settlements are now to be found in the valley of Doetor Brook but tin streaming here was so extensive that any settlement sited close to the river bank would probably have been destroyed. The bank of the Lyd has also been cut back, by more than 100 m in places, but two small settlements survive in a gap in the workings opposite the highest point of Great Nodden. Most of the west bank is too steep to have been suitable as a settlement site.

A crescent-shaped double-slabbed wall, **1**, just beyond the tinners' gully encloses a very small area open towards the river. A single hut (c. 5.0 m) outside the enclosure is attached to it by a wall. Downstream a tributary separates this from a larger settlement, **2** (fig. 43.1), 60 m from the river bank. A vague track passes through the centre of a roughly circular enclosure about 35 m in diameter with a pair of huts built across the perimeter wall, one of them with an entrance, 1 (6.3 m), being the largest in the settlement. Above the track the boundary is mainly double-slabbed but the lower half has become very indistinct. A further six huts (2.5 to 5.0 m) are to be found outside the compound, one of the latter having a short length of walling orientated towards a patch of surface stone. This may be part of the wall of another enclosure and the curved line of slabs on a slight bank a short distance upstream is the remains of a third one of similar size to the first.

MAP 43

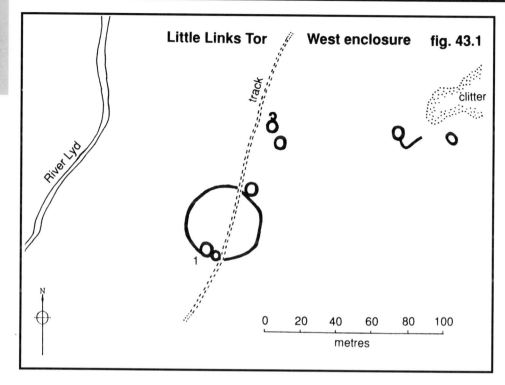

Little Links Tor   West enclosure   fig. 43.1

The most substantial settlement in the valley though lies on the lower slope west of Arms Tor, **3**. Numerous pits and fractured blocks show that stone workers have been active on this part of the hillside and many of the buildings have been considerably damaged. At least ten huts 5 to 7 m in diameter can be found here, some with exceptionally large wall slabs in proportion to their size, and others reduced to little more than circular platforms. One of the largest has an outer wall around one side increasing its diameter to an oval 11 m across. Short lines of stones attached to some of the huts reveal the former presence of enclosures.

4 Corn Ridge West enclosure and cairns

North of the Lyd watershed on the west flank of Corn Ridge are the slight remains of a small prehistoric enclosure. Little more than half the circuit wall is visible as a low bank, together with a single small hut (c. 2.0 m). A miniature cairn (3.0 x 0.2 m) a few metres from the hut may be the site of a burial, as may another oval-shaped mound (6.0 x 3.0 x 0.6 m) near the lower border of the enclosure.

5 Green Tor settlement

This pair of semi-lunate enclosures below Green Tor, which has the distinction of being the highest settlement site on Dartmoor, can best be viewed from the higher ground on the opposite side of the river. The lower sides of the enclosures are open to the river for about 100 m but the tinners have cut back the bank here reducing the area and perhaps demolishing a riverside wall. The double-slabbed perimeter wall is still continuous but the site is very overgrown and there may well have been more than the single hut (c. 4.0 m) now visible against the uphill side.

MAP 43

6 Sourton Tors stone circle

The probable remains of a stone circle lie inconspicuously on the ridge separating Sourton Tors from Corn Ridge. Apart from one or two stumps all the stones are flat, though many still seem to have one end buried in the earth. Some eighteen stones can be counted, lying 5.5 m apart and arranged in a circle about 32 m across around a flat interior. The stone-worker has been active on the Down as at least one stone has been fractured lengthways and the missing section carted away. A more interesting example of his labour lies about 40 m away: one half of the base of an apple crusher for cider making. They were often made in two halves[31] and this one seems to have been completed but then suffered some damage in transport and abandoned where it lies.

7 Great Nodden cairns (fig. 43.2)

The rounded mass of Great Nodden descends gradually southwards as a 2.5 kilometre spur alongside the River Lyd. A cemetery comprising sixteen cairns, all of them in battered condition, lies on the open land east of the ancient King Wall. Another, 17, was recorded on the summit in 1891 and two more show up only as crop marks on aerial photographs, 18, 19. Those that survive are composed of small stones and all of them lie in a prominent position on the western slopes or on the summit of the ridge. A number have the appearance of ring cairns, a circular bank around a flat interior, but some of these at least were probably cairns of normal shape from which all the interior stones have been carted away. Even allowing for destruction caused by the tinners, the valley of the River Lyd was comparatively sparsely populated and it seems likely from the position of the cairns that their builders settled within the enclosed lands further down the western slope.

Cairns 1-3 lie within the field south of the track from Nodden Gate, all well trampled and spread. Cairn 1 is a ring cairn, the circular bank 1.5 m wide surrounding an uneven interior about 8 m across. Two smaller and much pitted cairns 5 and 6 m across lie close to the field wall. A vague track mounts the slope north of the peatworks railway towards ring cairn 4 on the ridge. The slightly eccentric interior averaging 14.2 m across is surrounded by a bank 1.6 m wide which rises only slightly above the ground level outside. The low central mound has been dug into. Two hundred metres to the north is a group of six small cairns, (5-10) 4.5 to 5.5 m in diameter, none of which is more than 0.3 m high. Half of them have been trenched.

Northwards again two more circular banks which are probably prehistoric in origin lie on either side of the Nodden Gate track. Both have been much interfered with having apparently been used as quarries. East of the track, bank 11 is markedly eccentric, 11 to 18 m in outside diameter and 0.4 m high in places but much spread and with a very uneven interior. Thirty metres to the west a circular bank 9 m across, 12, surrounds a pit with a level floor well below ground level. Better preserved is the cairn on the flank of Great Nodden close to the railway embankment 350 m to the north, 13. Though much pitted at the centre it still stands a metre high and gives the appearance of originally being flat-topped. The pit with surrounding bank, 14, is also probably the remains of a robbed cairn. Cairn 15 at the north end of the ridge, though considerably damaged and only 0.3 m high at most, is still recognizable.

The large cairn 14 m across occupying the summit of Great Nodden, 16, has been considerably damaged like the rest, and nothing is now to be seen of another which once existed 6 m away, 17. When the latter was first described in 1891 only a cist of unusual type remained. It was roughly wedge-shaped with walls constructed of small vertically placed slate slabs. Its discoverer found two flints nearby.

MAP 43

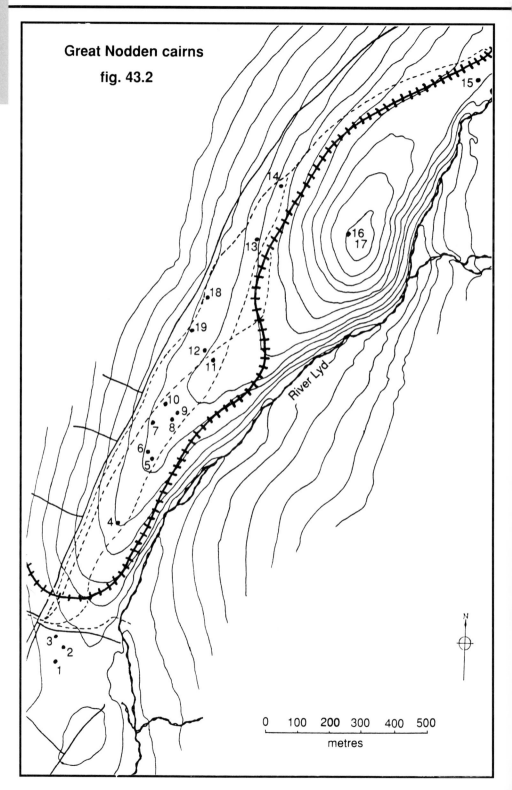

Great Nodden cairns

fig. 43.2

River Lyd

N

0   100   **200**   300   400   500
metres

MAP 43

8-12 Cairns on Corn Ridge and Sourton Tors

From Great Nodden the line of cairns continues northwards along the western slopes of Corn Ridge on to the plateau east of Sourton Tors. An easily identifiable pair 30 m apart lie just above the track which crosses the hillside in the direction of the eastern tor, **8**. The lower is a ring cairn 21 m across with a bank of small stones about 2.5 m wide, but much spread particularly on the eastern side. A number of vertically set slabs visible within the bank may once have formed an inner and outer facing, but the opposing gaps are no doubt modern. At first glance the other mound also appears to be a ring cairn and is a good example of the conversion of a cairn into one of this type. Stones have been removed from the interior down to ground level leaving an oval hollow 10 x 7 m across. An outer rim of unwanted stone has been left around half the perimeter whilst the rest of the mound remains intact. Three hundred metres downhill are a number of small stone heaps, maximum 5 m across, grouped closely together, that may also be prehistoric burial cairns[60].

At the junction of the tracks 250 m to the north, large slabs are visible within the disturbed interior of cairn **9**. A considerable portion of the south cairn at **10** has been carted away and its smaller neighbour 60 m to the north has also been thoroughly pillaged. The better preserved cairn 0.7 m high east of Sourton Tors, **11**, is one of the few of this group which still has evidence of a retaining circle, a single slab on edge at its base, but the siting is too exposed for it to have escaped intact.

The summit cairn on the northern end of Corn Ridge, **12**, is too remote for the removal of its stones to have been worthwhile and consequently it has kept its retaining circle and its original shape, disfigured only by a shallow central hollow. An unusual feature is an extra ring of small slabs forming a low kerb, with no obvious structural purpose, encircling the mound 2 m outside the retaining circle. For the same reason the ring cairn 40 m to the north-west is likely to be 'as built' rather than a robbed out cairn. The circular bank, 0.3 m high, surrounds an area 11.5 m across with a slight rise at the centre. Far less certain is the loose mound of stones which cover one of the low summit rocks in the direction of the curiously shaped stack known as Branscombe's Loaf, the name said to commemorate the thirteenth century Bishop of Exeter's temptation by the Devil. Someone appears to have thought it to be ancient as a trench has been driven across the centre.

13, 14 Cairns near Great Links and Green Tors

A large isolated cairn 16 m across and 1.4 m high lies about 250 m south-west of Great Links Tor, **13**, its bare stones conspicuous on the green hillside. A deep central crater contains a mass of displaced stones. The 1:25000 Ordnance Survey map shows a cairn at the head of a gully south-west of Lower Dunna Goat, but the structure here is far more likely to be a tinners' waste heap.

That rarity, a small but undamaged cairn, **14**, 6 m across, lies 30 m from Green Tor Water south-east of the Tor.

15 Homerton Hill Cairn Cemetery

A cairn cemetery similar to the one on Longstone Hill (**map 42**) a little over half a kilometre to the east occupies the northern tip of Homerton Hill. At least twenty round or oval cairns

MAP 43

can be found within 400 m, from 3 m to 7 m in diameter and all of them dug into. Curious features are the curved banks running through the cairnfield, not apparently enclosure walls and yet presumably of prehistoric date. The pit at the centre of one small cairn (3.5 x 0.3 m) at the north end of the group has exposed a cist 1.1 m long which takes up most of the mound. Two sides and an end slab remain in place, the flat stone nearby probably being the missing capstone.

Three hundred metres south of the cairnfield is an isolated mound (7.5 x 0.3 m), flat-topped and interesting only in that it appears to have been missed by the cairn diggers and seems to be undamaged.

16 Rattle Brook peatworks and tramway

Over the centuries peat has been cut for fuel both for domestic purposes and for use in smelting at the mines and streamworks around the moor, but in the nineteenth century a number of commercial ventures were undertaken to extract and process it on a much larger scale. Apart from its agricultural use a number of products could be extracted from the peat, including charcoal, gas, oil and various chemicals. One of the largest peat workings on the moor was at Rattlebrook Head, exploiting the thick deposits on Amicombe Hill. A licence for peat cutting here was granted by the Duchy of Cornwall in 1878 and the beds have been worked intermittently by a number of companies until the 1950s, but all their enterprising attempts failed in the end because of the high cost of transport or the difficulty and expense of drying the peat.[47]

A tramway for transporting the peat across the moor to the mainline station at Bridestowe was completed in 1879. This was one of three peat tramways on the moor, the others being Zeal Tor on the south-eastern side of the moor and Blackabrook (**map 30**). At first horses were used to haul the trucks up the incline to the turf ties but by the first world war the petrol engine had taken over[61]. The five kilometre moorland course of the tramway is now a levelled track, easy to follow along the flank of Great Nodden to Corn Ridge and then south-eastwards around Woodcock Hill to the workings at Rattlebrook Head. The rails and sleepers had been taken up by 1937 but the bridges are still intact. Little is to be seen at the far end of the tramway as the buildings, deemed to be a danger to livestock, were blown up by the Army in 1961. Vegetation has yet to enshroud the ruins, and stagnant pools now fill the hollows between the piles of masonry and rusting ironwork decaying amidst the surrounding bog. On the hillside beyond are the regular lines of turf ties, difficult to walk over, whilst half a kilometre downstream stands the gaunt shell of Bleak House, once the manager's dwelling, built on the debris discarded by the tin streamers.

Tin streaming along the Lyd and its tributaries

Vast streamworks disfigure the Lyd valley almost from its source down to its confluence with Doetor Brook, and the amount of sand and gravel released must have added significantly to the sandbanks on the Tamar. Below the tramway bridge the gully soon widens to over 100 m across and deepens to 3 m as the river alters course southwards before diverging altogether to follow the course of the original stream bed to the east. After a short gap an even larger gully up to 4 m deep opens up on the east bank, its floor covered with mounds of pebbles, continuing almost without a break to the junction with Doetor Brook. On the west bank just before the confluence are the remains of Wheal Mary Emma, a tin mine about which little is known, active for only a few years around 1860[8]. Filled-in pits and shafts

MAP 43

surround the mine buildings erected on the debris of earlier streamworks. A leat taken off the Lyd near Nodden Gate winds high around the hillside before descending steeply to a wheel pit beside the river just below the buildings. From the size of the pit, about 9 m by only 1 m wide, now without its superstructure, the wheel must have been exceptionally narrow. Nearby is the dressing floor with the well-preserved outlines of two round buddles and the remains of a third.

Doetor Brook is if anything more heavily streamed than the Lyd. The stream gushes out at Dick's Well but the workings start some 300 m further uphill in the direction of Great Links Tor. It appears the flow was not sufficient and a square reservoir 18 m across and 2 m deep was constructed west of the Well to supplement the supply, emptying via a leat through the south-west corner. Immediately downstream an enormous excavation, up to 6 m deep, opens out to east and west, forcing the track to the Rattlebrook workings to divert around the uphill edge. As the stream alters course southwards the excavation decreases in depth and the sides of the gully converge on the very well-preserved remains of Foxhole Mine on the west bank. The lack of any production records of this nineteenth-century mine suggest it was not particularly successful. A short leat is taken off the river upstream from a clapper bridge to a launder bank in almost perfect condition. Water flowed from the wheel pit below, 8 by 1.8 m wide, to a round buddle with central spreader still in place, before returning to the stream. The walls of the two-roomed mine building, each with a fireplace, stand to a considerable height with an entrance facing the river.

Downstream no less than five leats were taken off the Brook in the direction of the Walla Brook to the south as well as another serving Doetor Farm. The first two end at the river bank and were presumably cut before Doetor stream bed was lowered but the next continues down the side of the gully. Two more start 30 m apart just beyond the end of the streamworks downriver. The upper is fed from a pond above a reconstructed dam and water still flows along the first few metres of its course. The well-built bank of the other continues across the Down to an older tinners' pit near the Walla Brook which was utilized as a reservoir, the outlet being at a lower level. Apparently the supply from Doetor Brook was not sufficient and a leat 2.5 kilometres long taken off the Lyd above Smallacombe Stream was necessary to supplement the flow. This laborious undertaking, at one point running through the streamworks along the Lyd, is particularly well preserved below Brat Tor where it is still over a metre deep.

Tinning along the upper Rattle Brook

Streamworks begin to appear alongside the river a short distance above Bleak House, continuing downstream as a narrow band for 2.5 kilometres almost as far as Dead Lake Foot (**map 32**). A small two-roomed building (c. 7.0 x 2.5 m) opposite the upper end of the workings may well be a tinner's house. After 800 m the first gully opens out on the west bank in the direction of Lower Dunna Goat Tor, half a kilometre long, and a short distance below two openworks face each other on either side of the stream. This is the site of Rattle Brook Mine, another unsuccessful venture for which no production records are known. A leat empties into the top of the west bank gert, in the centre of which is a filled-in shaft, and just beyond are the foundations of at least one building on a shelf of the hillside. A second, lower leat carried water to a small wheel pit (c. 5.0 x 1.0 m) now choked by fallen masonry. Downstream the Rattle Brook enters flatter ground where it is joined by Green Tor Water and the Scad. Here the streamworks up to 2 m deep, expand enormously up the lower reaches of each of the tributaries.

MAP 43

a-g Boundary stones

The boundary stones between the commons shared by Bridestowe and Sourton and the parish of Lydford, **a-e** (*BS/L*), are as shown on the Ordnance Survey map except that pillar **a**, on the east bank of the Lyd has been moved 300 m to the opposite side of Nodden Gate. Stone **b** is sited on the hillside within the Arms Tor prehistoric settlement. The boundary with Okehampton is marked by post **f** (BS/9°) at Iron Gates where the old King Way Track from Tavistock to Okehampton crosses the ditch south of Sourton Tors. The tall unmarked pillar on the summit of Greak Links Tor also appears to be a boundary marker, perhaps of the Rattlebrook Peat Works.[13]

Another group of inscribed stones stand alongside Doetor Brook, **g**. The four north of the stream are lettered *TRDC* (Tavistock Rural District Council) and are set around the town's water intake.[11] The post on the south bank (*WD15*) is one of the series of forty-six set up by the Army around Willsworthy Range.

Widgery Cross

Brat Tor, prominent enough from the borderlands, has been made yet more conspicuous by the granite cross on its summit. It was erected in 1887 by William Widgery, the Dartmoor artist and father of the illustrator of the third edition of Rowe's *Perambulation*, to commemorate Queen Victoria's Golden Jubilee. Unlike the ancient Dartmoor crosses that were hewn out of a single stone this one is built up with granite blocks.

17 Sourton Tors ice works

Ice manufacture was one of the more curious of the industrial ventures initiated by the enterprising Victorians on the moor but, like so many of the others, ended as an expensive failure. Ice was in demand for preserving food, particularly fresh fish in transit from Plymouth and elsewhere, but unfortunately for the promoter, James Henderson, not only was artificial production becoming well established by this time but the weather proved a fickle partner in the business. The brief history of the ice works, opened in 1875 but abandoned after only eleven years in 1886 despite the twenty-one year lease, has been well described by Helen Harris.[62] The substantial remains lie on the slopes north-east of the scattered rocks which make up Sourton Tors, a series of long shallow ponds from which the ice was collected in winter and the foundations of the store house immediately below. Most of the stonework has been removed from the building which was constructed well below ground level to improve insulation and approached uphill through a cutting.

Indexed Lists of Settlements, Stone Circles, Rows, and Cairns

Gazetteer

Notes

References are either to early sources or provide additional information and are not otherwise included.

* plan in text

† reported excavation

Settlement list Area in hectares. Heights are above Mean Sea Level as printed on O.S. maps. Direction of gradient downhill. Later use of site to a significant extent: *ab fields* = fields long abandoned; *pres fields* = fields in recent or present use; *L.H.* = longhouse; *plant* = plantation.

Stone circle list Diameter is through centre of stones. Distance apart also through centres.

Stone row list Orientation is between the present ends of the row. Maximum deviation from the straight line between the ends. *E* = standing. *F* = fallen and approximately in place. *B* = buried but obviously part of row. Original number of stones calculated only where both ends are known. Intervisibility of one end from the other. Maximum gradient is of row, direction is that of slope, not always the same. Length is from centre of cairn or terminal at upper end. Distance between rows and between stones along row is a calculated average, two figures being given if there is a large variation.

Cairn list Dimensions are diameter (average of two directions) followed by present height, preceded by *c.* where not measured by tape or badly damaged. *C* = cist. LVG No. is the Parish and number in L. V. Grinsell's list (*DASP* 1978, No. 36). Barrow Report No. refers to the Series of 73 reports of the Barrow Committee published in the *Transactions of the Devonshire Association,* 1879-1958.

Settlements

map	no.	name	river	O.S. ref.	area (ha)	no. of huts	HMSL (m)	gradient down to	later use	references
24	1*	Challacombe Down W. A	Redwater	686 802	?	3	370	9°W.	tin works	–
	1*	Challacombe Down W. B	Redwater	685 804	?	6	370	9°W.	tin works	–
25	1	Birch Tor N.	Bovey	686 820	0.4	2	470	6°N.	–	–
	2	Birch Tor N.	Bovey	684 822	0.9	3	450	8°N.	–	38
	3	Birch Tor N.	Bovey	684 824	?	5	410	8°N.	–	–
	4	Birch Tor N.	Bovey	687 825	?	2	410	9°W.	–	39
	5*	Chagford Common	Bovey	678 831	3.0	4	380	6°E.	Ab. field	–
	6*	Chagford Common	Bovey	679 833	4.1	6	370	6°E.	Ab. field	–
	7*	Chagford Common	Bovey	680 836	?	5	360	6°E.	Pres. field	–
	8*	Chagford Common	South Teign	676 834	0.2	1	370	3°N.W.	–	–
	9*	Hurston Ridge	South Teign	673 825	2.8	7	430	5°N.E.	–	PPS 1983
26	1*	Kings Oven †	Walla Brook	674 813	0.3	1+	440	8°E.	Ab. field	TDA 1895
	2*	Assycombe Hill S.	Walla Brook	666 814	0.04	16	450	4°S.	–	DASP 1979
	3	Water Hill	Bovey	672 813	0.6	4	470	9°E.	–	–
27	1*	Broadun Ring †	East Dart	636 801	0.7	14	430	9°E.	Ab. field	23, TDA 1894
	2*	Broadun †	East Dart	635 799	6.0	33	390–420	10°S.E.	Ab. field	23, TDA 1894
	3*	Lower Broadun	East Dart	638 800	1.0	9	380	17°E.	Ab. field	–
	4*	Roundy Park	East Dart	639 796	0.8	4	365	3°N.E.	Ab. field	TDA 1891
	5*	Hartland Tor	East Dart	642 800	?	5	410	7°W., S.	newtake	TDA 1891
	6	Arch Tor 1–5	East Dart	6378	–	7	390	10°S.E.	–	–
	7*	Krapps Ring †	East Dart	644 781	1.1	13	400	6°N	–	TDA 1891, 1895
	7	Lakehead Hill N.2	East Dart	642 781	c.1.2	?	400	9°NW	plant.	TDA 1891
	7	Lakehead Hill N.3	East Dart	645 783	c.1.6	2+	390	6°N.W.	plant.	TDA 1891
	8	Lakehead Hill S. †	East Dart	645 773	?	1	410	8°S.	plant.	TDA 1896
	9*	Bellever Tor N.	Cherry Brook	644 768	3.1	4	400	4°N.	plant.	33
	9	Bellever Tor N.E.1	Cherry Brook	646 769	?	?	400	3°N.W.	plant.	–
	9	Bellever Tor N.E.2	East Dart	646 766	?	?	410	9°N.E.	plant.	–
	10*	Black Newtake	Cherry Brook	637 763	0.6	–	370	4°N.W.	–	–
	11	Smith Hill	Cherry Brook	632 758	?	1	350	2°S.	pres. fields	–
	12	Dunnabrook W.	Dunna Brook	639 756	?	3	350	5°S.E.	newtake	–
	12	Dunnabrook N.	Dunna Brook	641 758	c.4.0	1	360	6°S.	newtake	–
	13*	Laughter Tor N.	East Dart	652 759	0.4+	2	400	7°N.W.	–	–

map	no.	name	river	O.S. ref.	area (ha)	no. of huts	HMSL (m)	gradient down to	later use	references
28	14	Laughter Tor N.W.	East Dart	650 760	?	?	360	5°N.W.	plant.	–
	15*	Laughter Tor W.	East Dart	650 758	1.4	2	390	5°W.	–	–
	16*	Laughter Tor E.	East Dart	655 756	?	4	400	9°S.E.	Ab. fields	–
	1	Dunnabridge Pound	West Dart	646 746	1.0	2	330	6°S.W.	pound	10, 31
	2*	Laughter Hole	East Dart	661 753	0.7	2	350	5°N.E.	newtake	11
	3	Brimpts North	East Dart	664 751	0.3	2	330	11°E.	newtake	–
	4	Huccaby Ring	West Dart	658 738	0.2	–	325	6°S.	–	–
	5*	Outer Huccaby Ring	West Dart	655 744	0.7	1	350	6°S.W.	Ab. field	10
	6*	Cock's Lake	West Dart	654 745	?	2	350	4°S.W.	Ab. field	–
	7	Laughter Tor S.	West Dart	653 750	0.4	1	370	4°S.E.	–	–
	8*	Laughter Tor S.W.	West Dart	648 752	?	–	370	7°S.W.	–	–
	9	Brownberry S.	West Dart	648 741	?	1	280	4°W.	pres. field	–
	10	Brownberry E.	West Dart	653 738	?	1	320	8°S.W.	pres. field	–
	11	Lower Cherrybrook Bridge	West Dart	633 751	?	1	330	3°S.W.	–	–
29	1*	Littaford Tor S.	West Dart	613 765–612 778	–	80	380–440	10°W.	warren	–
	2	Beardown Plantation S.	West Dart	608 759	0.2	5	390	18°S.E.	plant.	–
	3	Beardown Plantation N.	West Dart	609 759	0.2	3	390	13°E.	–	–
	4	Beardown Hill E.	West Dart	610 764	?	5	400	11°E.	–	–
	5*	Beardown Tors E.	West Dart	610 775	0.7	8	410	13°E.	–	–
	6	Crow Tor S.E.	West Dart	609 786	0.2	–	460	7°S.E.	–	–
	7	Rough Tor S.E.	West Dart	612 794	?	2	470	9°E.	–	–
	8	Rough Tor N.E. †	West Dart	608 802	0.3	5	500	15°E.	–	TDA 1898
	9*	Muddilake Foot	Cherry Brook	628 752	?	7	350	9°E.	–	–
	10	Muddilake Source	Muddilake Brook	611 754	?	1	370	3°E.	newtake	–
	11	Stennen Hill	Cherry Brook	624 778	0.3	4	400	7°S.E.	–	–
	12	Higher White Tor	Cherry Brook	624 786	0.3	1	430	7°E.	–	–
	13	Conies Down Tor E.	Cowsic	592 788	0.3	5	450	9°E.	–	–
	13	Broad Hole E.	Cowsic	591 784	0.03	1	430	10°S.W.	–	–
	13	Broad Hole W.	Cowsic	591 783	0.03	1	430	9°S.E.	–	–
	14	Broad Hole S.	Cowsic	591 782	?	3	430	11°E.	–	–
30	1*	Dead Lake Foot	Walkham	564 781	0	14	420	10–14°S.	–	–

227

map	no.	name	river	O.S. ref.	area (ha)	no. of huts	HMSL (m)	gradient down to	later use	references
	2*	Langstone Moor †	Walkham	556 778	?	51	400–430	11°S.	–	TDA 1895, 1897, 1901
	3	Great Mis Tor W.	Walkham	555 772	?	5	390	5°W.	–	–
	4*	Little Mis Tor W.1	Walkham	556 763	1.6	40	360	7°W.	–	–
	5*	Little Mis Tor W.2	Walkham	557 761	2.0	17	370	7°W.	–	–
	6	Little Mis Tor W.3	Walkham	554 760	?	2	340	5°S.W.	Ab. fields	–
	7	Merrivale Bridge N.1	Walkham	554 754	0.3	2	320	9°W.	–	–
	8	Merrivale Bridge N.2	Walkham	552 751	?	3	300	8°W.	Pres. fields	–
	9*	Merrivale Bridge E. †	Walkham	555 750	0.6	41	340	8°W.	–	39, TDA 1895, 1902, 1934, 1943
31	1.1*	Cox Tor W.1	Tavy	528 760	0.07	1	390	11°S.W.	–	–
	1.2*	Cox Tor W.2	Tavy	527 761	0.2	0	390	12°S.W.	–	–
	2	Cox Tor W. Lower	Tavy	525 758	0.4	1	320	7°S.W.	–	–
	3	Cox Tor Farm	Tavy	522 762	–	1	300	10°W.	–	–
	4	Beckamoor Combe	Walkham	535 751	–	1	330	4°S.W.	–	–
	5	Barn Hill N.W.	Tavy	530 750	?	3	320	4°W.	–	–
	6*	Cox Tor N.E.	Colly Brook	535 765	?	24	350–400	8°N.E.	Ab. fields	–
	7*	Roos Tor N.W.	Colly Brook	539 772	?	73	320–400	11°W.	Ab. fields	–
	8	Roos Tor S.E.	Walkham	548 763	–	6	370	9°S.E.	Pres. field	–
	9*	Wedlake †	Colly Brook	540 777	c.1.8	16	350	7°S.	–	TDA 1905
	10*	Lower Godsworthy	Colly Brook	533 778	?	4	360	8°S.W.	–	–
	11	Smeardon Down	Colly Brook	521 781	c.0.9	1	320	11°S.W.	–	–
	12*	White Tor W. †	Tavy	536 785	0.6	7	390	8°W.	–	TDA 1899
	13*	White Tor Summit †	Tavy	542 786	0.8	10	460	level	–	18, 63, TDA 1899, 1965, DASP 1979
	13	White Tor S.W. Summit	Tavy	540 785	?	5	420	12°S.W.	–	–
	13	White Tor W. Summit	Tavy	539 787	c.0.2	5	430	8°W.	–	–
	13	White Tor N. Summit	Tavy	541 788	0.04	1	440	8°N.	–	–
	14*	White Tor N.	Tavy	543 788	0.6	25	440	10°N.	–	–
	15*	Cudlipptown Down E.	Tavy	544 792	?	4	390	11°N.E.	Pres. field	–
	16	Cudlipptown Down Central 1	Tavy	539 791	c.0.2	4	400	8°N.	–	–
	16	Cudlipptown Down Central 2	Tavy	540 793	?	2	370	7°N.	–	–
	17	Cudlipptown Down W.	Tavy	529 792	?	1	330	11°W.	pres. fields	–

map	no.	name	river	O.S. ref.	area (ha)	no. of huts	HMSL (m)	gradient down to	later use	references
	2*	Nattor Down	Tavy	541 830	?	6	330–420	9°S.W.	pres. fields	–
	3*	Hamlyn's Newtake	Willsworthy Brook	540 835	?	6	370	10°W.	–	–
	4*	Ger Tor	Tavy	549 833	–	10	420	9°S.E.	–	TDA 1894
	5*	Watern Oke.W. †	Tavy	564 835	c.0.4	78	430	7°S.W.	–	TDA 1906
	6	Tavy Cleave E.	Tavy	556 831	?	12	400–440	13°W.	–	–
	7	Lower Rattle Brook E.	Rattle Brook	562 845	?	15	440	10°W.	–	–
	8*	Deadlake Foot	Rattle Brook	561 842	?	16	430	10°S.E.	–	–
	9	Rattle Brook Foot	Tavy	559 838	?	4	430	6°S.E.	–	11
	10	Sharp Tor	Doetor Brook	547 848	0.5	10	440	8°W.	–	–
	11	Hare Tor W.	Walla Brook	538 841	?	5	370	3°N.W.	–	–
	12	Standon Farm	Tavy	546 818	?	4	320	9°W.	ab. fields	–
	13	Baggator Brook Upper	Baggator Brook	558 810	?	1	380	11°S.	–	–
	14	Baggator Brook Lower	Baggator Brook	554 808	?	3	340	12°S.	–	–
	15	South Common Plantation	Baggator Brook	557 805	?	1	380	11°N.W.	plant	–
33	1*	Watern Oke. Central †	Tavy	568 833	–	11	420	4°S.	–	TDA 1906
	1*	Watern Oke. E. †	Tavy	569 833	–	6	420	4°S.	–	TDA 1906
35	1*	Metherall †	South Teign	670 840	?	8	350	6°N.W.	pres. fields	TDA 1880, 1935, 1937
	2	Lowton Brook E.	Lowton Brook	665 836	?	4	380	9°N.W.	plant	10, TDA 1937
	3	Lowton Hill E.	South Teign	669 833	?	0	400	6°N.E.	–	–
	4	Lowton Brook W.	Lowton Brook	662 832	?	11	390	14°N.E.	fields/plant.	TDA 1902
	5	Assycombe Brook †	Assycombe Brook	659 825	?	8	400	14°W.	fields/plant.	23
	6	Fernworthy W.	South Teign	649 840	?	6	420	9°S.E.	plant.	–
	7	Hemstone Rocks N. †	South Teign	648 837	?	8	410	9°E.	plant.	TDA 1901
	8*	White Ridge N.	South Teign	646 828	0.3	4	440	10°N.	–	–
	9	Lade Hill Brookhead	South Teign	639 825	?	13	450	12°S.E.	–	DASP 1979
	10*	White Ridge S.W.1 †	Stannon Brook	647 816	4.0	5	460	10°S.E.	–	TDA 1894, 1895
	11*	White Ridge S.W. 2	Lade Hill Brook	643 816	1.8	3	460	8°S.W.	–	–
	12*	White Ridge S.W. 3 †	Lade Hill Brook	643 818	2.4	6	460	7°W.	–	TDA 1896
	13	Broad Down N.E.	East Dart	637 811	?	2	420	3°N.	–	–
	14*	Templers Newtake	East Dart	637 805	0.6	1	420	15°E.	–	–
36	1*	Kes Tor †	North Teign	665 868	c.50	38	320–430	12°W,N,E.	–	23, 27, 33 PPS 1954, TDA 1954

map	no.	name	river	O.S. ref.	area (ha)	no. of huts	HMSL (m)	gradient down to	later use	references
	2*	Kes Tor S.	North Teign	665 860	2.2	4	420	4°S.E.	–	–
	3	Frenchbeer Rock	South Teign	672 854	?	2	380	5°N.E.	pres. fields	–
	4*	Shovel Down Central A	North Teign	658 859	1.1	4	430	5°N.W.	–	–
	4*	Shovel Down Central B	North Teign	657 858	0.05	1	430	4°N.W.	–	–
	4*	Shovel Down Central C	North Teign	655 857	1.2	2	430	5°N.W.	–	–
	5*	Thornworthy Tor N.	South Teign	665 853	1.4	5	400	5°N.	–	–
	6*	Thornworthy Tor S.	South Teign	663 848	c.2.9	6	390	8°S.W.	–	–
37	1*	Stonetor Brook E.	North Teign	652 858	10	21	410	8°N.W.	wall	–
	2*	Stonetor Hill N.	North Teign	650 855	3.5	7	430	8°N.E.	–	–
	2	Stonetor Hill N. Farmstead	North Teign	649 858	0.5	1	400	9°N.	–	–
	3*	Stonetor Brookhead	North Teign	645 852	–	38	420	9°N.	–	–
	4*	Stonetor Brook W.	North Teign	647 860	1.2	8	390	10°N.E.	–	–
	5*	Shovel Down N.W. Corner	North Teign	646 865	2.3	5	380	4°N.E.	–	–
38	1	Scorhill	North Teign	657 874	–	1	395	6°S.W.	?	–
	2-7	Buttern Hill	North Teign	654 891	?	24	320–410	12°N.E.	newtakes	33, PPS 1952
39	1*	Throwleigh Common	Blackaton Brook	656 908	36	26	300–370	10°–14°E.	–	33, TDA 1986
	2	Kennon Hill N.E. 1	Forder Brook	649 901	–	5	400	8°E.	–	–
	3	Kennon Hill N.E. 2	Forder Brook	650 898	–	10	400	10°E.	–	–
	4	Kennon Hill N.E. 3	Forder Brook	647 897	–	1	420	6°E.	–	–
	5	Cosdon Hill E.	Blackaton Brook	652 917	?	3	320–360	22°N.E.	pres. fields	TDA 1953
40	1*	Small Brook 1	Small Brook	626 908	0.2	11	400	11°S.W.	–	–
	1*	Small Brook 2	Small Brook	626 907	0.15	1	380	7°W.	–	TDA 1890
	1*	Small Brook 3	Small Brook	626 906	0.6	5	380	9°S.W.	–	TDA 1890
	1*	Small Brook 4	Small Brook	628 905	0.45	7	420	17°W.	–	TDA 1890
	1*	Small Brook 5	Small Brook	628 904	0.2	3	410	11°W.	–	–
	1*	Small Brook 6	Small Brook	630 903	–	20	460	12°S.W.	–	TDA 1890
	2*	Cosdon Hill S.W.	Ivy Tor Water	628 912	?	9	460	9°N.W.	–	–
	3*	Cosdon Hill W.1	Ivy Tor Water	630 914	0.5	13	460	8°W.	–	33
	3*	Cosdon Hill W.2	Ivy Tor Water	631 915	0.45	6	460	8°W.	–	33
	4	Cosdon Hill N.E.	Cosdon Brook	647 923	?	3	340	6°N.E.	pres. fields	–
41	1	Kennon Hill	Gallaven Brook	641 890	0.9	14	460	7°S.W.	–	–
	2	Steeperton Tor N.E.	Steeperton Brook	621 890	?	18	460	11°N.E.	–	–
43	1	Great Noddon E.	Lyd	541 874	0.05	1	380	6°W.	–	–

map	no.	name	river	O.S. ref.	area (ha)	no. of huts	HMSL (m)	gradient down to	later use	references
	2*	Little Links Tor W.	Lyd	541 871	0.1	8	385	10°W.	–	–
	3	Arms Tor W.	Lyd	536 863	?	10	350	7°W.	–	–
	4	Corn Ridge W.	Crandford Brook	545 891	?	1	460	11°N.W.	–	–
	5	Green Tor	Rattle Brook	559 863	0.2	1	525	9°W.	–	–

Stone Circles

map	no. name	river	O.S. ref.	diameter	Av. ht. of stones	No. of stones	Orig. no. of stones	Distance Apart	Gradient and Direction	references
30	10* Langstone Moor †	Colly Brook	556 782	20.9	–	16	16	4.1	3°N.W.	23, 31, 64 *TDA 1895*
35	15* Fernworthy †	South Teign	654 841	20	0.57	27	29	2.1	level	38, 41, 63, 64, 65 *TDA 1871, 1898*
	16* Grey Wethers N. †	South Teign	638 831	32.2	1.15	20	30	3.3	3°E.	23, 31, 41, 45, 51, 64, 65 *TDA 1871, 1898, 1939*
	16* Grey Wethers S. †	South Teign	638 831	33.6	1.15	29	30	3.3	3°E.	23, 31, 41, 45, 51, 64, 65 *TDA 1871, 1898, 1939*
36	7* Shovel Down	North Teign	658 861	17.7	0.6	3+4?	13?	3.5	7°W.	*TDA 1932*
38	4* Scorhill	North Teign	654 873	27	1.06	33	c.60	var.	4°S.W.	2, 14, 23, 27, 39, 41, 65 *TDA 1932*
40	5* Buttern Hill	North Teign	649 884	24.8	0.5	18	c.40	c.2	1.5°S.	41, *TDA 1894, 1932*
	5* Little Hound Tor	Blackaton Brook	632 896	20.2	0.76	18	20?	3.17	1°S.	*TDA 1890, 1896, 1897*
43	5 Sourton Tors	West Okement	546 895	c.32	–	c.18	c.18	c.5.5	1°N.E.	42

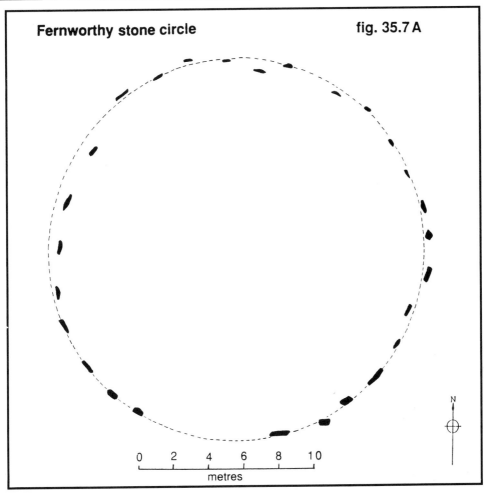

Fernworthy stone circle

fig. 35.7 A

0 2 4 6 8 10
metres

N

Stone Rows

Map	No.	Name	Number of Rows	River	O.S. Ref. Upper end	Orientation between ends (°T)	Maximum deviation (°)	Number of stones E	F	B	Original no. of stones	Terminals Upper End	Lower End	Intervisibility	Maximum gradient and direction	Length (m)	Distance between Rows (m)	Distance between stones along row (m)	Average height of stones (m)	H.M.S.L.	References
24	2	Soussons Down	3	W. Webburn	6767 7998	S	?	–	–	–	?	cairn	?	?	2°S.	c.62	?	?	?	410	TDA 1898, 1903
	3*	Challacombe Down	3	W. Webburn	6903 8073	158	0.5	64	4	–	?	standing stone	?	✓	8°N.	145.6	1.8/1.9	2.6	0.44	430	TDA 1892-3-4 1946-7
25	9*	Hurston Ridge	2	Bovey	6725 8242	025	0.5	99	–	–	99	cairn	blocking stone	✓	4°N.E.	143.3	2.0	2.77	0.41	440	TDA 1894, 1946-7
27	19.3*	Lakehead Hill Summit	1	East Dart	6438 7765	092	0	12	–	–	?	?	?	✓	level	19.9	–	1.2	0.25	425	TDA 1895, 1946
	19.4*	Lakehead Hill East †	1	East Dart	6449 7760	094	9.5	11	–	–	?	cairn	?	✓	4°E.	12.0	–	1.2	0.4	420	TDA 1895-6, 1946
	19.5	Lakehead Hill South 1?	1	East Dart	6434 7750	S.E.	?	4	–	–	?	cairn	?	✓	3°S.W.	–	–	?	?	410	TDA 1895-6
	19.6	Lakehead Hill South 2?	1	East Dart	6436 7747	S.E.	?	–	–	–	?	cairn	?	?	3°S.W.	?	–	?	–	410	TDA 1895-6
	19.7	Lakehead Hill S.E.	1	East Dart	?	N.W.	?	–	–	–	?	?	cairn?	?	?	?	–	?	–	?	TDA 1890, 1895-6, 1935
	19.14	Lakehead Hill S.W.	1	Cherry Brook	6418 7730	158	?	–	–	–	?	?	?	?	N.W.	c.123	–	?	–	400	TDA 1946
28	12*	Laughter Tor 1	2	East Dart	6521 7539	112	1.5	23	3	–	?	standing stone/cairn	?	✓	4°S.E.	164	1.7	1.2	0.23	395	TDA 1893, 1903, 1940, 1946
29	12	Laughter Tor 2	2	East Dart	6519 7539	119	?	10	–	–	?	?	?	✓	1°S.E.	c.10	c.1.0	1.4	0.05	395	–
	16*	Higher White Tor	2	Cherry Brook	6194 7842	014	?	12	5	19	?	?	?	✓	6°S.	95.4	1.4	?	0.3	490	31, TDA 1898
30	11*	Conies Down	2	Cowsic	5859 7905	010	3	21	20	–	?	cairn?	?	✓	6°S.W.	172.4	c.1.7	1.8–2.0	0.26	505	TDA 1893, 1946
	12*	Langstone Moor †	1	Colly Brook	5504 7885	003	0	13	14	–	?	cairn?	standing stone	✓	1°W.	118	–	2.64	0.19	430	TDA 1893-4-5, 1946
35	15*	Fernworthy 1	2	South Teign	6553 8429	016	0	45	1	1	?	cairn?	?	✓	1°E.	101	1.4	1.65	0.14	395	63, TPI 1830, TDA 1898, 1946
	15*	Fernworthy 2	2	South Teign	6551 8407	010	0	4	–	–	?	cairn	?	✓	level	20.5	?	1.13	0.1	395	63, TPI 1830, TDA 1898, 1946

Map	No.	Name	Number of Rows	River	O.S. Ref. Upper end	Orientation between ends (°T)	Maximum deviation (°)	Number of stones E	F	B	Original no. of stones	Terminals Upper End	Terminals Lower End	Intervisibility	Maximum gradient and direction	Length (m)	Distance between Rows (m)	Distance between stones along row (m)	Average height of stones (m)	H.M.S.L.	References
	15 *	Fernworthy 3	2	South Teign	6548 8410	007	0	13	–	–	?	cairn	?	√	level	31	1.3	1.28	0.15	395	63, TPI 1830, TDA 1898, 1946
	19 *	Assycombe	2	Assycombe Brook	6610 8263	061	1.5	129	3	1	144	cairn	blocking stone	×	8°W.	125	1.6	1.7	0.31	440	23, 64, TDA 1894, 1946
	20 *	White Ridge	2	Stannon Brook	6541 8165	007	3	41	5	13	?	cairn	?	×	4°S.W.	167	0.9–1.5	c.1.7	0.16	445	TDA 1946
	21 *	Stannon Newtake ?	2	Stannon Brook	6531 8111	134	?	4	–	1	?	cairn	blocking stones?	√	5°S.W.	c.18	?	?	0.5	410	TDA 1896
36	7 *	Shovel Down 1	1	North Teign/South Teign	6601 8586	171	19	89	6	4	?	?	?	×	8°E.	540	–	1.5	0.08	425	27, TDA 1932, 1946
	7 *	Shovel Down 2	2	North Teign	6595 8601	179	0	34	6	–	?	cairn	?	√	5°N.E.	182	1.4	1.5	0.49	415	14, 18, 27, 38, TPI 1830, 1858, TDA 1932, 1946
	7 *	Shovel Down 3	2	North Teign	6593 8604	159	2	67	2	2	?	?	?	×	4°N.E.	155	1.2	2.4–3.1	0.19	410	14, 18, 27, 38, TPI 1830, 1858, TDA 1932, 1946
	7 *	Shovel Down 4	2	North Teign	6599 8590	153	0.5	61	9	–	?	cairn	?	√	5°N.E.	118	1.4	2.2	0.32	425	14, 18, 27, 38, TPI 1830, 1858, TDA 1932, 1946
	7 *	Shovel Down 5	2	South Teign	6601 8582	178	4.5	71	7	–	?	?	standing stone	×	2°S.E.	148	1.4	1.35	0.12	425	14, 18, 27, 38, TPI 1830, 1858, TDA 1932, 1946
	7	Shovel Down 6	2	South Teign	c.6602 8567	c.180	?	4	–	–	?	?	blocking stone?	√	?	c.170	?	?	–	420	18, 27, 38, TPI 1858, TDA 1932, 1946
38	4	Scorhill	2	North Teign	6547 8720	c.177	?	10	–	–	?	cairn	?	√	3°S.	c.6.0	c.2.0	?	0.1	360	–
40	6 *	Cosdon	3	Blackaton Brook	6432 9159	277	3	107	19	1	?	cairn	blocking stone?	√	4°E.	146	1.4	1.32–1.57	0.31	435	TDA 1892, 1896, 1946
	–	Ramsley?	?	Taw	?	?	?	–	–	–	?	?	?	?	?	?	?	?	?	?	TDA 1896

235

Top: Langstone Moor stone circle
Above: Little Hound Tor stone circle

Langstone Moor stone row

Cairns

map no.		name	O.S. ref.	dimensions (m)	LVG no.	Barrow Report no.	Other refs
24	2.1*	Red Barrows †	6771 7963	20.0×2.0	Man. 5	–	TDA 1898, 1903
	2.2*	Red Barrows †	6770 7965	15.0×1.2	Man. 6	–	TDA 1898, 1903
	2.3*	Red Barrows †	6769 7967	21.0×1.3	Man. 7	–	TDA 1898, 1903
	2.4*	Red Barrows †	6769 7969	10.0×0.4	Man. 8	–	TDA 1898, 1903
	2.5	Soussons Plantation N. †	6767 7998	10.0×0.3	Man. 4	–	TDA 1898, 1903
	2.6*	Soussons Plantation S. †	6752 7868	8.6 C	Man. 9	22, 23, 45	TDA 1890
	4	Birch Tor Summit	6866 8163	17.0×2.0	N.Bov. 1	56	38
25	7	Chagford Common †	678 836	5+ cairns	Cha. 7, 8, 9, 10	–	TDA 1901
	9	Hurston Ridge Stone Row	6725 8242	6.5/7.0×0.5 C	Cha. 5	–	TDA 1894
	10	Hurston Ridge †	6700 8182	c.9.0×0.2	Lyd. 30	–	63, TDA 1901
	11	West Vitifer †	6757 8279	5.5×0.3 C	Cha. 4	16	42, 63, TDA 1897
26	1.2	King's Oven †	674 812	– C	Cha. 6a	–	18, TDA 1895
	4	Assycombe Hill S.1	6625 8116	8.0×0.5	–	–	–
	4	Assycombe Hill S.2	6624 8118	c.5.0×0.5	–	–	–
	5	Water Hill 1	6715 8128	18.0×1.3	Cha. 6	–	22, 38, 39
	5	Water Hill 2	6715 8129	5.0×0.3	–	–	–
	5	Near King's Oven	?	c.17.5 C	Cha. 6a	–	TDA 1871
27	4	Roundy Park †	6392 7967	5.5×0.3 C	Lyd.40	21	23, 39
	6	Arch Tor	6314 7782	8.0×1.2	–	–	–
	17	Rowtor Brook 1 †	6279 7863	8.5×1.4	Lyd.44	–	TDA 1890, 1891, 1901
	17	Rowtor Brook 2 †	6270 7866	8.5×1.0	Lyd.43	–	TDA 1890, 1891, 1901
	17	Rowtor Brook 3	6276 7880	7.0×1.0 C	Lyd.42	57	TDA 1890, 1891
	18	Chittaford Down 1	6350 7920	c.7.0×0.3	Lyd.38	–	TDA 1891
	18	Chittaford Down 2	6354 7921	c.4.5 C	Lyd.38a	–	TDA 1891
	18	Chittaford Down 3 †	6367 7946	7.0×0.5 C	Lyd.39	57	TDA 1901
	18	Archerton †	6385 7886	– C	Lyd.45	57	39, 63, TDA 1890, 1891
	19.1*	Lakehead Hill	6434 7777	6.0	Lyd.53	55	55
	19.2*	Lakehead Hill †	6425 7769	– C	Lyd.52	17, 55	63, TDA 1890
	19.4*	Lakehead Hill †	6449 7760	6.7? C	Lyd.54	–	TDA 1895, 1896

map no.	name	O.S. ref.	dimensions (m)	LVG no.	Barrow Report no.	Other refs
19.5*	Lakehead Hill	6434 7750	6.8	Lyd.55	54	*TDA* 1895, 1896
19.6*	Lakehead Hill †	6436 7747	5.6 C	Lyd.56	54	*TDA* 1895, 1896
19.7	Lakehead Hill	6470 7742	c.19.0×0.9 C	Lyd.57	54	*TDA* 1896
19.8	Lakehead Hill †	6468 7718	– C	Lyd.58	33, 55	–
19.9	Lakehead Hill	6466 7840	– C	Lyd.51	55	*TDA* 1891
19.10	Lakehead Hill	6504 7826	–	Lyd.51a	55	*TDA* 1891
19.11	Lakehead Hill †	?	–	Lyd.57a	–	*TDA* 1901
19.12	Lakehead Hill †	?	–	Lyd.57b	–	*TDA* 1901
19.13	Lakehead Hill †	?	–	Lyd.57c	–	*TDA* 1901
20.1*	Bellever Tor †	6408 7648	c.6.5×1.0 C	Lyd.59	54	23, *TDA* 1890, 1901
20.2	Bellever Tor	6413 7628	6.0×0.8	Lyd.59a	–	*TDA* 1890
20.3*	Bellever Tor	6391 7607	8.0×level C	Lyd.60	57	–
20.4*	Bellever Tor	6385 7605	11.0×0.5	–	–	–
20.5	Bellever Tor	6385 7603	6.0×1.0	Lyd.61	57	–
20.6*	Bellever Tor	6388 7587	7.4×level C	Lyd.62	57	*TDA* 1890
20.7	Bellever Tor	6386 7578	13.0×0.5	Lyd.63	57	–
20.8	Bellever Tor	6385 7573	– C	Lyd.64	57	*TDA* 1890
20.9	Bellever Tor	6357 7548	– C	Lyd.65	58	–
20.10	Bellever Tor	6408 7569	– C	Lyd.66	59	–
28 6	Cock's Lake †	6540 7476	7.2×0.4	–	22?	–
29 12	Laughter Tor Stone Row †	6521 7539	7.0×0.3	–	22	–
12	Laughter Tor S. (8)	?	var.	–	22	–
1	Littaford Tor	6142 7647	6.2×0.5	–	–	–
11	Stennen Hill 1	6259 7788	6.5×0.3 C	Lyd.47	57	*TDA* 1890
11	Stennen Hill 2	6262 7781	5.0×0.3 C	Lyd.49	57	–
14	Broad Hole S.	5910 7824	7.0×0.8	–	–	–
17	Lydford Tor E.	6035 7808	4.5×0.4	Lyd.41a	–	*TDA* 1901
18	Crow Tor †	6052 7866	4.0×0.4	Lyd.41	–	–
30 1	Langstone Moor cairn cemetery (c.6)	555 777	3–4.0×0.3	–	–	–
7	Merrivale Bridge N.	5527 7512	5.0×0.3	Pet.40	–	*TDA* 1898
10	Langstone Moor 1 †	5574 7811	5.5×0.3	Pet.39	–	63, *TDA* 1898
10	Langstone Moor 2 †	5573 7810	5.5×0.3 C	–	–	–

map no.	name	O.S. ref.	dimensions (m)	LVG no.	Barrow Report no.	Other refs
10	Langstone Moor 3 †	5571 7809	c.5.0×0.2	Pet.40a, 41a	–	*TDA* 1898
11	Conies Down Stone Row	5859 7905	c.3.0×0.2	–	–	–
11	Conies Down Summit	5882 7941	23.0×1.0 C?	Lyd.32	–	31, *TDA* 1895
12	Langstone Moor Stone Row	5504 7885	?	Pet.41	–	–
13	White Barrow	5685 7930	21.0×1.7	Lyd.31	–	–
14	Cock's Hill W.	5618 7913	16.0×0.8	Pet.38	–	–
15	Youldon Brookhead	5671 7984	9.0×0.8	–	–	–
16	Greena Ball 1	5684 7784	8.0×0.6	Lyd.35	–	10, 39, *TDA* 1905
16	Greena Ball 2	5685 7782	8.0×0.9	–	–	–
16	Greena Ball 3	5689 7784	11.0×1.0	Lyd.36	–	10, 39, *TDA* 1905
16	Greena Ball 4	5694 7783	11.0×1.5	Lyd.37	–	10, 39, *TDA* 1905
17	Little Mis Tor S.E.	5692 7595	22.0×0.4	Lyd.37a	–	*TDA* 1906
31 1.3	Cox Tor Summit	5306 7618	–	Pet.37a	–	*TDA* 1898
1.4	Cox Tor N.	5303 7635	18.0×1.6	Pet.37	–	*TDA* 1898
1.5	Cox Tor N. †	5302 7642	17.0×0.8	Pet.35	–	*TDA* 1898
1.6	Cox Tor N. †	5304 7642	10.0×0.7	Pet.36	–	*TDA* 1898
1.7	Cox Tor N.	5305 7652	c.5.0×0.3	–	–	
1.8	Cox Tor S.E. †	5316 7613	c.4.0×0.3	–	–	*TDA* 1898
1.9	Cox Tor S.E. †	5318 7614	c.5.0×0.3	–	–	*TDA* 1898
7	Roos Tor Cairn cemetery (c.20)	541 772	3–6.0×0.3–0.5	–	–	–
11	Smeardon Down	5228 7814	c.12.0×0.3	–	–	–
13	White Tor Summit	5422 7862	27.0×3.5	Pet.22	–	22, *TDA* 1899
16	Cudlipptown Down 1	5351 7904	3.0×0.2	–	–	–
16	Cudlipptown Down 2	5350 7904	4.5×0.2	–	–	–
17	Cudlipptown Down N.	5337 7946	5.0×0.3	–	–	–
18	Wedlake E.1	5428 7756	c.11.0×0.8	Pet.34b	–	–
18	Wedlake E.2	5444 7767	18.0×0.4	Pet.34a	–	–
19	Langstone Moor S.1 †	5484 7763	c.15.0×0.4	Pet.33	–	*TDA* 1899
19	Langstone Moor S.2 †	5488 7765	5.8×0.3	Pet.34	–	*TDA* 1899
20	White Tor S.S.E.1 †	5434 7836	10.5×0.5	Pet.30	–	*TDA* 1899
20	White Tor S.S.E.2 †	5435 7834	4.8×0.4	Pet.32	–	*TDA* 1899
20	White Tor S.S.E.3 †	5435 7837	4.5×0.4	Pet.31	–	*TDA* 1899
20	White Tor S.S.E.4 †	5438 7843	4.6×0.4	Pet.23	–	*TDA* 1899

32

map no.	name	O.S. ref.	dimensions (m)	LVG no.	Barrow Report no.	Other refs
20	White Tor S.S.E.5 †	5448 7825	c.7.5×0.3	–	–	*TDA* 1905
20	White Tor S.S.E.6 †	5436 7820	6.0×0.2	–	–	*TDA* 1905
20	White Tor S.S.E.7	5470 7822	4.5×0.4	–	–	–
21	White Tor S.S.W.1 †	5400 7830	13.0×5.7	Pet.29a	–	*TDA* 1899
21	White Tor S.S.W.2 †	5402 7831	c.5.0×0.2	Pet.29	–	*TDA* 1899
21	White Tor S.S.W.3 †	5399 7828	?	Pet.29b	–	*TDA* 1899
22	White Tor E.1 †	5459 7869	7.8×0.2	Pet.24	–	*TDA* 1899
22	White Tor E.2	5458 7866	9.4×0.3	Pet.25	–	–
22	White Tor E.3	5460 7866	12.5×0.3	Pet.26	–	–
22	White Tor E.4 †	5469 7869	6.3×0.3 C	Pet.27	55	39, *TDA* 1889, 1899
23	White Tor N.W.1 †	5372 7900	9.0×0.3	Pet.20	–	*TDA* 1899
23	White Tor N.W.2	5372 7895	16.0×0.3	Pet.21	–	–
23	White Tor N.W.3	5373 7885	2.5×0.2	–	–	–
1	Standon Hill N.1	5550 8255	4.8×0.3	–	–	–
1	Standon Hill N.2	5551 8256	5.8×0.3	–	–	–
2	Nattor Down 1	5390 8267	13.0×0.4	–	–	–
2	Nattor Down 2	5366 8253	c.10.0×0.8	–	–	–
2	Nattor Down 3	5393 8286	6.3×0.5	Pet.12	–	–
2	Nattor Down 4	5410 8295	4.6×0.5	Pet.13	–	–
2	Nattor Down 5	5409 8286	5.7×0.3 C	Pet.14	–	–
2	Nattor Down 6	5429 8298	c.4.5×0.3	–	–	–
4	Ger Tor Summit	5465 8333	6.0×0.4	–	–	–
16	Standon Hill Summit	5553 8146	18.5×2.0	Pet.19	–	–
17	Standon Hill W.	5473 8136	c.5.0×0.3 C	Pet.15	–	10
18	Limsboro	5654 8053	15.0×2.5	Lyd.14	–	22
19	Hare Tor S.E.	5547 8368	7.5×0.6	Pet.16	–	–
19	Hare Tor S. †	5520 8366	3.4×0.5	Pet.17	25	–
19	Western Red Lake W. †	5639 8289	1.2×0.6	Pet.18	25	–
20	Hare Tor N.1 †	5518 8457	10.0×1.3	Lyd.13	24	–
20	Hare Tor N.2	5509 8446	10.0×1.0	–	–	–
21	Doe Tor E. †	5438 8484	5.0×0.4 C	Lyd.12	24	–
22.1	White Hill	5294 8368	19.0×0.3	Pet.1	–	–
22.2	White Hill	5300 8366	c.13.0×1.0	Pet.2	10, 13	–

map no.	name	O.S. ref.	dimensions (m)	LVG no.	Barrow Report no.	Other refs
22.3	White Hill †	5302 8366	c.9.0×0.2	Pet.3	10	–
22.4	White Hill †	5305 8365	c.9.0×1.2	Pet.4	10	–
22.5	White Hill †	5310 8365	c.10.0×0.7	Pet.5	10	–
22.6	White Hill	5315 8364	c.7.5×0.5	Pet.5a	–	–
22.7	White Hill	5316 8364	c.5.0×0.2	Pet.5b	–	–
22.8	White Hill	5321 8370	5.0×0.2	Pet.6	–	–
22.9	White Hill	5344 8390	16.0×0.1	Pet.9	–	–
22.10	White Hill	5371 8419	8.0×0.6 C	Pet.11	–	–
22.11*	White Hill W. cairn cemetery (c.24) †	526 838	2.0–6.0×0.1–0.4	–	10	*DASP* 1980
22.12*	White Hill N.E. cairn cemetery (c.24)	535 840	2.0–5.0×0.1–0.4	Pet.10	–	*DASP* 1980
22.13*	White Hill S.E. cairn cemetery (c.11)	534 838	3.0–6.5×0.3–0.4	Pet.7	–	*DASP* 1980
34						
1	Quintin's Man	6210 8386	17.0×1.8	Lyd.15	–	31
1	Near Quintin's Man	?	?	Lyd.15a	–	–
1	Teignhead Newtake 1 †	?	?	Lyd.15b	–	*TDA* 1902
1	Teignhead Newtake 2 †	?	?	Lyd.15c	–	*TDA* 1902
2	Marsh Hill	6214 8243	c.10	–	–	–
3	Sittaford Tor S.	6348 8258	6.0×0.3	–	–	56
35						
7	Hemstone Rocks N.1 †	648 838	?C	Lyd.17	–	*TDA* 1901
7	Hemstone Rocks N.2 †	648 838	?	Lyd.17a	–	*TDA* 1901
7	Hemstone Rocks N.3 †	648 838	?	Lyd.17b	–	*TDA* 1901
7	Hemstone Rocks N.4 †	648 838	?	Lyd.17c	–	*TDA* 1901
9	Lade Hill Brookhead †	638 824	?	Lyd.16a	–	*TDA* 1898
11	White Ridge S.W.	6414 8160	5.0×0.2	Lyd.19	–	–
13	Broad Down N.E.	6370 8101	6.5×0.5	Lyd.18	–	–
15.1	Fernworthy	6553 8429	?	Lyd.20	–	*TDA* 1898
15.2	Fernworthy †	6551 8407	7.0×0.3 C	Lyd.23	–	*TDA* 1898
15.3	Fernworthy †	6548 8410	6.0×0.3	Lyd.21	–	*TDA* 1898
15.4	Fernworthy †	6549 8405	8.0×0.3	Lyd.22	–	*TDA* 1898
15.5	Fernworthy †	6556 8408	c.6.0×0.6	Lyd.24	–	*TDA* 1898
16	Grey Wethers E. †	6411 8321	5.0×0.4	Lyd.16	–	*TDA* 1898
17	South Teignhead	6408 8282	8.0×14.0×0.5	–	–	*DASP* 1986

map no.		name	O.S. ref.	dimensions (m)	LVG no.	Barrow Report no.	Other refs
	19	Assycombe Hill Stone Row	6610 8263	8.0×0.4 C	Lyd.26	–	31
	20	White Ridge Stone Row	6541 8165	c.8.0	Lyd.27	–	*TDA* 1898, *DASP* 1986
	21*	Stannon Newtake E.	6545 8108	3.9×0.3 C	Lyd.29	57	*TDA* 1905
	21*	Stannon Newtake W. †	6531 8111	6.0×0.7	Lyd.28	15	–
	22	Thornworthy †	6674 8434	11.5×0.6 C	Cha.3	56	*TDA* 1880
36	4	Central Settlement	6576 8585	5.0×0.3 C?	–	–	–
	4	Central Settlement	6570 8624	6.5×0.3	–	–	–
	7*	Fourfold Circle	6595 8601	c.9.0	Gid.3	–	27, *TDA* 1932, 1941
	7	near Fourfold Circle?	6595 8599	4.0	Gid.3a	–	*TDA* 1932
	7	Shoveldon Rows 4	6599 8590	7.0×0.3 C	Cha.1	–	27, *TDA* 1932
	7	Three Boys?	6603 8550	? C?	Lyd.9a	–	39, *TDA* 1932
	7	Thornworthy Corner N.	6612 8547	? C?	Cha.2	–	*TDA* 1932
	7	Thornworthy Corner W.	6599 8550	c.6.0×0.3	Lyd.9	–	–
37	2	Stonetor Brookhead E.1	6534 8558	7.0×0.6	–	–	–
	2	Stonetor Brookhead E.2	6528 8560	? C?	Gid.1.?	–	–
	5	Shoveldown N.W.1	6438 8640	4.5×0.3 C	–	–	–
	5	Shoveldown N.W.2	6435 8626	4.5×0.3	–	–	–
	5	Shoveldown N.W.3	6436 8625	4.5×0.3	–	–	–
	5	Shoveldown N.W.4	6438 8626	4.5×0.3	–	–	–
	5	Shoveldown N.W.5	6438 8624	4.5×0.3	–	–	–
	5	Shoveldown N.W.6	6435 8593	5.8×0.4	–	–	–
38	4	Scorhill S.1	6553 8726	c.7.5×0.8	–	–	–
	4	Scorhill S.2	6547 8720	c.7.0×0.5 C?	–	–	–
	6	Scorhill N.1	6573 8770	11.0×0.4	Gid.4	–	–
	6	Scorhill N.2	6574 8774	12.0×0.4	Gid.5	–	–
	7*	Buttern Hill Chambered Cairn 1	6566 8855	8.0×6.0×0.5	–	–	*DASP* 1980
	7	Buttern Hill Chambered Cairn 2	6586 8897	?	–	–	*DASP* 1980
39	1	Throwleigh Common 1	6540 9067	7.0×0.3	–	–	–
	1	Throwleigh Common 2	6542 9053	5.0×0.3	–	–	–
	1	Throwleigh Common 3	6546 9055	5.0×0.3	–	–	–
	1	Throwleigh Common 4	6546 9056	3.5×0.3	–	–	–
	1	Throwleigh Common 5	6554 9044	7.4×0.3	–	–	–

map no.	name	O.S. ref.	dimensions (m)	LVG no.	Barrow Report no.	Other refs
40						
6	Shilley Pool N.	6505 9143	8.9×0.3	ST 5a	–	–
5	Little Hound Tor Stone Circle	6330 8954	8.5×0.8	ST 7	–	–
6*	Cosdon Hill Stone Row †	6432 9159	7.0×0.3 C	ST 5	–	TDA 1892, 1896
6	Cosdon Hill E. †	?	?	ST 5b	–	TDA 1896
7.1*	Cosdon Beacon	6362 9150	27.0×3.0	ST 3	–	14, 39
7.2*	Cosdon Beacon	6366 9151	c.25.0×0.6	ST 4	–	14, 39
7.3*	Cosdon Beacon	6371 9159	c.18.0×0.4	ST 2	–	14, 39, TDA 1905
7.4*	Cosdon Beacon	6372 9164	6.5×0.6 C	ST 1b	–	14, 39, TDA 1905
7.5*	Cosdon Beacon	6370 9171	16.0×1.5	ST 1	–	14, 39
8	Cosdon Hill N.1	6360 9330	c.5.0×0.3	–	–	–
8	Cosdon Hill N.2	6356 9315	?	ST 8	–	10, 59
8	Cosdon Hill N.3	6357 9306	?	ST 9	–	–
9	Cosdon Hill N.4	6335 9246	c.7.0×0.4	ST 10	–	DASP 1980
10	Cosdon Hill N.W.	6305 9265	c.7.5×0.5	–	–	DASP 1980
10	Cosdon Hill N.W.	629 927	3–4.5×0.2–0.3	–	–	–
	Cairnfield (7+)				–	
11	Little Hound Tor	6328 8993	8.0×0.4	ST 6a	–	TDA 1890
12	Watchet Hill	6151 9305	c.14.0×0.8	Bel.3	–	10, TDA 1890
13*	Nine Stones	6124 9284	7.2×0.6	Bel.1	42	41, TDA 1890
14	Cullever Steps	6078 9195	c.4.5×0.4 C?	Bel.2	–	TDA 1890
15	Higher Tor S. †	6110 9134	8.5×1.0 C	Lyd.1	–	10, TDA 1890
c	Tor Marsh S.1?	6212 9048	5.0×0.3	Lyd.2	–	–
c	Tor Marsh S.2?	6217 9043	3.5×0.3	Lyd.2a	–	–
41	Kennon Hill S.W.	6389 8897	6.0×0.7	–	–	–
3	Watern Tor S.	6291 8607	24.0×3.5	Lyd.8	–	–
4	Watern Tor	6287 8688	4.5×0.4	Lyd.7	–	–
5	Hangingstone Hill	6169 8611	c.18.0×1.8	Lyd.6	–	–
5	Hangingstone Hill N. †	6172 8643	?	–	–	OS 1:25000
6	Wild Tor N.E.	6290 8810	6.5×0.5 C	Thr1, 2	–	TDA 1902
	Ramsley Hill	6518 9306	10×0.7	–	–	–
42	Yes Tor 1	5796 9021	29	Oke.1	–	10
1	Yes Tor 2	5803 9091	20+	Oke.2	–	10

map no.	name	O.S. ref.	dimensions (m)	LVG no.	Barrow Report no.	Other refs
2	High Willhays?	5804 8938	22	Oke.5, 5a	–	–
3	Forsland Ledge	5757 8888	10×0.4	Oke.4	–	10
4	Harter Hill	6013 9192	10×0.6	–	–	–
5	Black Down	5846 9233	7.5×0.8	–	–	–
6	Black Down W.	5738 9153	6.5×0.6 C	–	–	–
7	Yes Tor N.W.1	5723 9100	5.0×0.3	–	–	–
7	Yes Tor N.W.2	5724 9102	c.5.0×0.2	–	–	–
7	Yes Tor N.W.3	5728 9100	6.5×0.3	–	–	–
8	Langstone Hill Cairn Cemetery (c.24)	568 908	2–7.0×0.2–0.6	–	–	DASP 1980
9	Langstone Hill S.	5690 9055	13×0.9	–	–	10
	Okement Hill N.	?	small	–	–	10
	Okement Hill Summit	?	large	Lyd.5a	–	–
43						
4.1	Corn Ridge W.	5463 8916	3.0×0.2	–	–	–
4.2	Corn Ridge W.	5455 8925	6.0×0.3×0.6	–	–	–
7.1	Great Nodden	5306 8620	11.0×0.3	–	–	–
7.2	Great Nodden	5308 8625	5.0×0.3	–	–	–
7.3	Great Nodden	5306 8628	6.0×0.3	–	–	–
7.4	Great Nodden	5324 8620	17.5×0.3	–	–	–
7.5	Great Nodden	5333 8678	5.5×0.3	–	–	–
7.6	Great Nodden	5331 8680	4.7×0.3	–	–	–
7.7	Great Nodden	5333 8687	5.5×0.3	–	–	–
7.8	Great Nodden	5339 8689	4.5×0.3	–	–	–
7.9	Great Nodden	5340 8691	4.5×0.3	–	–	–
7.10	Great Nodden	5336 8693	4.5×0.3	–	–	–
7.11	Great Nodden	5350 8706	c.15.0×0.4	–	–	–
7.12	Great Nodden	5348 8708	9.0×0.3	–	–	–
7.13	Great Nodden	5360 8739	16.5×1.0	Bri.6	–	10
7.14	Great Nodden	5367 8755	7.5×0.3	–	–	–
7.15	Great Nodden	5425 8788	8.5×0.3	Bri.5	–	–
7.16	Great Nodden	5388 8741	14.0×0.5	Bri.7	–	–
7.17	Great Nodden	538 874	? C	Bri.7a	13, 21	–
7.18	Great Nodden	5345 8723	?	–	–	–
7.19	Great Nodden	5341 8713	?	–	–	–

map no.	name	O.S. ref.	dimensions (m)	LVG no.	Barrow Report no.	Other refs
8	Corn Ridge W.1	5441 8884	21.0×0.3	Bri.3	–	–
8	Corn Ridge W.2	5443 8887	14.0×0.4	Bri.4	–	–
8	Lake Down cairn field	542 888	3–5.0×0.3	–	–	*DASP* 1980
9	Corn Ridge W.3	5446 8914	10.0×0.3	Bri.2	–	–
10	Corn Ridge N.W.1	5459 8943	11.0×0.3	Bri.1	–	–
10	Corn Ridge N.W.2	5461 8948	7.5×0.3	–	–	–
11	Sourton Tors E.	5474 8982	11.0×0.7	Oke.3	–	–
12	Branscombe's Loaf 1	5515 8917	15.5×1.8	Bri.9	–	10
12	Branscombe's Loaf 2	5511 8920	14.5×0.3	Bri.10	–	–
12	Branscombe's Loaf 3	5520 8918	c.10.0	–	–	–
13	Great Links Tor	5490 8650	16.0×1.4	Bri.8	–	–
14	Green Tor	5642 8610	6.0×0.8	–	–	–
15	Homerton Hill Cairn cemetery (c.20)	561 905	3–7.0×0.2–0.5	–	–	*DASP* 1980
15	Homerton Hill N.	5616 9065	3.5×0.3 C	–	–	*DASP* 1980
15	Homerton Hill S.	5636 9015	7.5×0.3	–	–	–

BIBLIOGRAPHY AND REFERENCES

T.D.A.   *Transactions of the Devonshire Association.*
P.P.S.   *Proceedings of the Prehistoric Society.*
D.A.S.P.   *Devon Archaeological Society Proceedings.*
T.P.I.   *Transactions of the Plymouth Institution.*
M.A   *Medieval Archaeology*

2.   Fleming, A. 1988. *The Dartmoor Reaves.*
7.   Fleming, A. 1983. 'The Prehistoric Landscape of Dartmoor, Part 2. North and East Dartmoor'. P.P.S. 49.
8.   Burt, R. et al., 1984. *Devon and Somerset Mines.*
10. Crossing, W. 1912. *Guide to Dartmoor.*
11   Hemery, E. 1983. *High Dartmoor.*
13. Brewer, D. 1986, *A Field Guide to the Boundary Markers on and around Dartmoor.*
14. Croker, J.G. 1851. *A Guide to the Eastern Escarpment of Dartmoor.*
18. Baring-Gould, S. 1900. *A Book of Dartmoor.*
19. Gill, C. (Ed.). 1970. *Dartmoor: A New Study.*
20. Linehan, C.D.1966 'Deserted Sites and Rabbit-Warrens on Dartmoor, Devon'. M.A. 10, 113–144.
22. Mrs. Bray. 1879. *The Borders of the Tamar and the Tavy.*
23. Burnard, R. 1986. *Dartmoor Pictorial Records.*
27. Ormerod, G.W. 1876. *Archaeology of Eastern Dartmoor.*
30. Hamilton-Jenkin, A.K. 1974. *Mines of Devon. Volume 1: The Southern Area.*
31. Worth, R.H. 1953. *Dartmoor.*
32. Broughton, D.G. 1968/9. 'The Birch Tor and Vitifer Tin Mining Complex'. Trans. Cornish Inst. of Engineers. 24.
33. Greeves, T. 1985. *The Archaeology of Dartmoor from the Air.*
34. Greeves, T. 1986. *Tin Mines and Miners of Dartmoor.*
35. Baring-Gould, S. 1908. *Devonshire Characters and Strange Events.*
36. Ogilby, J. 1675. *Britannia.*
37. Ormerod, W.G. 1876. 'On the Traces of Tin Streaming in the Vicinity of Chagford'. T.D.A. 1, 110-115.
38. Page, J.L.W. 1889. *An Exploration of Dartmoor and its Antiquities.*
39. Rowe, S. 1896. *A Perambulation of Dartmoor.*
41. Chudleigh, J. 1893. *Devonshire Antiquities.*
42. Pettit, P. 1974. *Prehistoric Dartmoor.*
43. Greeves, T. 1987. 'The Great Courts or Parliaments of Devon Tinners 1474-1786'. T.D.A. 119, 145-167.
44. Risdon, T. Rep. 1970. *The Chorographical Description or Survey of the County of Devon.*
45. Thom, A., Thom A.S., Burl, A. 1990. *Stone Rows and Standing Stones.*
46. Harris, H. 1981. 'Nineteenth Century Granite Working on Pew Tor and Staple Tor, Western Dartmoor'. T.D.A. 113, 33.
47. Harris, H. 1968. *Industrial Archaeology of Dartmoor.*
48. Greeves, T. 'Wheal Prosper - A Little Known Dartmoor Tin Mine'. Plymouth Mining and Mineral Club Journal Vol.6 No.1.
49. Greeves, T. 'Merrivale Bridge Mine, Wheal Fortune & Staple Tor Sett, 1806-1887'. Plymouth Mining and Mineral Club Journal Vol.6 No.3.
50. Robins, J. 1988. *Rambling On.*

51. Starkey, F.H. 1984. *Odds and Ends from Dartmoor*.
52. Worth, R.H. 1941. 'Dartmoor: 1788-1808'. T.D.A. 73, 217.
53. Le Messurier, B. 1965. 'The Phillpotts Peat Passes of Northern Dartmoor'. T.D.A. 97, 161-170.
54. Le Messurier, B. 1979. 'The Post Prehistoric Structures of Central North Dartmoor'. T.D.A. 111, 59-73.
56. Breton, H. *Beautiful Dartmoor*. Part 3.
57. Costello, L.M. 1981. 'The Bradford Pool Case'. T.D.A. 113, 59-77.
58. Greeves, T. 1985. 'Steeperton Tor Tin Mine, Dartmoor, Devon'. T.D.A. 117, 101-127.
59. St. Leger-Gordon, D. 1954. *Under Dartmoor Hills*.
60. Fleming, A. 1980. 'The Cairnfields of North-West Dartmoor'. D.A.S.P. 38, 9-12.
61. Hemery, E. 1983. *Walking the Dartmoor Railroads*.
62. Harris, H. 1988. 'The Sourton Tors Iceworks, North-West Dartmoor'. T.D.A. 120, 177-200.
63. Burnard, R. 1906. 'Early Man'. Victoria County History.1, 341-372.
64. Falcon, T.A. 1900. *Dartmoor Illustrated*.
65. A.Z. c. 1870. *Dartmoor Sketches*.
66. Roberts, P. 'Standon Hill and Wapsworthy'. Plymouth Mineral and Mining Club Journal, Vol.12. No.2.